LAW AND DISORDER

LAW AND DISORDER

by
James D. Forman

THOMAS NELSON INC.
Nashville / Camden / New York

Second Printing, September 1972

Library of Congress Catalog Card Number: 72–169035

International Standard Book Number: 0–8407–6148–1

This one is for the Forman lawyers—

Alexander A.
Leo E.
Robert S.
and W. John Kennedy,
who chose to follow the same thorny path.

Contents

Introduction   9
Chapter One   The Tribal Beginnings   11
Chapter Two   Civilizing the Law   18
Chapter Three   Sources of Our Common Law   41
Chapter Four   Great Systems of the Law Today   54
Chapter Five   Humanizing the Common Law   72
Chapter Six   Civilizing Punishments   94
Chapter Seven   Freedom of Speech and Press   107
Chapter Eight   Privacy and the Police   125
Chapter Nine   Civil Rights   151
Chapter Ten   Law Among Nations: War and Its Control   161
Chapter Eleven   The Future of the Law   180
Appendix:
   A Reference Note on Case Citations As They Appear in
     Chapter Notes   205
   Chapter Notes   206
   Bibliography   211
   A Glossary of Legal Terms   215
   Index   221

Introduction

LAW HAS BEEN ENDLESSLY DEFINED BY JURISTS, THEOLOGIANS, PHI-losophers, poets, and cynics. Seldom is there agreement. To the average person, it is an occult discipline as baffling as nuclear physics. Except for Perry Mason or the headlines of a celebrated murder trial, we seem to live day by day quite apart from the law; but the fact is, we live with it. Savages have at times managed to survive without it, but only if all men were saints could civilized society exist without laws and a system to amend and enforce them.

Behind almost every newsworthy event, laws are operating, be it the plane crash, the society wedding, the natural disaster, the big business failure, the traffic accident, or the natural death. Take as an example the following (which would probably not make headlines). A man with no thought on his mind of the law or its permutations gets up in the morning, starts for work in his car, and on the way runs over and kills a stranger. The legal ramifications are endless. Was the driver drunk? Had he forgotten to put on his glasses? Was he driving recklessly? In short, was he negligent? Or did the victim somehow contribute to his own death by running out into the street, or by walking against the green light? Perhaps the car was defective. The steering may have failed or a new tire may have blown out for no apparent reason.

In such a case, the manufacturer may be held responsible. Insurance companies most certainly will become involved, and the terms of their insurance contracts will be read to the last detail. Finally, there are questions concerning the victim's property. Who gets it? Is his will valid? In this way, an accident will involve many people and a vast array of laws. Too complicated? Perhaps, but the alternative is to leave matters to the goodwill of the car's driver or the vengeance of the victim's relatives, an alternative to law and order which is not unknown in the world today.

Although laws are designed for application in the individual case, law in another sense must consider the general social welfare. It must guarantee fair play between people who are fallible and who rarely behave like saints in situations that may never before have been contemplated. Law, then, must have an eye on the future and a hand on the pulse of the times. Law, though rooted in the past, must change, and does; too rapidly for some, too slowly for others.

Negligence law has evolved with the automobile. Treatment of the criminally insane and of prisoners in general has responded to the influence of modern sociology and psychology. Divorce laws and treatment of pornography alter with more liberal social views. Entirely new problems, such as drug addiction, pollution, and a growing social consciousness of the rights of minority groups require new laws or the drastic modification of old ones. In a world grown small through communications and the population explosion, the once utopian dream of international law has become a growing necessity.

To keep itself alive on this rapidly changing planet, the law must grow, redefine itself and its function, and constantly prune back deadwood. The objective here is to examine this process of growth from the law's most fragile roots in primitive and savage times into the vast and diverging legal systems of today. The concentration will be upon the evolving common law of the United States, particularly upon those areas of present abrasion and flux. Finally, there will be a few tentative suggestions of what directions the law may take in the future.

CHAPTER ONE

The Tribal Beginnings

As LONG AS MAN HAS INHABITED THIS PLANET, EVER SINCE CAIN or his anthropoidal equivalent killed his brother, it is safe to say there has been disorder. As Thomas Hobbes remarked, "In a state of nature, the life of man is nasty, brutish and short." [1] Throughout human history, law inherently lags behind, if indeed it ever comes into play at all. Even today, societies remain with no fixed way of settling crimes. Among the Andaman Islanders, if a man goes wild, attacks people for good reasons or bad, or destroys property, there is no predetermined social formula for dealing with him. The abused or his relatives may take private vengeance, or they may not. Neighbors may ostracize the disorderly person to the point of exile within the community, or they may not. But there exists no tribal authority to whom resort may be taken, no one with a duty to act in behalf of the community.

This law of the jungle, which of course is no law at all, lasted among all men for thousands of years. Law as we define it today has certain requirements. There must be predetermined and binding rules of conduct within the human community that are regularly enforced by some impartial agency within that group. In the beginning, the agency with power existed in the tribal leader, usually the strongest and most clever male. Later, it was transferred to a council of elders, and the sanctions they imposed were arbitrary at best. Custom within a perpetuated community might

11

in time channel the application of power so that the potential offender would think twice before acting. Another strong force for shaping group behavior was, of course, religion, once it had emerged from the purely primitive. Within the context of the Bible, the first disorderly person may have been Eve, but the first criminal was Cain, and his punishment was taken entirely from human hands. He was marked, lest other men attack him, and sent into exile, a fate perhaps acceptable to the Andaman Islanders, but rarely applied under the laws of modern society.

Between Cain with his stone and the wrath of God, and today's towering hierarchy of courts applying their myriad and imperfect laws, there is no clear line of development. There are steps, forward and back, along the paths of civilization. There are examples casting a haphazard and glowworm light upon a dark and uncertain history. Where laws were not recorded, little can be ascertained about the tribal laws of the past, but much can be surmised from observing primitive societies as they exist today.

The Sunda Islanders punish an habitual liar by having passersby heap twigs on the spot where the dishonesty occurred. This is bad publicity, in other words, but not law, for the twig piling is not undertaken by a sheriff at the direction of a court applying a law to the effect that liars shall be embarrassed in such manner. This is purely a customary remedy, which seems to work, as does the so-called Eskimo song duel. Given a grievance, the hostile parties sing at one another before an audience. A quarrel involving domestic relations might go as follows:

> "What is rumored about this family?
> Why do they not agree?
> Why does the wife steal her husband's furs?
> Why does he take their kayack and row away?
> Oh, yes, all who are listening
> what do you think? . . ."

Where real malice is involved, the verses are interspersed with the butting of heads, and approval generally goes to the harder skull. More legalistic are the Gringai, an aboriginal tribe in Australia.

For serious disorders the offender must dodge a number of flung spears, the number to be determined by the magnitude of the offense. In this case, the punishment for the crime is predetermined and enforced by the tribal elders; a state of simple law has been achieved.

Among the Comanche Indians of the nineteenth century, no law of domestic relations existed, but their family customs were elaborate and often violent, reflecting a society that gave its closest attention to war and the aggrandizement of the warrior. The main objectives of a Comanche male's life were stealing horses, counting coups, and killing enemies. No man was drafted into the tribal army; braves followed their war chief out of respect alone. If that respect failed, the brave might withdraw from the war party and nothing was said against him. As individual as their warring was their treatment of women. If a woman committed adultery, a man might respond variously. If the scandal did not become public knowledge, he might simply give her a good thrashing and forgive and forget; but once the word was out, ridicule, as among the Andaman Islanders, became a weapon to force the husband to act. He could, if equal to his rival, simply put an arrow into the man's favorite horse and call the matter square, a horse and a woman being of like value to the Comanche. He might cut off his wife's hair, whip her through camp to her lover's tent, and there demand various possessions in compensation, but the situation was rarely this simple. Perhaps the wife denied her husband's accusations. Then the third degree was in order, and the husband could take his wife to a lonely spot, hold her face over a fire, and coerce a confession. He might follow this up by cutting off her nose in order to spoil her appearance forever and so make her unattractive to anyone else. A less painful but no more civilized variation on this treatment was the conditional curse, whereby a woman denying her husband's charge of adultery would place her hands on the ground and call on the powers of nature: "May I perish when the buffalo come from the north if I have betrayed my husband." The seriousness and psychological importance of this curse are not to be underestimated. Very often the woman died at the appointed time, and her death was called a "sun killing."

Still the rival remained to be dealt with, and in some cases he was a man of greater war honors than the husband. He might choose to protect his horse and his possessions, or to ridicule his accuser as a man unable to stand up to him in a fair fight. If this did not end the matter, a fight might follow. More often the inadequate plaintiff had recourse to a war chief who would act in his behalf. Outside the tepee of the defendant a bargaining session would take place. Damages would be discussed and often paid where fear was mutual. If this failed, the aggrieved might muster his kin, initiating *escalation* in modern terminology, to the point where tribal war was not impossible nor, in fact, undesired.

A final variation sometimes occurred, when wife and lover absconded. Honor accrued to the husband who pursued, but if he was old or weak or cowardly, he might seek out a *tekniwap*. Rather like the medieval champion, the *tekniwap* was a war leader who could not admit fear and was thus honor bound, not merely as arbitrator but as demander of recompense: damages and the wife, or a fight to the death. This way the husband very often came away with his wife and a bonus in horses or other goods, but lost stature in the community. Jokes and ridicule might follow him, and his rival, though dead at the hands of a champion, would leave behind him a fairer reputation. In short, the Comanche tribes of the nineteenth century lived without law. However, along the warlike lines of their society, they contrived customs that may have favored the brave but did give a rough justice.

Although the Comanches lived in a state of warfare with outsiders and of lawlessness among themselves, custom at least left a path for arbitration. Not so with the Jibaro Indians of eastern Ecuador who, reduced to about twenty thousand souls, show every sign of eventual self-extermination. The world will little miss them. These fear-ridden people live in small family groups, inhabiting fortified hilltop homes, the approaches to which are set with pit traps. Formerly, each community had a wooden war tower, rising as high as forty yards, with a lookout platform on top. These towers are now diminishing, made indefensible by the trade gun. They are apt to vanish along with the Jibaro, whose way of life is simply not compatible with the killing capacity of modern weapons.

Each Jibaro household is ruled absolutely by the father. There are no chiefs, only war leaders, and the nearest approach to justice exists within clan groups, which adhere to the rule of an eye for an eye. A violent death in one household deserves a death in the household of the killer, and revenge is undertaken without remorse. "He has killed himself" is the saying.

Among distinct clans there is neither law nor justice and but one custom: war to extermination. Cause for war and the taking of heads is eagerly sought and easily found. When a family member becomes ill, witchcraft is regularly blamed. If death ensues, divination is resorted to, which in turn confirms suspicion. With the offending wizard identified and subsequently murdered, a blood feud is initiated or renewed. A raiding party sets out with the objective of taking an enemy stronghold by surprise. Honor figures not at all in this, for it would only obstruct efficient killing and the joyful taking of heads. After much elaborate cutting, scraping, heating in hot sand, and sewing back together, the tsantsas, or shrunken heads, for which the Jibaro are notorious, are produced. Home again, a feast rewards their efforts, and to protect the victorious warriors from the revengeful spirits of the slain, the headman blows a mixture of tobacco juice and saliva through the nostrils of the shrunken heads. Meanwhile, a counterexpedition may already be setting out, bent on blood. So, without benefit of law or mitigating custom, the Jibaro go their grim and dwindling way.

Such institutionalized lawlessness is by no means limited to the Indian past or the jungles of South America. Until very recently, elaborate ritual lent a glamorous tone to the Albanian blood feud. Within a family, an injury to one was taken as an injury to the entire clan, and the burden of revenge fell on all. To maintain the spirit of revenge, the relatives might sit glaring at a bottle of blood. Hopefully, they would at last cock their skullcaps over one ear for resolution, seize their guns, and set out to kill. If their blood failed to boil, blood money might be accepted, but usually the murderer was hunted. Meanwhile, the killer made no bones of his deed. He went about the usual business of farming, though taking the precaution not to answer a knock on his door. At night he would sleep on the second floor, while the women slept below. In the fields he might dress in women's clothes, for women were forbidden as victims of revenge. As a rule, the formula was biblical, "'one for one," but sometimes double revenge was taken, and as often as not, this perpetuated the feud. The victim need not be the murderer so long as he was a member of the murderer's family, but he must not be too old or feeble-minded or too frail to carry a gun. To kill such as these would be to lose caste. Neither could he be a child, fifteen to twenty years being the usual cut-off age for victims. Sometimes a time limit was set for retaliation, in which case it was imperative that the murderer quickly inform members of his family of his crime so that they could be prepared to protect themselves.

Here indeed were elaborate and predetermined rules of conduct, but scarcely the impartial social agency to enforce them. Often, justice was rough indeed. For example, in one community the custom was to allow revenge within twenty-four hours of the crime; that is, during a period of "boiling blood." A man of one family promised a shepherd of another a rifle cartridge if he found a lost lamb. The lamb in due course was found, but the cartridge was withheld, so enraging the shepherd that he murdered the lamb's owner. All this took place on Easter Eve, and the following day both brotherhoods converged for the Easter festival. Blood of course was boiling, and within an hour, fourteen men had died for the sake of a single cartridge.

Slaughter was not the only solution to the Albanian blood feud. Blood often cooled. Public opinion might press for reconciliation, especially if the original homicide had been accidental. Then the murderer might go silently to the house of the aggrieved. If a cup of coffee was offered him by his host, it meant that blood money would be accepted as indemnity. But if the murderer was turned away, the feud was on. Then the murderer had to either stand his ground or accept voluntary exile, an act that branded him a coward and saw his goods dispersed and his house burned. At times a crime might be so vile as to enrage the community beyond family limits. In such a case the criminal could be forced to set the torch to his own home, saying, "On my head be the ill luck of the village and tribe." Then, like the scapegoat of old, he would be drummed by Gypsies to the frontier, never to return.

More primitive, and yet more civilized, is the drumming practiced by the Tiv tribesmen of central Nigeria. Here, when a dispute arose among family or tribe, the aggrieved would begin to beat a drum at night, and when this attracted attention he would begin to sing his complaint. Presently, his opponent would drum and sing a rebuttal. If either man tired or felt his imagination for scandal failing, he hired a songmaker to prepare scurrilous songs. Night after night the contest proceeded, enhanced by home-brewed beer furnished by the opponents to attract supporters and dancers. Such tuneful contests at slander sometimes went on for two weeks or more, and usually ended in a fight or free-for-all, with the winner in fact being the winner in principle as well. More recently, it has been customary for the district officer to finally take notice of the tumult and persuade the local chief to get the musical factions together and settle the matter.

CHAPTER TWO

Civilizing the Law

PRIMITIVE CULTURES, EXISTING TODAY AND IN THE PAST, HAVE RELIED
upon strength of arm, speed of wit, religion, custom, and sometimes
law to achieve order. No modern state today exists without
written laws demanding certain patterns of behavior, courts to
apply the law to the facts of each disorderly situation, and some
court- or state-directed agency with the coercive power to see that
the judgments of the court are carried out. Coercive power is as
old as the fist. Some forms of tribal court or council must be nearly
as old as human speech. A zoologist might fairly see it in the conduct of baboons; but what is relatively recent, and the possession
of civilized man alone, is recorded law.

Perhaps the earliest fragment of written law to be preserved are
the Laws of Lipit-Istar, King of Isin, circa 1800 B.C. Four of the
first six provisions form an interesting and one-sided view of
domestic relations in this Sumerian kingdom:

> If a son says to his father, "Thou art not my father," he may shave
> him, he may put the slave-mark on him (and) sell him.
> If a son says to his mother, "Thou art not my mother," they shall
> shave half his head and lead him round the city and put him out of
> the house.
> If a wife has hated her husband and says, "Thou art not my hus-

18

band," they shall throw her into the river. (Bear in mind that very few of these ladies could swim.)

If a husband says to his wife, "Thou art not my wife," he shall pay one half maneh of silver by weight.

The most famous of the early legal writings dates from about a hundred years later. It comes from Babylonia and is known as the Code of Hammurabi. The code was unearthed at Susa and comprised 3,600 lines of cuneiform writing cut into a diorite column. Harsh and uncompromising, it had an eye-for-an-eye justice, which was repeated in the Bible. At least the potential offender, if he was literate, should have harbored no illusions about the consequences of his conduct. A few of the more illuminating provisions follow:

> I, Hammu-rabi the shepherd, called of Illil, who gathers together abundance and plenty, who accomplishes everything for Nippur, "bond of heaven," the reverent [prince] who cares for Ekur, the able king, restorer of Eridu, cleanser of the shrine of Eabzu, who has stormed the four quarters [of the world], who magnifies the fame of Babylon, who gladdens the heart of Marduk his lord . . .

It continues on in this vein for several of our pages, without pause or period, and concludes as follows:

> . . . when Marduk commanded me to give justice to the people of the land and to let [them] have [good] governance, I set forth truth and justice throughout the land [and] prospered the people . . . at that time:
>
> 1. If a man has accused a man and has charged him with manslaughter and then has not proved [it against] him, the accuser shall be put to death.
>
> 2. If a man has charged a man with sorcery and then has not proved [it against him], he who is charged with the sorcery shall go to the holy river; he shall leap into the holy river and, if the holy river overwhelms him, his accuser shall take and keep his house; if the holy river proves the man clear [of the offense] and he comes back safe, he who has charged him with sorcery shall be put to death; he who leapt into the holy river shall take and keep the house of the

accuser. [This provision constitutes an interesting parallel to trial by ordeal, which was a staple in the courts of Europe during the Middle Ages.]

7. If a man buys silver or gold or slave or slave-girl or ox or sheep or ass or anything else whatsoever from a free man's son or a free man's slave or has received [them] from safe custody without witnesses or contract, that man is a thief; he shall be put to death. [Punishments were uniformly severe and corporal. Imprisonment did not develop until much later times and even then was not popular.]

14. If a man kidnaps the infant [son] of a [free] man, he shall be put to death.

21. If a man has broken into a house, they shall put him to death and hang him before the breach which he has made. [Clearly not only vengeance, but the deterrent effect upon others is here intended.]

53. If a man has been slack in maintaining [the bank of] his [field] and has not maintained [his] bank and then a breach has occurred in his [bank], and so he has let the waters carry away [the soil on] the water-land, the man in whose bank the breach has occurred shall replace the corn which he has [caused to be] lost. If he is not able to replace the corn, he and his goods shall be sold and the tenants of the water-land, whose sesame the waters have carried away, shall divide [the sum to be obtained]. . . .[1]

A landmark English case, *Rylands v. Fletcher*,[2] decided in 1868, offers an interesting parallel to the above. Defendants were millowners who, without any negligence on their part (negligence is implied above), constructed a reservoir. The water from the reservoir broke into an abandoned mine, passed through, and flooded the plaintiff's adjacent coal mine. The defendant in this case, although free of blame, was held liable for damages to the plaintiff on the theory that one who collects on his property anything that, if it escapes, is likely to do mischief, must keep it at his peril. Subsequently the decision has been narrowed in its application and generally applied only when the nature of the activity is inherently dangerous, such as the transportation and use of high explosives, and the like.

Ancient Greece, cradle of democracy and the civilization to which we are inclined to trace our cultural roots, has left very little in the way of recorded laws. Much, however, can be gleaned from its literature and mythology. King Minos of Crete, for instance, has come down to us as a great judge and framer of laws, though no contemporary records remain. Draco, an Athenian lawgiver of the seventh century B.C., set out so severe a code of laws that the word "draconian" means harsh or cruel, and is still in popular use. Preserved in stone are certain "Profane and Sacred Laws," together with the family laws of the city of Gortyn in Crete from 400 B.C. Surviving orations furnish further legal evidence, but no comprehensive code or body of law survives.

More important than her laws of conduct was Greece's democratic contribution to legal procedure, for with Solon (639–559 B.C.) began the popular court of Athens. Formerly, justice had been in the hands of the sovereign and his appointed officials, but Athens introduced what might be called a jury system. It was in many ways more democratic than our own, and subject to the same virtues and vices. The most famous case so tried was that of the philosopher Socrates, who was accused in 399 B.C. of worshiping new gods and corrupting the minds of the young. This was a time of Spartan supremacy in Greece. It was a period of political and religious chauvinism, much like the McCarthy era in the United States, and old laws prohibiting impiety had just been revitalized. Though ill defined, impiety was a capital crime.

At each such trial, as many as 5,000 jurors were present. In Socrates' case, there were 501 in loud attendance. Pay was less than that of a day laborer, and the general intelligence of the unruly mob was low and subject to waves of prejudice. All trials were limited to one day, and when the single session was over, the jury did not retire for deliberation, but voted by passing between two large amphorae. One received counters indicating guilt, the other innocence, and a tabulation was immediately made and a verdict rendered.

During the trial proper, the prosecutors, who were Socrates' original accusers and subject to heavy penalties should their cause prove frivolous, presented evidence in the form of affidavits prepared before a magistrate at a preliminary hearing. Witnesses testified only to authenticate their oaths and could not be cross-examined. As defendant, however, Socrates could interrogate his accusers. He could also bring witnesses in his defense, though actually he called but one. Primarily he spoke alone in his behalf, calling on friends in the audience to attest to the truth of his words. With the evidence and arguments complete, the jury voted 281 to 220 against him. This meant guilty. However, the defendant was always entitled to propose an alternative to the death penalty. Normally this would be banishment, which in the case of a close vote followed almost automatically. But Socrates, unlike two other famous martyrs, Jesus and Joan of Arc, experienced no misgivings on the way to death. At first he humorously proposed that his penalty should be free board for life in the city hall. Then, hardly more serious, he suggested a fine of thirty minae, by today's measure about five hundred dollars. Such mockery achieved the inevitable result, and this time the death penalty was voted overwhelmingly. There was no appeal under Athenian law, and usually execution followed immediately. On this occasion, all executions were suspended while the city awaited the return of a sacred boat from the island of Delos. Socrates was to spend thirty days in prison, during which time an escape plan by friends was developed and declined. Socrates reasoned that he had transgressed only improper laws; if he fled, he would violate the obligations of a citizen and for the first time be guilty of a crime against the city. So the ship returned, and Socrates accepted his self-inflicted death, a draft of hemlock, with his usual composure.

Across the Mediterranean, laws were developing among the tribes of Israel, based on a nomadic background wherein conduct responded to custom, religion, and patriarchal command. The first efforts at codification are recorded in the Bible, Exodus 20–23, and have to do with the covenant, religious matters, theft of property, and violence punishable by death. In content and tone they are reminiscent of the thousand-years-older Code of Hammurabi, and there can be little doubt that they were also influenced by the more advanced civilizations of Babylon and the Canaanites.

The way administration of law changed can to some extent be gleaned from the Bible. In earlier times the elders, made up of tribe and family leaders, served as judges in criminal cases. They held informal court in the open air, with both sides pleading their case under oath. Bearing false witness was harshly punished. Over the years the priests, whose original function was to keep the sanctuary, assumed a more political aspect and took over the elders' role in court. With the development of a settled state, during the years of Greek domination, the king became a supreme court of appeal, rendering decisions in Solomon's hall of judgment. When the Roman Empire took over from the Greeks, a council of leading men, the Sanhedrin, administered Hebrew justice in the local courts, their jurisdiction being limited to religious crimes.

Throughout this turbulent millennium, during which Israel rose to statehood, then fell under the sway of numerous conquerors, the rabbis preserved a growing legal tradition, verbal at first and then written, which in A.D. 600, long after a Jewish nation had ceased to exist, resulted in the Talmud. The Talmud, comprising the Mishna, or oral law, and the Gemara, a commentary on the Mishna, was preserved through the centuries of exile as the spirit of a personal religious law. It remains an influence in modern Israel.

What of Hebrew crime and punishment? From the beginning, crimes fell into three categories: (1) injury to property, such as theft; (2) injury to persons, which ran the gamut from lying and bearing false witness to manslaughter and murder; (3) offenses against the moral order, which included blasphemy, adultery, prostitution, and the like. Punishment, as in the Code of Hammurabi, was based on the idea of strict retribution with the goal of deterrence and the extirpation of evil. Capital punishment was commonplace, and the method normally was public stoning. Then the Romans introduced death by hanging and the sword, not to mention crucifixion, an oriental adaptation reserved for the vilest criminals. From the torment of crucifixion Roman citizens were exempt. Lesser punishments involved beating, usually with a cat-o'-nine-tails type of flail, its thongs armed with bits of lead, which was called a scorpion. Slaves were commonly branded. Imprisonment was unknown or rare in the early days but appeared toward the end of the Empire. Fines were unknown, but restitution in kind fitted very well under the notion of "an eye for an eye."

As in Greek legal history, so with the ancient Hebrews one

judgment alone has been remembered in detail: the trial and punishment of Jesus Christ for high treason. As with Socrates, the background was prejudicial, for the Roman province was threatened by seething Jewish nationalism. Thousands of rebellious Jews had already been crucified. Socrates had been disposed of on religious grounds for political reasons; Jesus was tried on political grounds for religious motives. On the one hand was the conservative aristocracy of the Sadduccees, who were comfortably satisfied with the Roman system and opposed to the persistent notions of a Messiah who would reestablish the old ways. On the other hand, supporting such notions, were the Zealots and, less fanatically, the Pharisees, who regarded the coming Messiah as an earthly king of the line of David, who would restore Israel to political power. Whether or not Jesus saw himself in this militant light or as a purely spiritual force, his arrival in Jerusalem for the Passover feast was variously anticipated, and after he caused a disturbance in the forecourt of the temple by overturning the tables of the money changers, he was quickly arrested and brought to trial before a quorum of the Sanhedrin. As mentioned, their jurisdiction was limited to religious crimes. To establish guilt, two agreeing witnesses were necessary, and Jesus, knowing the practice of hiding eavesdroppers (a practice anticipating our electronic microphones), kept silent. Nonetheless, two witnesses were eventually found who testified that Jesus had said he would destroy the temple and rebuild it "without hands" within three days. This alone did not constitute blasphemy, a technical crime amounting to an insult to the majesty of God, so Caiaphas asked Jesus outright whether he was the Messiah. Rather than deny his mission, Jesus replied, "I am he." This still fell short of the capital crime desired by his accusers. When further questioned, Jesus refused to say "Jahweh," the sacred name of God revealed to Moses, but continued to refer only to "the Power." Sufficient evidence to convict on religious grounds was lacking, though such a judgment would have received the rubber-stamp approval of the Romans and a sentence of stoning by the mob. Instead, Jesus was turned over to Pilate, and the Romans then tried him for treason under their statutes. At this time Roman law provided elaborate guarantees of fair trial, but such niceties were reserved for Roman citizens. So Pilate tried Jesus summarily, and the conviction hung upon one question: did Jesus regard himself as king of the Jews? Jesus remained silent. His refusal to comment was taken as an admission of guilt; and Pilate surrendered him to the soldiers.

A curious footnote to the story of the crucifixion has always been the detail of calling on the crowd to choose one criminal for release at Passover. Apart from the biblical account of the release of Barabbas, there is no authority for such a practice, and it seems unlikely that the Romans would have risked the escape of a known and dangerous revolutionary.

Long before the crucifixion of Jesus, Roman law had reached its first flower. By 753 B.C., Rome was already a primitive monarchy, but her great legal contribution to future ages began during the Republic, approximately 450 B.C., with the Twelve Tables. These constituted a kind of Magna Carta which regulated relations between patricians and plebeians, the upper and lower classes. Although most of these statutes were destroyed when Gaul sacked Rome, a number remain, and they are sufficient to indicate a wide range of legal attitudes. Some were very primitive, such as "Law LXVIII: Whoever casts an evil spell or puts a spell upon crops shall be restrained," somewhat anticipatory of the yet unthought-of Inquisition. Some were sternly patriarchal and reminiscent of Hammurabi: "Law I: Sons shall be under the jurisdiction of the father"; and "Law XLIII: Women shall not lacerate their cheeks; nor shall they lament at funerals." Others were surprisingly modern: "Law XIII: No one shall exact interest at more than a twelfth of the principal yearly"; and "Law XXVII: If a person is insane, there shall be jurisdiction over him and his finances by his relatives and kinsmen." Of ominous portent for future times was "Law LXIII: The charge of treason is punishable by death." [3] Fair enough on its face, perhaps, the meaning of treason would later be interpreted by Ulpian, a third-century Roman jurist, to mean acting with hostile intention against the state or emperor. This would come to include any criticism, direct or in veiled satirical form, so that under the emperors, free speech and press as we think of them today virtually disappeared.

Civil actions under the developing Roman system would begin with a praetor if the parties to the action were citizens. If the parties were peregrines, that is, free people but not Roman citizens, the jurisdiction lay with a peregrine praetor. If the praetor deemed the action worthy of adjudication, he would issue a formula containing a statement of the question to be tried. An example of this would be, "Let Marcus Brutus be judge. If it seems that Romulus ought to pay Remus ten Didrachms and there has been in the case no fraud on the part of Remus, for the ten Didrachms condemn Romulus to Remus; if any fraud does appear, absolve Romulus." Thus the praetor would set out the law of the case, and the judge, who might be any citizen, could hear the facts from both sides without any clear rules of evidence and render his decision like a jury of one empowered to give execution. In the early days a successful plaintiff had to obtain his awarded damages personally. Often the convicted party would not comply, so it became the practice for the plaintiff to appeal to the praetor again and bring an action of the judgment whereby the debtor might be imprisoned and his property sold.

Under the early praetor system, each praetor framed his own law, and the pressure to match a case to earlier similar cases, which we call case precedent, scarcely existed. However, with the philosophical influence of Greece and the development of a legal tradition, digests were kept and complex legal situations considered. An example from Digest II, considering such modern doctrines as negligence and assumption of risk, goes as follows:

> Mela says, if some people were playing a ball game and someone knocked the ball harder than usual and sent it against a barber's hand, so that a slave under the barber's hand had his throat cut by a jerk of the blade, that the action lies against whoever was to blame. Proculus says it is the barber; and certainly if he was shaving people in a place where people normally played games and where many people passed by, the blame is his; but one might also reason that a man who commits himself to a barber who has his chair in a hazardous place can only blame himself.

The criminal law was slow to develop, for the praetor could deal summarily with anything he regarded as infringing on state interests. It was not until the last century B.C. that written codes were set down defining various crimes, and even then discretion filled in the gaps. Although this method continued for the lower classes, under Greek influence a kind of jury system evolved, with the Senate trying aristocrats for treason. The usual criminal courts became the so-called standing-jury courts, each one dealing with a particular statutory crime. These juries were large, and the verdict of the majority was binding, without appeal. The court had no discretion regarding the sentence, which was set out in the statute.

During the early Republic, penalties were simple and generally mild, usually the payment of a fine. If the offense was serious, beheading could be avoided by the standard practice of going into exile, forfeiting both property and citizenship. With the Empire, penalties became diversified and often savage. Possibilities included labor in the mines or becoming a gladiator, with even crueler methods, such as crucifixion, reserved for noncitizens. Patricians often avoided trial altogether by suicide. This was considered honorable, and it prevented confiscation of the criminal's property, which followed as a natural consequence of a guilty verdict.

Apart from the procedural laws, at the heart of Roman substantive rights was the law of status. This began in the family with the *pater familias,* the all-powerful father who alone held property and, in early Republican times, the power of life and death within the family. He could decide whether a newborn child would be reared or exposed to die. This strict concentration of rights, stemming from early peasant community life, dissipated somewhat with the Empire, and practices such as *filius familias* developed, which allowed even a slave to administer family funds.

Outside the family, rights were caste oriented. At the top of the privileged scale were the freeborn Roman citizens, with senators and important soldiers at the pinnacle. Beneath them were the citizens by adoption, the freeborn noncitizen, manumitted slaves, and slaves. A good example of how this pigeonholing of caste affected rights occurred in the case of death resulting from a wrestling or boxing match. A slave could be prosecuted, but not so a citizen. The damage was held in the citizen's case to have been done for the sake of valor and glory, virtues considered totally alien to the role of slave.

This does not mean that the role of slave was all bad. Although a father had the right of life and death over his sons, to kill his slave was murder, and slaves in important houses achieved such high positions of trust—as accountants, for example—that freemen often willingly passed into slavery to gain these posts. Education for slaves was also encouraged, and often they amassed considerable fortunes before being manumitted.

One interesting legal doctrine operating between status equals and related to our currently controversial "good Samaritan" law, was that of negotiorum gestio. This implied that in another's absence a friend might gratuitously announce himself as his agent and take steps in his behalf, such as repairing his roof after a storm or giving medical aid to his slave, and expect compensation for these unasked-for deeds. This practice was common during the Republic, but with the Empire, gratuitous services between equals and the paid services of inferiors began to merge under the law.

Roman law as a living force today is not an adaptation of the law as it was applied during the years of the Republic and the early Empire, but a result of the later imperial codifications during Rome's decline. Christians, during the first centuries of the movement, were considered mali homines (wicked men); they had few rights and were occasionally persecuted. The major codifications began with Constantine the Great (A.D. 288–337), who established the Council of Nicaea. They were largely motivated by a desire to bring the Christian faith into power. Emperor Theodosius II published a code in A.D. 438 which, among other matters, defined the judicial authority of Catholic bishops and thus pushed the church further along the road to authority over the law. But the code that is remembered today is that of Flavius Anicius Justinianus, known as Justinian, who succeeded to the throne in Constantinople in A.D. 527. He appointed a commission led by the jurist Tribonian to collect and organize the Roman laws. The ponderous result of these labors was Corpus Juris Civilis, made up of four parts. First was the Codex, setting out imperial constitutions since the time of Hadrian. Second came the Digest, taking selections from classical jurists such as Paulus Ulpian. The *Institutes* based on the work of Gaius followed, and finally there were the *Novellae*, comprising later additions to the Code.

A prime function of the Justinian Code was religious, bolstering the Church, and the third preface stated,

> We order all those who follow this law to assume the name of Catholic Christians, and consider others as demented or insane. We order that they shall bear the infamy of heresy; and when the Divine vengeance which they merit has been appeased, they shall afterwards be punished in accordance with our resentment, which we have acquired from the judgment of Heaven.

Thus the compilation by Justinian was an artificial creation of Roman scholarship and not the functioning law of the Empire. It remains the essential legacy of Roman law, which can be traced through the Middle Ages to the present, and it is reflected in the Code Napoléon of France, for which it was a model.

With the collapse and splintering of the Roman Empire, the Code survived in the Eastern Empire and in the monastic libraries of western Europe. Occasionally it was adapted by energetic kings, as in the Visigothic codes of the sixth century A.D. Here the preamble is startlingly philosophical for an age considered barbaric. Subtitle II outlines how the lawmaker should conduct himself: "The maker of laws should not practice disputation, but should administer justice. Nor is it fitting that he should appear to have framed the law by contention, but in an orderly manner. For the transaction of public affairs does not demand, as a reward of labors, the clamor of theatrical applause, but the law destined for the salvation of the people." A definition of the law follows. "The law is the rival of divinity; the oracle of religion; the source of instruction; the artificer of right; the guardian and promoter of good morals; the rudder of the state; the messenger of justice; the mistress of life; the soul of the body politic." Down-to-earth, practical, and current reasons for laws are then given: "That human wickedness may be restrained through fear of their execution; that the lives of innocent men may be safe among criminals; and that the temptation to commit wrong may be restrained by the fear of punishment." [4]

Couched in a less serious vein was a short medieval digest supposedly written by a judge called Caratnia the Scarred and brought into question by King Conn of the Hundred Battles. A few examples read as follows:

[Section 4] "I decided a bondwoman wife must share the cost of her child's upbringing." "You decided wrongly," said Conn. "I did it wisely, for the child's father was himself a bondman."

[Section 19] "I decided harm by an animal is payable like harm by a human." "You decided wrongly." "I did it wisely, for here the animal had been kept by its owner after once doing harm and was notoriously vicious."

[Section 46] "I decided, for a bard's song composed on the spot and therefore inadequate, the regular fee must be paid." "You decided wrongly." "I did it wisely, for this was a song to invoke magic and must therefore be extemporized."

[Section 51] "I decided, no head-money is payable for a treacherous killing." "You decided wrongly." "I did it wisely, for here there was a set-off for seven deeds of violence on the other side." [5] [This latter seems to anticipate the Albanian blood feuds.]

With the gradual emergence of Europe into more settled times and the growth of commerce in the Middle Ages, the Code of Justinian became once again the living law of continental Europe. In the eighteenth century, Robert Joseph Pothier (1699–1772) began a reunification of the law, taking the Code of Justinian and blending it with French customary law and the philosophy of natural law. This monumental work was continued into the nineteenth century by Jacques Régis Cambacérès and resulted in the French Civil Code of Napoleon (1804), which exists in France to this day and which has become the model for other European countries.

An influence upon the law equal to that of Rome during the Middle Ages was the Roman Catholic Church. Politically, the Pope manipulated kings and barons through papal decrees and excommunications, just as he stimulated the Crusades. Legally, there was the Inquisition, devoted to the punishment of heretics and persons guilty of offense against the Catholic orthodoxy. Authority could be found in Deuteronomy, which provided for stoning those who abandoned the true faith. Occasional heretics were burned during the latter days of the Holy Roman Empire, but it was Pope Innocent III, in 1198, who gave life to the antiheretical movement in the secular world. His successor, Pope Gregory, announced his intention of employing friars to travel throughout Europe to discover heresy and repress it. So the Inquisition began to travel, and continued to do so for the better part of six hundred years, until Napoleon conquered Spain in 1808 and extinguished its last vestiges.

The right of the individual to fair trial is a major concern of democratic governments today, and there is no better example of the evils that can follow the loss of such a right than the methods used by the court of the Inquisition. Bound by no ordinary rules of procedure, the court could imprison on suspicion, and the guilt of the defendant was presumed from the start. The judge was also the accuser, and the names of those who had denounced the defendant were withheld. Women, children, and slaves could be brought as witnesses by the prosecution, but could not speak for the defendant. If the defendant refused to give evidence, he was treated as a heretic. He might become reconciled with the Church if he denounced his alleged accomplices and confessed his guilt, a process encouraged by torture. An interesting canonical law indicated that torture could only be applied once, but no time limit was set. To ensure cooperation, witnesses, too, might be tortured. Needless to say, the Church ran up an admirable rate of convictions. If confession was achieved, the defendant might be let off with due penance or public scourging. If he remained impenitent, the Church would not want to bloody its hands. As had been done with Jesus, he was turned over to a secular judge who rubber-stamped him along to the stake.

Originally, such convictions were infrequent. But when it became customary for the court to confiscate the worldly goods of heretics, the incentive to convict was ensured, and the Inquisition moved into high gear. When heresy was largely weeded out, the Inquisition turned to sorcery, and in Spain, where the Church felt itself threatened by other established religions, such as Islam and Judaism, these, too, were purged.

Though the Inquisition is usually associated with Spain for its excesses, it was in France that the most famous trial took place, that of Joan of Arc. Like the cases of Socrates and Jesus before her, the trial was politically as well as religiously motivated, with even less chance of the defendant's getting off. For centuries England and France had been battling over Continental territories. How an international court might have settled their claims no one will ever know. Geographically France had the stronger claim but, until the arrival of Joan, the less inspired army. With Joan's faith, the tide of battle turned against the English, and when she was captured they wanted her dead, either as a heretic before the court of the Inquisition, or, failing this, as a witch convicted by their own military court. The Inquisition, led by Couchon, Bishop of Beauvais and Grand Inquisitor of France, rose to the occasion. Joan had no counsel, and her admission that she had responded to divine voices was taken as private revelation and against the judgment of God's representatives on earth—in a word, heresy. Faced with death by fire, she did briefly recant, but under pressure and the threat of life in solitary confinement, again asserted her personal faith. Wearing a paper cap shaped like a bishop's miter inscribed, "Heretic relapse, apostate, idolatress," she went to the flames calling on Jesus. In 1456, over twenty years after her death, the Inquisition repudiated its own trial, set Joan on the road to sainthood, and thereby wrote its own death warrant in France.

Religion's involvement with the law was by no means limited to the Inquisition, but entered into purely personal contests. Accused and accuser might direct their appeal to God and stand before the cross, arms lifted, while a divine service was performed; the judgment went to him who could keep his arms aloft longest. Ordeal by fire and water was a more widespread practice. The very elements involved, water for the Deluge and fire for the Day of Judgment, implied divine approval. The normal procedure was for the accused to find a small pebble within a caldron of boiling water. After the plunge, the hand would be enveloped in a cloth and sealed with the judge's signet, to be unwrapped again within three days. Guilt or innocence was determined by the condition of the hand.

Although England was somewhat isolated from the mainstream of the Inquisition and Church influence, the ordeal was for some time a fixture in criminal trials. In English procedure it is customary for the clerk to ask the defendant whether he pleads guilty or not guilty. Upon a plea of not guilty, the clerk formerly would ask further, "And how will you be tried?" to which the correct response was, "By God and my country." In its original form, this answer went back to a time when the defendant had a choice, God or his country, meaning the ordeal or a jury trial. If the defendant settled for the ordeal, he might have to walk barefoot over scalding plowstones or be thrown into a lake. Curiously, if he floated to the top, he was being rejected by the element and was guilty. A demonstration of innocence was scarcely more satisfying, but it is to be assumed that after a reasonable submersion he would be pulled out and perhaps resuscitated.

In early times, to be tried "by my country" was quite rare and obtainable only on payment of a fee to the king. In A.D. 1215, Pope Innocent III ordered the clergy to stop giving religious sanction to the ordeal, and with this decision use of the ordeal quickly diminished, leaving no alternative to jury trial in England. A problem developed when the defendant refused to plead at all. Shorn of the ordeal, the jury had to deal with a mute defendant somehow, and it was left to them to decide whether his silence came from malice or the visitation of God. If the latter, the trial was allowed to proceed; otherwise the defendant went to prison to think it over. If he thought too long, he would starve to death, for no food was provided. Sometimes, to encourage a decision, weights sufficient to kill were laid on his body until he pleaded guilty or not guilty, or until he died. Many men chose death, not through pure stubbornness but with the same motive as the Romans who committed suicide rather than stand trial: a guilty verdict would forfeit his worldly goods to the crown; a silent death before trial would leave them to his family.

Although the ordeal, having lost its religious sanction, died out centuries ago in Europe, it has not entirely disappeared. In Liberia there remains the trial by sasswood, during which the accused drinks a draft made deadly by the poisonous sasswood bark. Theoretically the poison will catch the guilty; if innocent, the stomach will acquit. And there is a core of psychological sense in this, for the innocent person may drink with eager confidence and quickly throw up the lethal dose, while the guilty may sip slowly, absorb the poison, and die.

A savage practice popular among the Germanic tribes of the Dark Ages and given religious sanction and ritual by the Church was the wager of battle. From the time of David and Goliath, God presumably had decided such affairs in favor of the right, and so trial by combat spread throughout Europe at the expense of more civilized adjudication. It was unknown in Anglo-Saxon England, but William brought it along with his Conquest.

As a legal recourse it came to be used in matters both civil and criminal. Property claims were settled by the sword, and in any criminal proceeding the defendant might claim perjury and exclaim, "Thou hast lied against me. Grant me the single combat, and let God make manifest whether thou hast sworn true or false." Nor was this an institution reserved for the aristocracy. It was regular practice for a trained and royally employed champion to encounter common robbers in single combat. If their predictable drubbing was not itself fatal, they were hanged. Some few might claim exemption from the lists. Men of the cloth, women, and those who were physically incapable might resort to other justice or seek a champion. Even here there were exceptions. What, for instance, physically exempted a male? The loss of a limb, debilitating illness, old age, extreme youth, surely; but what if his only claim to unfitness was missing teeth? Clinging to legality in the midst of madness, at least one court decided that the lack of a molar was no excuse, but the lack of incisors, since they might be considered weapons of offense, was sufficient cause.

Then, too, there are thirteenth-century records in Germany of women taking part in such trials. The system was elaborately thought out and handicapped. Her male opponent was made to stand in a pit three feet wide with his left hand behind his back. His armament consisted of three clubs; she had three rocks fastened to ropes. Once the fight began, if the man, in delivering a blow, touched hand or arm to earth, he lost a club. After three such blunders he was adjudged defeated and the woman could order his execution. On the woman's part, each time she struck the man while disarmed she also lost a weapon, and if she lost all three she could be buried alive.

A more usual recourse was to a substitute, gratuitous and reminiscent of Ivanhoe in some cases, but more often a hired killer. In the early days a gentleman might volunteer to fight for honor and the right in behalf of a lady or the Church. Such was the case when the Priory of Tynemouth's ownership of a certain manor was questioned by a neighbor, Gerard de Widdrington. The priory called on Sir Thomas Colville to champion its claim, and so feared was his challenge, the manor went to the priory by default.

More common was the professional champion, a hired ruffian who ran the risk of losing hand or foot, the immemorial punishment for perjury, should his talent in battle fail. By the thirteenth century, in fact, the occupation of champion was so undesirable that they were deprived of the right to bear witness or to inherit property.

Once wager of battle was decided upon, time was set aside to train for the contest and to put one's affairs in order. Usually a month or more passed before the appointed day. This was time enough in which to vanish, but if one did fail to appear, shame, banishment, and the confiscation of possessions followed. Even the natural death of a contestant was frowned upon. In the Scottish Marches, if a man died before the contest the body had to be brought to the field, for "no man can essoin himself by death" (excuse oneself for not appearing).

Once the contestants were on the field, an oath was repeated, somewhat as follows:

"Hear ye, justices, I have this day neither eaten nor drunk, nor have I upon me any enchantment or sorcery through which the power of God may be increased or diminished and the devil's power increased, and that my cause is true, so help me God and his saints."

Yet attempts to influence God's judgment were common. In 1355, when the Earl of Salisbury and the Bishop of Salisbury contested the ownership of a castle, the champions were examined before the contest, and it had to be aborted when charms and prayers were found inside the armor of the Bishop's man. Judgment went to the Earl.

Initially, a choice of weapons was allowed to the appellant, but as sentiment became hostile to wager of battle, the choice shifted to the defendant, in the hope that such contests would thus be discouraged. Usually the fight took place bareheaded and on foot, with the contestants clad in tunics, simple gloves, and no defensive armor apart from a wooden buckler. Champions usually were assigned clubs only, but private individuals might resort to swords, and nobles often chose to fight on horseback. Even they were deprived of defensive armor apart from a wooden shield, though weapons of attack—lance, sword, or dagger—were available. When neither man was bested, the contest was called off at sunset or when the stars were first visible. Such a draw was decided in favor of the defendant, since no charge had been proved.

With death or dishonor at issue, chivalric courtesy was not expected, however noble the contestants. When Charles the Good of Flanders was murdered in 1127, a knight named Herman challenged one of the assassins, whose name was Guy. Both were noted warriors, and they chose to fight on horseback in the classic manner. Herman was promptly unhorsed with the lance, but resourcefully he managed to disable Guy's horse with his sword, after which they fought to exhaustion on foot. Finally Guy threw Herman down and leaped on him to deliver the death thrust, but Herman was ingenious to the end. With his last strength, he shot a gauntleted fist beneath his opponent's coat of mail, grasped and twisted off his scrotum, at which point Guy toppled over, gave up the ghost, and was adjudged guilty as charged.

If the loser survived in a trial by combat, other consequences followed. In a criminal case, a vanquished defendant would suffer the appropriate punishment, a vanquished plaintiff would be subject to the harsh penalties due perjury. Thus strength of arm, not justice, was weighed in the scales. Even when the issue began in a courtroom, fact-finding could at any time give way to the judgment of force, for a party seeing that the evidence was piling up against his cause could accuse an inconvenient witness of false swearing and challenge him to a fight, thereby throwing out the trial entirely. An honest litigation became virtually impossible, with witnesses challenged or intimidated before they even testified, so it is not surprising that church and king alike began to apply pressure to eradicate the practice.

By 1300, trial by combat had become rare, though it remained on the statutes in England until the trial of *Ashford v. Thornton* in 1817. Mary Ashford had been murdered, and Abraham Thornton, a large and formidable bricklayer, was brought to trial. He pleaded not guilty, ". . . and I am ready to defend the same with my body." Miss Ashford's only possible champion was her small, frail brother, who reasonably declined the challenge. In fact, Abraham Thornton was finally acquitted by a jury, and to avoid the repetition of such awkward situations, trial by battle was at last formally abolished.

Although the divinely and legally sanctioned trial by combat died early, its informal counterpart survived for centuries. Queen Elizabeth I of England tried to stamp it out by restricting the fencing schools. Oliver Cromwell made the acceptance of a challenge a crime punishable by six months in prison, but still the practice flourished. Among "gentlemen of honor" it blossomed with renewed vigor in the latter portion of the eighteenth century, when the dueling pistol was introduced. Although by this time to kill in a duel was legally murder, only two men were ever tried and executed, both in Ireland, and both because they fired before the signal was given, not because they had participated in a duel.

Based on the premise that "if a gentleman evades a justifiable call, he puts himself outside the pale of honour, and notification of this fact to honourable society produces his exclusion from it," an elaborate and compulsive extralegal code developed. Challenges were possible only among social equals, usually gentlemen too dignified to settle matters with their fists. When a man quailed at a challenge, however trivial its cause, his name was likely to be posted in his favorite club or coffeehouse as a coward; a kind of drumming the scandal. And causes were often trivial, if not absurd. In 1804 in Holland Park, Kensington, Lord Camelford was shot dead by one Lieutenant Best of the Royal Navy because his lordship had been tardy in removing his hat during the singing of "God Save the King" at a circus performance. The years made little difference. In 1840 on Wimbledon Common, Lord Cardigan, who later would lead the equally dubious charge of the Light Brigade at Balaclava, wounded Captain Harvey Tuckett. The issue at stake was whether Moselle wine should be served to the officers of the 11th Hussars in its own bottle or from a clear glass decanter.

The ritual of the duel itself was elaborate and well documented. The contest invariably took place at dawn. Each man had his attendant, called a second, and generally a doctor stood by. The pistols came from a matched pair and fired a lead ball of a specified size from a smooth-bored barrel of no more than ten inches in length. Rifling was a French practice that left too little to chance and was duly frowned upon. Experts differed widely on whether challenger or challenged should get off the first shot, or whether both should fire at the same time. A hit, however minor, usually ended the matter, and quite often as a token of reconciliation the guns were fired harmlessly into the ground. Should three fires take place without a hit, the seconds were usually empowered to hurry their principals away lest continued inaccuracy subject them to ridicule.

Upon occasion the shedding of blood was not enough. In 1830, two Philadelphia physicians fought for reasons neither reported nor remembered. At eight feet both missed on the first fire, but Dr. Jeffries was determined to fight to the death and managed on the second exchange to hit Dr. Smith in the arm. A respite was taken until Smith recovered himself, and on this fire Jeffries was wounded in the thigh. Following a last dizzy pause, the weakened combatants tottered to within six feet of each other and let fly once again. Smith fell dead on the spot, and Jeffries breathed only long enough to declare what a gentleman and one-time good friend his deceased opponent had been.

Less bloody but more famous was the duel between Alexander Hamilton and Aaron Burr. Business and political rivals, their mutual bitterness had developed over Burr's obtaining a charter for the Chase Manhattan Bank, which became a direct threat to Hamilton's banking interests. Later, Hamilton thwarted Burr's attempts to become President of the United States, and when in 1804 Hamilton called Burr a dangerous candidate for the governorship of New York State, Burr gave his challenge. Hamilton promptly borrowed a set of pistols from his friend Colonel John Church, a pair which two years before had brought about the death of Hamilton's son Philip in a duel. Weehawken, New Jersey, was chosen for the contest, and the parties rowed there at dawn on July 11. Ten paces were walked off, the men turned, Burr fired, and Hamilton, hit in the side, discharged his gun as he fell. It was the end for both men. Hamilton died the next day and Burr fled the city, his career ruined.

It was by no means the end for dueling, which flourished for another ninety years if one counts the romanticized Western shootouts, but resistance to the custom was growing. Causes were trifling at best. Fire-eating bravos were using the duel as an instrument of extortion. It had gone on too long. Even its adherents were growing bored. Why else but in a search for novelty did two Parisian dandies, for the love of a ballerina, elect to square off from balloons, as reported in the Paris newspapers of June 22, 1808:

A very modest wind was blowing from the northwest, and so far as could be determined the balloons kept about thirty meters apart. When they rose to a height of about nine hundred meters, M. le Pique discharged his blunderbuss without effect. Almost immediately the fire was returned by M. Granpree, thereby puncturing his adversary's balloon, with the result that it fell rapidly and M. le Pique and his second were dashed to bits on a rooftop.

The victorious Granpree descended at leisure some miles away, and it is to be presumed that the charming ballerina pirouetted into his arms.

But the applause was dying, and by 1826 a Mr. Mann of Andover was able to turn ridicule about in a written reply to the challenge of a fellow solicitor and bachelor named Fleet.

> I am honoured this day, Sir, with challenges two.
> The first from Friend Langdon, the second from you.
> The one is to fight and the other to dine
> I accept his "engagement" and yours must decline.
> And frankly my life be it never forgot
> Possesses a value which yours, Sir, does not.
> So I mean to preserve it as long as I can
> Being justly entitled a family man
> With three or four children, I scarce know how many
> Whilst you, Sir, have not (or ought not) to have any.
> Besides that, the contest would be too unequal
> I doubt not will plainly appear by the sequel
> For e'en you must acknowledge it would not be meet
> That one small Mann of war should engage a whole Fleet.

Still, courts were reluctant to prosecute. Duels dragged on, particularly among army officers, but the glory was gone from it. Very often the challenger now was ridiculed, and to kill in a duel, though still uncondemned in court, could mean social ostracism and cashierment from the service. Before 1860, dueling in the United States and England had died a natural death due to social pressure without major benefit from official law or its enforcement.

Perhaps if we are, as some anthropologists believe, descended from an extinct form of killer ape, then dueling might well be the proper, socialized expression of a natural instinct. Seeing more basic sense in the song duels of the Eskimo, one is inclined to hope otherwise, and put reliance on the courts of law.

CHAPTER THREE

Sources of Our Common Law

THE FIRST REMEMBERED SOURCES OF ENGLISH LAW ARE ROMAN. UNDER Roman influence, Britain emerged from barbarism during the first century A.D. It flourished for several civilizing centuries. Then, with Rome's decay, Britain held out briefly against Nordic invasion under such legendary leaders as Arthur. Although in Continental Europe the Holy Roman Empire kept its legal roots intact, Roman law in England gradually lapsed into disorder and illiteracy. All that survived of it was a blend of immemorial customs, dealt out separately and summarily by the lord of each manor. Roman texts survived in Continental monasteries, but in England very little was written down and less has survived. The earliest-known Anglo-Saxon laws were those of King Aethelbert, king of Kent, who was baptized by Augustine in A.D. 597 when Britain still had Roman ties. These laws were supplemented by the subsequent kings of Kent and compiled in a manuscript, *Textus Roffensis*, by Ernulf, Bishop of Rochester, between A.D. 1115 and 1125.

The following examples are typical, and about as sophisticated as laws ever became in those savage times:

If a man seize hold of the breast of a Ceorlish woman, let him make bot [payment] to her with five shillings: if he throw her down, and do not lie with her, let him make bot with ten shillings: if he lie with her, let him make bot with sixty shillings. If another man had before

41

lain with her, then let the bot be half that. If she be charged therewith, let her clear herself with sixty hides, or forfeit half the bot. If
this befal a woman more nobly born, let the bot increase according to
the Wer. [King Alfred, 11]

If a man strike out another's eye, let him pay him nine shillings,
and six shillings and six pennies, and a third part of a penny as bot.
If it remains in the head, and he cannot see aught therewith, let one-
third part of the bot be retained. [King Alfred, 47]

If a man strike out another's tooth in front of his head, let him make
bot for it with eight shillings; if it be the canine tooth, let four shillings
be paid as bot. A man's grinder [molar] is worth fifteen shillings.
[King Alfred, 49]

These codes go on at length, listing almost every type of injury
it is possible to inflict; noses and great toes struck off, windpipes
pierced. The loss of a fingernail was worth five shillings, a bruise,
nothing to the victim.

Overall order returned with King William I, who conquered the
Anglo-Saxon King Harold in 1066. His invading Normans brought
with them a kind of Roman gift for administration and a desire to
milk the vanquished for what they were worth. William held
court at Gloucester, and to facilitate the division of the land and
the apportionment of local contributions to his treasury, the Domes-
day Book was prepared by 1086. Besides the King's "Bench,"
William established other courts. The Exchequer was concerned
principally with finance, and for the purpose of enforcing royal
rights against royal vassals at local level there were circuit courts
called eyres. After a time they enforced not only the crown's fiscal
pleas but "common pleas" of the local people. The law applied at
this level was nominally the customary law as it had existed before
the Conquest, for William promised to his English subjects the
rights they held in the days when Edward the Confessor was
alive.

William I subjugated England, but it remained for Henry II,
crowned almost a hundred years later, to pull it out of feudalism.
Young Henry Plantagenet ascended the throne in 1154 to find
his land torn by anarchy, and the work of his conquering ancestor
largely undone. During a reign of over thirty years, Henry worked

tirelessly. He crushed the last purely feudal revolts, demolished unlicensed castles, and substituted a form of payment called "'shield money" for the old knightly service. Subsequently, he could hire mercenaries rather than rely on knightly loyalty.

In the area of law, his reforms were many and lasting. Previously the customary law had been strictly local; it was now strengthened by the uniform system of royal courts, the eyres, which moved on regular circuits throughout the country shires. During the twelfth and thirteenth centuries, these eyres, made up of royal judges, developed a primitive jury system by which sworn bodies of local people informed the court of the circumstances of a dispute. Questions were put to them, and they were sworn to give true answers upon which the court based its decisions. Although only testimony and not part of the court's judgment, it was from this practice that the jury verdict evolved, and it was from such testimony regarding local customs that the king's judges, meeting between circuits in London, began knitting various local customs into one enduring system of law.

A rare example of the interworking of local custom, juries, and the royal courts is a case reported in 1295, wherein one Joan, daughter of William of Alconbury, sued the local lord abbot for damages due to the appropriation of eight acres of land. The trial report reads as follows:

> The jurors say upon their oath that the said Joan was of full age according to the usage of the manor (when she surrendered the said land, and the full age of a woman is thirteen years and a half and the full age for males is fourteen years and a half) and that the said Joan has no right in the said land but it is the proper escheat of the lord abbot. Therefore it is considered that she take nothing by her writ, and be in mercy for the false plaint. She is pardoned on the ground of poverty.[1]

For a time, the old Anglo-Saxon local courts continued in operation, but they were gradually buried in such Norman tribunals as the seignorial courts, dealing with lord-and-vassal relations; the Curia Regis, law between the king and his personal vassals; not to mention the all-important royal courts of the common law and chancery (the royal secretariat), which were to assume a shifting balance of power in years to come.

The royal courts of the common law got a good one-hundred-year jump on chancery as far as making law was concerned, and the device employed for welding customs into common law was a document called a writ. When the royal judges agreed that a general rule of law could be distilled from a number of related customs, they let it be known that an order from the king addressed to a county sheriff would be issued commanding him to bring the complained-of party into the king's court on a certain day. The writ set out the principle of laws on which the case would be tried, and was issued via the royal chancery for a fixed fee. Where a situation was not covered by one of the writs, local custom prevailed, and if it was the habit in Cornwall to recover a stolen crumpet by personally lopping off the thief's head, no one could complain of it.

However, the common-law judges of the twelfth and thirteenth centuries were energetic in providing against such injustices. Writs by the hundreds were prepared, each one amounting to a law, giving damages to the plaintiff whenever he could fit the facts of his situation to the stipulations of a particular writ. The system was reminiscent of the early Roman praetorian system, but more rigid in practice. If a plaintiff had a valid grievance under one writ but carelessly brought his complaint under another one, he was thrown out of court.

At first, apart from the writs, there was little law reporting. Individual cases were forgotten, or only roughly recorded with so little system that they could rarely be referred to as sources for future decisions. Then Henry of Bracton, a judge on the King's Bench in the mid-thirteenth century, prepared his *De Legibus et Consuetudinibus Angliae* (*Concerning the Laws and Customs of England*) and this began a systematic approach to the rapidly emerging common law. Before the end of the century came the first annual reporting of cases, the "Year Books." Circulation was at first small, but the demand was great, and with the promulgation of the Year Books grew a belief that courts must follow former opinions dealing with the same set of facts unless overruled by a higher tribunal or by parliamentary legislation. The idea was to declare rather than make law, and it evolved into the rule of judicial precedent which is acknowledged, if often sidestepped, to this day.

By the end of the thirteenth century, the imaginations of the common-law judges began to lag. Few new writs appeared until impetus came from a fresh source, the King's Chancellor of the Exchequer. The exchequer, literally the treasury, derived its name from the chequered cloth upon which revenue was sorted. Initially the chancellor functioned solely as a finance minister, but when the king needed money—as he generally did—it was not convenient to go to common law, and the chancellor began to assume his own legal jurisdiction and to issue writs without court authorization. Conflict arose. The courts would jealously refuse to enforce the chancellor's demands until the Parliament called upon him, as keeper of the Register of Writs, to extend the breadth of the law by making new writs to meet the needs of new circumstances. Such remedies were called "actions on the case," and the chancellor began giving judgments to plaintiffs who complained of "defects of justice" in the common law. Eventually this lawmaking was called equity, and its flexibility added much to the development of English law. It eased courtroom procedure, for under common law there had been such a narrow formula for pleading that if a word was misplaced it might cause a case to fail. Also, all parties who stood to lose or gain by the court's decision were excluded from the witness box, which often excluded evidence entirely. The chancellors disregarded these tedious rules. As recompense for wrong, the common law offered only money damages. Equity put pressure on the defendant to act. An example might involve a piece of personal property. Perhaps the defendant had agreed under an honest contract to sell it to the plaintiff, or perhaps he had unlawfully taken it. The common law offered the plaintiff only damages, not the object involved, which might have personal or other value not measurable in money. Equity, with its bills for restitution and specific performance, provided for its delivery.

So the common law of England was carried along first by the courts, then by the chancellor, and then for bitter centuries by the two together, each seeking supremacy, until James I decreed in behalf of equity whenever conflict arose. Subsequently the common law and equity were merged, but the marks of the struggle have been left on procedure and doctrine, and law schools still offer a separate course in equity, an area where ethics and fairness overlay strict, often harsh, law.

The unique quality of English common law is that it is made in court by the piling up of one trial decision upon others. This does not mean, however, that the English kings overlooked the more traditional form of law pronouncement, the statute. The law of the case theoretically is declared only at the end, thereby allowing the parties to a dispute to be surprised, but a statute hopefully sets up a precise rule of conduct to be observed in future. Its purpose is not, like the court, to declare the law, but to change it.

The first Norman monarchs of England ruled by court and royal decree, and it was not until the establishment of Parliament in the thirteenth century that statute making became a regular practice. King John, ruling from 1199 to 1216, got things rolling. A cruel, devious, and mistrusted man, he campaigned tirelessly and ineffectually to regain Norman territories in France. These expeditions were resisted by his nobles, particularly when John demanded a fee called scutage, which amounted to a money payment in lieu of active military service. This feudal service was legally owed to the king by those noble vassals who held land grants direct from him. Refusal to pay meant prison. Still, resistance grew when John planned his second campaign, and rebels, behind Robert Fitzwalter, marched on London. The frightened king presented them with a document known as the Articles of the Barons. From this grew the Magna Carta, a careful resuscitation of the old Anglo-Saxon principles which had been suppressed by the Normans. The king guaranteed certain customs and rights to the people, including trial by jury, and promised freedom to the Church. Best remembered is the passage which states: "No free man shall be taken or imprisoned, or disseised, or outlawed, or banished, or anyways destroyed, nor will we pass upon him, or commit him to prison, unless by the legal judgment of his peers, or by the law of the land." This section, wrung from John in 1215 along with the rest, has subsequently been interpreted as a guarantee of the right to due process, and as a part of the Constitution of the United States it remains a lively Supreme Court issue.

Although the Magna Carta limited royal powers, it left the king as head of state, and he would remain so for over four hundred years. Not without question, however. King Henry III was another squanderer, and the barons, under Simon de Montfort, brought their grievance to arbitration before Louis IX of France. Quite predictably, he decided in favor of the divine right of kings. The barons, although they had agreed to abide by the decision, broke their oaths, defeated King Henry in battle, and took him prisoner. Simon de Montfort called a Great Parliament, later a model for the House of Commons, although at the time it came to nothing. The following year, 1265, de Montfort was killed in battle by the royalists. The baronial share in making the laws seemed doomed.

Now it was time for Edward I to leave his mark on history. A strong man, known as The Hammer of the Scots, he was also a great king; the English Justinian, some called him. Though a royalist at heart, he was willing to compromise with his lords to gain his ends, and often summoned parliaments to obtain the support of his subjects. To carry on taxation of the clergy and the barons for the support of his European campaigning, he repeatedly confirmed the Magna Carta, and each confirmation rooted it deeper in the common law. Not only did he reinforce the Magna Carta, he established the various Statutes of Westminster, which strengthened and defined the role of the courts. To instill local responsibility, these statutes provided that any county which could not bring its felons to justice would itself stand liable for damages.

The further evolution of the common law can best be seen as a power struggle between the kings, the church, and the law itself as representing the rights of the people. William I had landed in England as conqueror and king with divine powers, but he brought along certain obligations to his warrior barons which has as their eventual outgrowth the Magna Carta and later statutes. He also had obligations to the church, for he had paid for papal blessing on his intended conquest by promising to set up a separate system of ecclesiastical courts in England. This meant a church hierarchy from archdeacon's tribunal through bishop's and archbishop's courts direct to the Pope in Rome. Its jurisdiction was wide, for the church claimed superiority to earthly monarchs in all things "spiritual." For several centuries this included matters of worship, morals, clergy, marriage, legitimacy, wills of personal property, and the distribution of the goods of the deceased.

The first real clash between church and king came when Henry II appointed his Chancellor, Thomas à Becket, Archbishop of Canterbury in 1162. The object of this nomination was to fix the king's control over the church, but Becket switched his staunch loyalty to Catholicism. The resulting contest, though it brought death and subsequent martyrdom to Becket at the hands of royal assassins, humbled Henry, who was obliged to walk as a barefoot penitent to Becket's tomb in Canterbury. Lost to the common law were a quantity of potential defendants, for the king was obliged to surrender to ecclesiastical courts jurisdiction over members of the clergy. This was benefit indeed for any member of the cloth, since the ecclesiastical courts not only imposed no "judgment of blood" on their members, but offered a way to acquittal via the process of purgation, whereby the accused swore to his own innocence. If twelve compurgators believed him, he got off, without witnesses being called in prosecution. Not only priests were included under this protection, but even secular clerks, which meant anyone who could read or feign reading the opening of the Fifty-first Psalm: *"Miserere mei Deus . . ."* "Have mercy upon me, O God, according to thy loving-kindness: according unto the multitude of thy tender mercies blot out my transgressions."

For several hundred years there was little change in the relationship of church and king. Then came Henry VIII with his marital problems. To clear the way for his alliance with Anne Boleyn, he cast out the Roman clergy and set the Church of England in its stead. Despite his political mastery of religion, under the law, "benefit of clergy" continued to expand. In 1707 the literacy test, too, was dropped, so that the British soldiers who were tried after the Boston Massacre for killing members of the rioting public were permitted to avail themselves of the plea. Following the American Revolution, the united colonies abolished the privilege entirely, though it survived in England until repudiated by statute in 1826. The law, not the king, had prevailed. In 1857 the church's last legal stronghold was surrendered. Probate (the administration of the property of the dead) and matrimonial questions were transferred by an act of Parliament to the secular courts.

It had taken seven centuries for the law to move the church down from the judge's bench. It took as long a time to overcome the king. Initially the struggle was a feudal one involving the king and his powerful lords. The issue involved neither law nor morality, simply power, and culminated in the bloodletting remembered as The Wars of the Roses. This intermittent war began in 1455, two years after England's adventures in Europe were foreclosed and the island was full of restless soldiers. King Henry VI was not only weak but witless, and the houses of York and Lancaster both put forward aspiring successors. York bore the white rose on its banner and Lancaster the red. Civil war lasted for thirty years. Eighty princes of the blood, countless nobles, and over one hundred thousand common soldiers, both mercenary and volunteer, died in the dispute. Edward IV of the house of York, with few kingly virtues besides his generalship, won the throne in the Battle of Towton (1461) in a blinding Yorkshire blizzard, and, except for the temporary restoration of Henry in 1470–1471, remained King till his death in 1483. He was succeeded by his brother, Richard III. Remembered perhaps unfairly as Crookback, a man for whom his people were ashamed to fight, Richard was cut down in a minor skirmish at Bosworth Field, on August 22, 1485. His demise led to a reconciliation. Henry Tudor became king and took as his device the united roses of the warring families. Thus ended a lawless age, and it brought forth an era of strong monarchs that included Henry VIII and Elizabeth I.

Superficially the king had never been more secure, and yet Parliament, submerged during the long struggle, had been needed and had survived. Though it could not wrest the power from the king during the long wars, it had been vital as a mechanism for raising taxes to support the armies in the field. Even before The Wars of the Roses began, Parliament had made bold to impute to Richard II upon his deposition the crime of having declared the laws to be "in his own breast." Here the divine right of kings had been questioned in word if not in fact. Under the Tudors, no great legal issues arose. The law went its quiet way and the monarchs seemed divine indeed. England prospered. Then came the weaker line of Stuart kings. Charles I's problems were, once again, financial. In 1627, when certain lords refused under pressure to advance him a loan, the King had them imprisoned under a warrant signed by his Attorney General alleging their refusal to contribute. The imprisoned lords, in what became known as The Five Knights Case, appealed to the King's Bench for a writ of habeas corpus to show cause why they were being detained. Although the original purpose of a writ of habeas corpus was to ensure that a defendant was brought before the court as a preliminary step before confinement, the knights urged that under the Magna Carta even a king must show legal cause for committing his subjects to prison. King Charles's argument and firm belief was that he could do no wrong and his acts could not be questioned. Momentarily he prevailed, and the prisoners remained in jail. Protest was instant and loud. Cowed, the King released the men, but the issue continued in parliamentary debate until he agreed to abide by the Magna Carta, and not to levy illegal taxes. In the excitement that followed, a grateful Commons voted the King the funds he had wanted from the beginning. In practice he later repudiated his concessions, and it was not until 1679, during the reign of his son Charles II, that habeas corpus as the knights defined it became law.

With The Five Knights Case, Charles I's troubles were just beginning. Not only was he having money trouble and dissension with upstarts in the House of Commons, but he was suspected of Catholic partiality. Catholicism had been bloodily excluded from the realm by Henry VIII. Now a reverse purge was anticipated, and this unified the Scottish Presbyterians against the King. In 1639 he invaded Scotland, while at his back Parliament boiled. He brought charges of treason against parliamentary leaders, and within three years a people's army of merchants and burghers united behind Parliament. The supremacy of divine monarchy at last was face to face with the supremacy of popular law, and if the King had God on his side at first, Parliament had the purse and a general named Oliver Cromwell. Initial victory for the King was followed by defeat and finally capture. On New Year's Day in 1649, a half-empty Commons voted that levy of war against Parliament and the people on the King's part was treason. Five days later a court of 135 commissioners tried Charles at Westminster Hall. The King, steadfast in his God-given rights, refused to acknowledge the court's jurisdiction. To his traditional mind, he was the law, or above it. With hopeless dignity, Charles became the defender of due process, asking what had become of England if power without law could make law. No matter; the trial was political, and death, not justice, its objective. On January 30, Charles went to the headsman, and if law's triumph was the result of its grotesque misuse, certainly no king thereafter could feel beyond its reach. On that occasion was born the notion that there could be treason against the laws and institutions of a country, and not merely against the ruling power.

This concept has remained alive ever since, though it has been threatened. With the restoration of the monarchy in 1660, thirty-two of the surviving participants in Charles's trial were condemned to death, though only thirteen were executed. Twenty others, already dead, were tried. This included Cromwell, whose body was, exhumed and hanged, then reburied in an unmarked grave at the foot of the scaffold. Yet Charles II did not challenge Parliament, and his brother James II, who began mumbling once again about the divine right of kings, was driven into exile. Parliament offered the crown to William and Mary of Orange, accompanied by the Declaration of Rights, asserting the "true, ancient, and indubitable rights of the people of this realm." Written in 1689, the Declaration, like the American Bill of Rights, limited the power of the ruler and procured the rights and liberties of the people. No king thereafter dared think aloud in terms of his God-given powers, except perhaps George III, and as even his people knew, poor George was mad.

During this latter period of the common law's emergence, the American colonies were growing fast. Implements of war and commerce came with the settlers, as did the law. In 1618, the Leyden Agreement was drawn up by the Pilgrims, assuring their loyalty to the King (of England) on their application for a patent to land in Virginia. Upon arrival in the New World (and far north of Virginia), their leaders drew up the Mayflower Compact, on November 11, 1620. This set out in simple words an agreement among the settlers to abide by the laws of God, king, and all just and equal ordinances. In this respect the Pilgrims were not innovators. The only law they knew was the common law, shorn now of the ordeal and trial by battle, and it was adapted over the years to suit the rough civil and political conditions of the frontier. Case reporting was haphazard at best and circulation erratic, but undeniably the common law of England had been transplanted and was thriving in her colonies. In fact, Blackstone's *Commentaries on the Laws of England* (1765–1769) was more avidly followed in the American colonies than in England.

Following the Revolution of 1775–1783, America's shores were shed of British soldiers and tax collectors, but not of British laws. The Declaration of Independence states that "all men are created equal, that they are endowed by their Creator with certain unalienable Rights . . ." This is reminiscent of the Magna Carta, with one noteworthy new element more influential in theory than in practice, the so-called natural law. Natural law was a revolutionary force in the eighteenth century. Philosophically it reached back to the Stoic school of Zeno in ancient Greece with the idea that a law of nature binds ruler and subject alike. The notion was preserved in Rome and by the church fathers, Saint Augustine and Saint Thomas Aquinas; though of course in the Christian era it was associated with the wisdom of God. Later, Newtonian ideas of a world functioning as a well-oiled machine were equally destructive to the doctrine. Man was held to have the right to live as an individual, and any law destructive to this right denied natural justice. Such a theory was very adaptable to the backwoods courthouse where it could fill the all-too-wide gaps in the general law. The English Stamp Act, which was so critical in sparking the American Revolution, was an unpalatable purse-picker, and it was denounced as against natural law. In practice, of course, almost any law could be defended as natural or attacked as unnatural. This impossibility of consensus left natural law as a revolutionary force, but only a vague incentive and ethical guide when it came to the nitty-gritty task of framing specific rules of courtroom law. There the common law survived.

Beginning as a simple scheme for exploitation by the powerful, the common law had become the bulwark of popular rights. The early writ system was gone, but its principles remained embedded in the law. The rule of law, the growth of the law through court-made precedents, the evolved jury, and the distinguishing of causes of action upon which plaintiffs might rely—all these were a legacy distilled from early days and preserved in modern practice. Such continuity can be found in none of the other European legal systems.

This survival of the common law has depended on its practitioners' ability to adjust it to new circumstances. Old decisions have been ignored when new circumstances make them irrelevant, unpopular holdings have not been extended, and throughout runs the very flexible doctrine of the "reasonable man." Time and time again the court has put it to jury deliberation whether or not a party to the action acted as a reasonable man would have acted under the given circumstances. What was reasonable one hundred years ago may no longer be deemed so, and vice versa. The elasticity of such doctrines gives life to the common law. However, there is a very literal price to be paid. Flexibility comes at great expense, long trials, appeals, uncertainty as to result. How much easier it is to apply fixed rules in advance than to pay legal experts to argue, and to wait for a jury to decide! Because of this time-consuming expense on the one hand and the rapidly changing demands of the twentieth century on the other, many question the virtue of perpetuating the common-law system. Certainly a much wider understanding of legal rights is needed. Modifications must come if social and economic justice is to be done by the courts as we know them. There are no easy answers, and it is not the purpose here to give them; only to raise some of those questions that are better understood by lawyers than laymen.

CHAPTER FOUR

Great Systems of the Law Today

BEFORE PROBING THE LEGAL SYSTEM OF THE UNITED STATES FOR strengths and weaknesses, it might be well to set it in context by touching lightly on its major competitors. As a preamble even to this, one might fairly ask, What is law? Can it be defined? The answer, of course, is a qualified affirmative.

Law has been variously defined; sincerely, sarcastically, rarely with much degree of harmony. Some love the law. Voltaire said, "Where law ends, tyranny begins," and Samuel Johnson remarked, "The law is the last result of human wisdom acting upon human experience for the benefit of the public." Benjamin Franklin thought that "law is the greatest blessing society has given to the individual." Others had nothing but contempt. Thoreau said, "I think the law is really a humbug, and a benefit principally to the lawyers." Jonathan Swift concurred. "Law is a bottomless pit, a harpy that devours everything." Ambrose Bierce wrote that law was "a machine which you go into as a pig and come out of as a sausage." Casting no such value judgment, a dictionary might define law as a body of rules prescribing social conduct and judiciable in court.

A sheriff in the Old West would have preferred to regard "law" as five bullets in the cylinder, and "judgment" as the one under the hammer. Plato, one of the first philosophers dealing with law, stressed its moral aspect, and Cicero in his *De Republica* said,

"True law is right reason, consonant with nature, diffused among all men, constant, eternal." Here natural law enters. More recently, law has been detached from morality on the theory that morality is what ought to be, but law is simply what the courts in fact decide. According to Justice Oliver Wendell Holmes,

> The life of the law has not been logic; it has been experience. The felt necessities of the times, the prevalent moral and political theories, institutions of public policy, avowed or unconscious, even the prejudices which judges share with their fellow men, have had a good deal more to do than the syllogism in determining the rules by which men should be governed.[1]

Today the influences of psychology and sociology have entered the picture, and they demand that legal rules be evaluated in terms of their actual or potential social consequences. Clearly, even the definition of law itself shifts with time and place, so it is hardly surprising that the systems which try to apply it are even more various in structure and method.

Yet always, when the law is not hindered by politics or prejudice, the end results converge, seeking justice. Take, for example, the judgment of Oka Tadasuke, a Japanese magistrate of Yedo holding court in the eighteenth century. Before him came a mother who was employed as a servant and consequently had been forced to put her child out with a nurse. When the child reached the age of ten, the woman had completed her service and sought her child's return, but the foster parent refused. The dispute came before Tadasuke. Both women claimed to be the child's mother, so the judge put the child between the two, and told them each to take hold of one of the child's hands and pull. Whoever yanked the child free was to be declared the mother. The foster mother won easily and claimed the child, to which Tadasuke retorted, "You are a fraud; the real mother, fearing to harm her own flesh and blood, relaxed her grip." How distant in time and place, and yet how similar to the judgment of Solomon.

Modern law, like modern science, tends to have an international flavor. Most early systems were closely bound to religion and took the form of maxims, variously adopted and interpreted through the ages. However much these moral rules still serve as a guide to personal conduct, two systems of law have left their imprint throughout large portions of the modern world.

First there is the Code Napoléon, Roman-based, adopted throughout the Continent and modified according to the needs of each country—France, Switzerland, Germany, and many others. Take, for example, modern Greece. Though regarded as the cradle of Western civilization, ancient Greece left no legal heritage to its modern counterpart. Dominated for centuries by Turkish Moslems, Greece won its independence in a savage struggle that lasted from 1821 to 1829. Once freedom was gained, Greece was immediately Europeanized. The first Greek king, Otto I, was imported from Bavaria. His successor, George I, came from Denmark, and with these kings came laws based on the French model, the Code Napoléon. The Code was further spread by the nineteenth-century period of European colonialism. It continued to be emulated when these former colonies became independent in the twentieth century.

The second system referred to is that of the common law. Though less easily transported, thanks to the former worldwide scope of the British Empire its influence is nearly as widespread as that of the Code Napoléon, particularly in North America, Africa, and Asia.

An example of mixed law covers the 400 million Hindus who live principally in India and Pakistan, but also in Burma, Malaysia, Singapore, Aden, Kenya, Uganda, and Tanzania. As part of a religious community, each Hindu carries with him a personal law coexistent with the local law, whether the latter has an English or a French coloration. Historically, the roots of Hindu law can be traced back to the Vedic literature of 1500 B.C., which dealt with mercy, charity, the treatment of elders, and good government. Among the Brahmin caste, there gradually developed a discipline called The Science of Righteousness, or Dharmasastra. This, in practice, was made up of maxims and poetical moral precepts and became the bedrock of judicial interpretation. Jurists referred to it as smriti, or memory, and it was treated with the sanctity of holy scripture. Commentators over the centuries added explanations and relevant quotations, and such terse admonitions as "Inequal things should not be treated as equal" were extended and given practical application. For instance, if the penalty for minor theft was the loss of a hand, then death should only be meted out to persistent offenders. Another maxim, baffling on its face, states that a crow has only one eye. A dubious statement, but defended by the argument that no one has seen more than one eye at a time. Its legal extension is the notion that a sentence given an interpretation at one time cannot be altered to fit another occasion.

Then, in the middle of the eighteenth century, along came the East India Company, and right behind it the red coats of the British Army and the flowing robes of the British courts. Baffled by the age-old Dharmasastra, the British injected a dose of common law, and especially of equity, into the system, with a nod to native professors appointed to the courts for their views on local personal laws. The result was Anglo-Hindu law. Some early maxims were abandoned as no longer applicable to modern times, such as the rule that when a deceased left no son, his widow must cohabit with his closest relative so as to provide the line with a male heir. In other situations the laws commingled. When the question arose whether a murderer could succeed to a victim's estate, the Indian Sanskrit texts were silent. However, they did indicate that disobedient children could not inherit. This latter was a bit too much for the British, who would not set out just what measure of disobedience deserved disinheritance, but by combining the English common-law rule with the Indian principle, they concluded that parricide constituted gross filial disobedience and thus denied the murderer the estate.

Following the Second World War, the British withdrew from India. A Hindu code was adopted which in some elements reflects the French model, but where the new code is found lacking, the courts still return to the older Anglo-Hindu law. Nor is the influence of Dharmasastra totally dead, for in India there has never been any active separation of church and state and no ruler such as Henry VIII who purported to master religious institutions. Dharmasastra remains a possible argument in the courts and a guide in personal and religious matters.

Not far away on mainland China, legal systems developed independently beginning about 500 B.C. during what has been called The Age of Warring States. A philosopher named K'ung Fu-tzu lived during those chaotic times, better remembered now as Confucius. Though the kingdom of Ch'n emerged supreme from the strife and law was simply a matter of royal decree, the ideas derived from Confucius were spreading. At their core was the principle that man and natural forces are interspersed and work upon one another, so that any harmonious human conduct out of step with natural order will tend to upset the cosmic balance. The tyrannical Ch'n emperors were seen as violating this balance. In a series of revolutions they were overthrown, and from the ashes rose the Han dynasty, imbued with the Confucian idea that a ruler had a natural mandate to rule until he acted against nature. Then it became a citizen's duty to rebel, a theory not dissimilar from the natural-law ideas that prompted our own Founding Fathers to act against England in the eighteenth century.

So Confucian philosophy became the basis for customary law in old China. It functioned well enough for centuries, but brought with it certain harsh abuses that would have shocked the gentle philosopher who believed not in punishment but in good example. For instance, in accord with the great concern for natural order, the male-female principles were seen as a harmonious balance, and, unlike the case in most early societies, women in China had what amounted to equal rights. Children, however, had no rights. A child's acts against family tranquillity could be harshly dealt with within the home. An unfilial child might, in fact, be buried alive by his parents, for private law was left up to the family or the clan.

Until the seventh century A.D. this customary adherence to a natural order resisted any notion of state-imposed law. When such legislation arrived with the T'ang dynasty, there remained great pressure to settle disputes outside the courts. Due to Confucius, litigation was considered virtually immoral, and Emperor K'ang Hsi stated in the seventeenth century,

> Lawsuits would tend to increase to a frightful amount if people were not afraid of the tribunals, and if they felt confident of always finding in them ready and perfect justice. As man is apt to delude himself concerning his own interests, contests would then be interminable, and the half of the Empire would not suffice to settle the lawsuits of

the other half. I desire therefore that those who have recourse to the tribunals should be treated without any pity, and in such manner that they shall be disgusted with law, and tremble to appear before a magistrate.[2]

To go to law was not only a disgrace but a hazard to plaintiff and defendant alike. Failure to prove a case often meant severe punishment, and torture was used to get confessions of guilt from the accused or of malice on the part of the petitioners. When questioned by the magistrate, parties were forced to kneel before his table while attendants harassed them with threatening gestures. If the defendant was found guilty, the array of penalties included flogging, death by strangulation, or beheading with the sword. Particularly villainous crimes were punished with the so-called Death of a Thousand Cuts. From such practices has come the legend of inscrutable Oriental cruelty, but even this slicing to death isn't any more atrocious than England's former practice of hanging, drawing, and quartering, or France's method of breaking highwaymen on the wheel.

Private justice among the Chinese was similar to that of more primitive societies, such as the ordeal in which dissident parties stuck their heads into a cage containing a poisonous snake. Presumably the snake, being in harmony with nature, would bite whoever was at fault. Another proceeding, not limited to China and reminiscent of the test of fire and water, was the practice of snatching a coin from a jar of scalding oil. And akin to the Comanche sun killing was an oath taken over the body of a freshly slaughtered chicken that called down a similar fate on the person who was lying.

Traditional Chinese law began to vanish with the intrusion of Western influence during the past hundred years. After the fall of the emperors in 1912, attempts were made to institute legislative codes following the European models of Switzerland, Germany, and France. Locally, old customs continued as the anarchy of war and revolution tore China. Under the Communist regime today the old customs exist in a clandestine way with the overlay of a Soviet model of justice, which at root is nothing but the old Code Napoléon of France.

A final influence of Chinese law, comparable in influence to the

Hindu science of righteousness or the comments of Confucius, are the writings of Chairman Mao Tse-tung. Take, for instance, the following, a delight to any women's rights movement: "Men and women must receive equal pay for equal work in production. Genuine equality between the sexes can only be realized in the process of the socialist transformation of a society as a whole." [3] The legal applications and ramifications of such a statement in terms of labor and family law are enormous. Another observation would seem basic to freedom of the press and free speech. "The Communist Party does not fear criticism because we are Marxists; the truth is on our side, and the basic masses, the workers and the peasants, are on our side." [4] It is not known whether any living Chinese has treated this statement as a constitutional guarantee of his rights to speak out.

Although most of the more modern and complex legal systems have all but abandoned their religious base, two that have not exist in hostile opposition: Jewish and Islamic law. Traditional Jewish law is the far older of the two, and its age, in terms of vitality, is beginning to show. Rooted in the customs of the nomadic tribes that settled in Palestine, Jewish law served as an adjunct of Jewish religion. Its most vital function, once the kingdom of Israel had ceased to exist and its people had been scattered, was to provide a cohesive element without which Judaism would long ago have vanished from the earth.

This enduring religious-legal heritage has been preserved in a series of writings, first of which is the Mishnah, collected from earlier books about A.D. 200 and for the first time systematically arranged under six headings:

1) seeds or agricultural commandments
2) festivals
3) women (meaning domestic relations)
4) torts or civil crimes
5) sacred things
6) ritual cleanliness.

The Palestinian and Babylonian academies were the spiritual centers of Judaic thought after the destruction of the Temple in A.D.

70. They kept copious records of their studies of the Mishnah, which form what is known as the Talmud today.

Like the Chinese law, the strength of this law is ethical and personal. Under local rabbinical leadership, it depended on no great power structure for application, but could move with the Jewish communities as they settled in exile throughout Europe and the East. Subjected to the legal dominion of other states, whether the common law of England or the Inquisition of Spain, Jewish law persevered as an all-embracing body of religious duties that regulated life within the Jewish community. Where disputes arose outside the family, the community rabbi might act as arbitrator, imposing excommunication (*cherem*) or fines (*qenas*), with the main concern being offenses against God, such as disrespect to parents, sexual deviations, and blasphemy. Each small community, more often than not surrounded by suspicious, if not hostile, strangers, tried to settle its own affairs by reference to and interpretation of the Talmud and other religious writings. Via this self-regenerating isolation, Judaism and its domestic laws endured through the centuries.

An early threat to this survival came in 1807, when a group of upper-class French Jews found their traditional ways an obstacle to progress. With Napoleon's blessing, they convoked a Sanhedrin to deal with problems of emancipation and absorption of the Jewish community. More recently, ironical or appropriate as one may regard it, the threat to the Orthodox Jewish community and its Talmudic laws has come from the modern state of Israel. There, older, less worldly ways clash with a modern and militant state, and if the traditional laws are to survive at all in a community which has adopted legal codes similar to those of Continental Europe, they must find new dynamic leadership capable of bringing them into harmony with the emergent nation. Otherwise Israel may well grow impatient and declare itself a purely secular community.

Although hostile today, young by comparison, and never displaced from the area of its birth, Islamic law has a source and evolution not unlike the traditional laws of its Jewish neighbors. In the seventh century A.D. the Prophet Mohammed, like Moses before him, set down the commandments of his God. Submission

to the will of Allah, as expressed through the revelations of his messenger, was the basic rule, and from this radiated Mohammed's
admonitions for fair dealing, temperance, and other virtues.
Such statements, called Qur'an (Koran), provided a religious ethic,
but no rule of law setting forth rights and duties. Traditionally a
man could divorce his wife simply by denying her. The Koran does
not strictly deny this right, but urges that it not be abused and that
the husband make fair provision for the repudiated woman. After
the Prophet's death it became the task of the caliphs to adapt
these moral urgings to customary law.

Sometimes the Koran, particularly in family matters, is quite
specific. The following quotation is similar to the United States
law of intestate succession:

> God bids that, in distributing an estate, a son receive as much as two
> daughters; if only daughters remain, and more than two, they receive
> two thirds of the estate; if only one, the half. Father and mother shall
> have each one sixth, if there is a child; if none, and parents take, the
> mother has one third; if brothers survive, the mother takes one sixth,
> provided that legacies and debts be first paid.[5]

Under the Umayyad dynasty, Islam became a vast military
empire and a diversity of legal practice developed, for as the empire spread, so did the diversity of customary law and the schools
of interpretation. On the one hand was the idea that in each
generation the consensus of qualified legal scholars should be
deemed infallible, a practical notion which has remained popular
since medieval times. On the other hand, against this approach
was cast the method of Shari'a, which insisted that certain knowledge of Allah's laws could only come as it had come to Mohammed,
through divine revelation. Law was not to be *made*, as with the
consensus theory, but *discovered;* a sort of common-law theory
which, though influential, does not furnish sufficient flexibility for
modern demands.

For a time the law remained static. Jurists were merely imitators,
following the doctrine of Shari'a. Gradually the cumbersome nature
of this theory began to break down, particularly in the areas of
criminal and land law. Legal authority was delegated to secular

officials called masters of complaints. Some old areas of offense, such as wine drinking, theft, fornication, highway robbery, slander, and apostasy, were left to the old ways. The rest went to the judge for decision and punishment.

Today, with the Moslem empire broken up among many separate nations, the ties of religion, language, and law still tend to unite them. However, Western European systems have had influence. Continental criminal codes have generally been adopted, though the old Shari'a family law remains except in Turkey, which in 1927 adopted the Swiss domestic code. Between one Moslem nation and another, as well as between the more Westernized upper-class minorities and the conservative masses, gaps widen with regard to how the law shall be applied. If not a cause, this disunity is certainly a symptom of the disharmony that exists among Arab countries today.

An area of the world unique in its background is Latin America. Here was a vast wilderness occupied by savage tribes as well as by several magnificent and completely independent Indian cultures, such as the Aztec, the Toltec, and the Inca. Spanish intrusion began in 1492, the very year that Spain itself finally shed the Moslem yoke after some seven hundred years of Moorish subjugation. Within half a century the conquest was complete, and a Spanish viceroy governed the land with the help of the Catholic Inquisition, which held jurisdiction over violations of religious faith and morality. Justice otherwise was left to the council courts, called the *audiencias,* and their subdivisions. For nearly three hundred years, Mexico, taken perhaps unfairly as an example to represent the whole, was governed as a Spanish province—until Napoleonic troops invaded Spain in 1808. Though Napoleon held the mother country for only a few years, Spain's dominion in Mexico was permanently weakened and ripe for democratic revolution. A priest named Miguel Hidalgo, who was a great admirer of both the French and American revolutions, began the struggle with a policy of agrarian reform, returning the land to the Indians. When Hidalgo was captured and shot, another revolutionary, José Morelos, picked up his banner in 1811 and suffered the same fate. Chaos reigned in the now independent country. Governments rose and fell, none lasting more than a year, until the popular leader Benito Juárez emerged in 1857. His program consisted of destroying the temporal power of the Catholic Church in Mexico by a forced sale of church real estate for the benefit of the dispossessed masses. The church threatened excommunication and encouraged France to send its troops. The Catholic emperor, Maximilian, was imported from Austria, and held the crown for a few years. Then Juárez, with the people behind him, defeated the emperor and had him shot. Juárez did not live long with his triumph. He died in 1872 and was replaced by Porfirio Díaz, a popular and efficient leader. His motto, "Bread or the club," meant not rule by law but by the police and the prison warden. Public works boomed. Foreign investors prospered. But the communally held Indian land was turned over to big speculators, so that by 1910, 85 percent of the rural population of Mexico was landless. The people had become serfs, subject to the hacienda owners. Again came revolution. This time it raged for a decade, leaving a million dead, haciendas gutted, and churches pillaged; but in its fires was forged a new Mexico, one nation, blending the Indian and the Spanish past.

At the core of reform was the constitution of 1917. As always, the concern was the fair distribution of land, which was taken from the control of church and hacienda and placed in the hands of the individual peasant family. The first twenty-nine articles of this constitution were a bill of rights guaranteeing freedom of speech, press, and religion, and the right to work. It also included the unique writ of *amparo*. The goal of this writ was to restrain arbitrary executive action from infringement of the individual's constitutional guarantees, and it included in its omnibus nature the effect of habeas corpus, mandamus, and certiorari.

The actual court structure under the new republic is not dissimilar to the United States model. At the top is a federal system of six circuit courts and one supreme court. The latter, however, has three distinct chambers to deal separately with civil, criminal, and administrative matters. Beneath the federal courts are the various distinct state courts. The substance of the law, however, follows the French model of the Code Napoléon, which had been adopted in Spain and brought to the New World during the colonial period. The task of the judge, therefore, is not to make rules of law but simply to match the facts of the case to the statute law as it exists. Even the supreme court of Mexico has no power to declare a law unconstitutional.

In short, Mexico's approach to law and order is a polyglot of adoptions from other systems. To fairly represent the laws of any nation, a vast library is necessary. This is particularly true throughout Latin America, which has endured long years of Spanish or Portuguese domination and the heavy hand of the church. Most of the countries have struggled through periods of lawlessness into independence without achieving stability, and as often as not their laws are more paper and print than practical application. Apart from Mexico, few have yet achieved stability, and a future of disorder and turmoil seems inevitable before a status quo based upon sound constitutions can be envisioned.

An interesting bridge between the primitive and the modern exists in Africa. Perhaps it is inaccurate to speak of "African" law, but there is a similarity of pattern throughout: ritual practice based on ancestral customs and supernatural beliefs and an overlay of European colonial influence which is still evident in spite of recent independence. Typical of these people, thrust head over heels into the twentieth century, are the Kikuyus of Kenya. With the arrival of Europeans, older ways continued to be applied, much as the Normans applied Anglo-Saxon customary law. Chiefs or family heads still adjudged cases with oaths and ordeals, and normally continued to achieve reconciliation. Unlike the Chinese, however, Africans have never been discouraged by litigation. They enjoy it as an entertainment and a challenge, and they continue to do so in the Europeanized courts. When settlement fails within the family group, the plaintiff may lodge his complaint with his own headman. If settlement is still not achieved, the case may reach the formal courts. Thus far, Kenya, apart from its Mau Mau struggle for independence, has been a model of adjustment under the law, both old and new.

The Code Napoléon spread north and east as well as south. Though Russia brought about the downfall of Bonaparte and his empire, the final victory in a way belonged to France. In Czarist circles, no love was lost upon the Russian peasant. All admiration was for France and England, and those languages were spoken in court circles to such an extent that the last Czar, as he stood facing a Bolshevik firing squad, could not speak a word of Russian in his own behalf. Along with language, the French legal code was readily borrowed, and though the French language died on Russian lips along with Czar Nicholas, the law survived the violent days of Communist revolution. Initially the Communist revolutionaries cast aside the old ideas of law and order. The writings of Marx, prophet of world communism, were searched for applicable law and found wanting in practice. Government by decree followed, with enforcement in the hands of so-called People's Courts. Under Lenin, the ideal was a Soviet system featuring the dictatorship of the common man, in which eventually the need for law would die out. Such notions derived from the belief that private property thrust envious relationships upon people, which required laws to enforce ownership. Without property, such clashes of interest would vanish.

In the hope of attaining this state of bliss, brutal means were applied. A political assassination in 1934 set off a growing pattern of arrests, confessions, and executions. The Soviet army alone disposed of 80 percent of its marshals and generals. These were Stalin's Moscow Trials of 1936 through 1938, conducted in the supper room of the nobles' club of Czarist days, now known as the House of Trade Unions. The accused offered no defense, but stood and listened to a recording which played back months of interrogation. Complete confessions, clearly coerced, were obtained in most cases. Nikolai Krestinsky, former Vice-Commissar of Foreign Affairs, shocked the court by denying his former confession. Hustled back to his cell, he returned the following day rather the worse for wear and pleaded guilty. In his, as in most cases, the firing squad followed, without appeal.

Since those dark days, codes based on a European model have "temporarily" been reactivated. Law, like its relative, morality, has been taken as an expression of the will of the whole people. In fact, law is an offspring of morality, which in turn is the prevailing view of the people as it is shaped into a statute and accorded the power of the state for its enforcement. More than simple physical coercion, law is a tool for influencing the individual conscience of the good citizen as well as the citizen gone bad. The Russian view is that the criminal must not merely be punished. His soul must be wrestled with in the hope that he will see the light and move along in harmony with the Soviet community toward a more perfect tomorrow.

Naïve, perhaps, but there is much to commend the present Soviet system, which has moved far from the black days of the Purge. At the lowest level of jurisdiction, more funny than frightening, are the Big-Brother-is-watching tribunals known as Comradely Courts. Here the concern is to eradicate "unhealthy social attitudes" and signs of "capitalistic decay." The only sanction is public influence, "drumming the scandal," so to speak, and the court is conducted informally by neighbors and fellow workers of the disputing parties. Issues may vary from drunkenness to child neglect to sloppy work habits. Any convenient room will do for the hearing, and anyone present may speak out, usually urging the quarreling parties to resolve their differences in a graceful Soviet spirit.

Failure in the Comradely Court may lead in time up the ladder to the People's Court, which handles both civil and criminal trials in the first instance. This court, like the other Russian courts, is to some extent a political instrument, and it is not intended as an impartial buffer between the citizen and the state. But it is no longer military in nature, as it was during the Stalin era, and confession alone can no longer condemn a man. As with other European court systems, the judge, acting with lay jurists, serves as judge, jury, and, in most minor instances, as impartial prosecutor. Much, in other words, depends on the judge's integrity, but no more so than in our system, where a decision may go astray due to a judge's prejudice, a lawyer's greed, or a prosecutor's ambition. In Russia, the ruble can seldom buy partial justice.

In more important cases, a procurator takes part. He resembles our district attorney, though his functions are wider in scope, covering investigation of certain civil suits. He is a protector of the law as well as an accuser. When the procurator is present, the defendant must have an attorney.

The general manner and setting of the court is informal. There are no rigid procedures to be followed, no technical phrases to be enunciated. The courtroom is homespun at best, often resembling a warehouse or a run-down office. The judge wears no official garb and is set apart by no class distinction, no "your Honor" this or that. He is simply another worker, bound to a tedious task. Civil cases take place in the same room before the same judge as criminal trials. Parties are examined and witnesses are called by the judge. Witnesses may speak from their seats and spectators may throw in their two cents' worth. The judge may soothe a distraught witness, fetch her water, tongue-lash a party for his thoughtlessness and un-Soviet-like character. Deliberations are brief, and the judge usually gives judgment within a few minutes. When large sums of money are involved, lawyers appear, and a dragging air of bourgeois legalism prevails.

The most prevalent trial is criminal. A judge and two lay assessors preside. The hearing normally considers the findings of a preliminary investigation. Police may retain a possible criminal on reasonable suspicion and hold him for up to three days on the procurator's decision. This pretrial inquiry is usually more decisive than the trial itself, for, unlike the United States system, the trial does not ideally begin with a blank mind. The investigation is thorough, and it concerns not only the crime in question but the prisoner's entire life history. As in our juvenile courts, concern is for the whole social man. During the period between investigation and trial, the defendant will be released unless there is reason to believe he will vanish. As the investigation is entirely in police hands, there is little chance that the defense will spring evidential surprises at the trial. Without a jury, the attorney can expect to gain little from his own cleverness or appeals to sympathy and prejudice. Clearly such a system makes for simplicity and clarity at the trial, though it does allow for earlier injustice. At the preliminary investigation, witnesses sometimes have been rigged, and though the justification for denying the defendant an attorney at this point is based on the theory that the investigator is only a researcher after impartial truth, in psychological fact it is hard to be both accuser and defender. It is human nature to go one way or the other, and injustice is often done.

Since the trial is little more than the restatement of investigated and established facts, the accused is rarely acquitted. Usually guilt is admitted, and the question is only one of the degree of punishment. Before passing sentence, the judge will admonish the criminal. "What are you doing with your life, comrade? Aren't you ashamed? You, a trained factory worker, a valuable asset to Soviet society? Why do you drink? Why do you neglect your good wife? Why did you steal?" Sometimes members of the defendant's family or work community will appear in his behalf, describing his good and reliable character and work record, the misfortunes of his youth, or his heroic war record—all in the hopes of mitigating the inevitable sentence.

An offense constantly appearing is hooliganism, a catch-all for various social disorders all the way from drunken rowdiness to expressing disrespect for Soviet society. In such a vague doctrine there lies the potential of abuse, and the United States Supreme Court would probably strike it down as unconstitutional due to vagueness. Not so the Soviet Union, where the molding of conduct to a more perfect state is put ahead of the individual's right to deviate from the pattern. Individualism is not encouraged.

Appeals from the criminal decisions of the People's Court are possible, but rarely do they alter the judgment and rarely are they attempted except in the most serious crimes. An appeal is not limited to the defendant. A dissatisfied procurator may appeal the decision which he regards as too mild or too harsh. Another means of review is initiated from above, and may be instigated, after the sentence has been effected, by the chairman of a higher court or by a higher-ranking procurator. This provides a means for a court to correct earlier mistakes and is as likely to lead to heavier as to lighter sentences. An example of this occurred in the 1950's, when a gang of money speculators were first sentenced to prison for eight years. After sentence, a new code of penalties was established which extended the term to fifteen years, and when a death penalty was made applicable to the crime, the procurator-general obtained a special decree under which the defendants were shot. This is as terrifying an example of ex post facto legislation as one can find. Unfortunately for the condemned, they were the victims of a political storm that began with their trial and developed into a nationwide witch-hunt for money speculators, the lowest form of parasite in the Communist book. In a climate not unlike that which existed during our own McCarthy era, politics spilled over—as it theoretically never should—into justice, and so the men died.

Most serious crimes such as murder do not begin in the People's Court but in a court called the *Oblastnoi*. Procedure does not vary materially. The court, not the prosecution or the defense, calls the witnesses. Suppose the defendant is accused of killing his wife with special cruelty, an aggravated circumstance which means the death penalty. In this case the defendant has beaten his wife to death. He stands mute while his factory work record is brought in and examined pro and con. There are no subtle tactics of defense, no arguments over the admissibility of hearsay evidence. The judge methodically interrogates witnesses, then turns them over to the procurator and the defense attorney. The concentration is upon the defendant; not merely upon his crime, but upon his worth as a citizen. The decision is quick to follow. There are no hung juries in Soviet Russia, where it is the firing squad, not the noose, that sends the offender on his way.

Over the entrance to a Soviet court it is customary to see the following inscription: "The smallest crime, the slightest violation of our legal order, is a crack which is instantly employed by the enemies of the Soviet workers." Lenin said it; the courts apply it literally and with harsh regularity: two years for stealing a shoe; five for taking a joyride in someone else's car; two for a waitress who pours each glass of wine short so that after a fortnight she has saved a bottle's worth for herself. One ameliorating factor is the nature of imprisonment, which usually is more inevitable than severe. Most offenders are sent to a labor colony, where life is primitive but open. Families may be present, and the prisoner works at a respectable job rather than rotting in jail. In the most minor of offenses, the court will sometimes not even remove the offender from his usual work, but dock him a portion of his wages for a given time. Another device amounts to banishment, under what is known as the "parasite law." This law is applied to drunks, prostitutes, and other vagrants, and it provides for work at a specified location, generally away from urban centers. The law may be in the social interest but, like other Soviet inventions, it is dangerous. What if, as has happened in the past, avant-garde painters and writers are considered vagrants and removed?

For most serious crimes, there is the firing squad. In 1917, with the first rosy flush of revolution, it was abolished. It was promptly restored the following year, abolished once again, and once more restored in 1920. After World War Two it was abolished, then reinstated seven years later. Generally it is applied to treason, acts of terrorism, banditry, and violent murder, but in 1961 it was extended to such purely economic crimes as counterfeiting and speculating in currency.

In general, Soviet justice works well. Where it is harsh, it is so in the belief that the courts have a duty not only to punish the individual but to root out crime for the betterment of society and thereby mold responsible citizens. If the man is basically healthy, capitalism and the lust for property has made him ill. It is up to the court, then, to provide a cure. In practice, everything is locked up. Factory doors are guarded by security police, windshield wipers are locked inside cars to remove temptation, and crime, where it does exist, as a "relapse into capitalism," is cut out, so that the perfect society of the future may be born. At least this is the theory.

CHAPTER FIVE

Humanizing the Common Law

BEFORE WE CONSIDER THE EVOLVING SUBSTANCE OF THE COMMON LAW, notice must be taken of the enormous structure that applies it. In the United States, each state has its hierarchy of courts, beginning with trial courts of limited and petty jurisdiction, up through two or more levels where the trial record may be taken on appeal. When constitutional issues are involved, appeal may be carried into the federal district court. At the top is the Supreme Court of the United States.

The Supreme Court has achieved powers unprecedented in English common-law history, and unanticipated by its founders. The decisive year was 1803, the Chief Justice John Marshall, and the unprepossessing case at issue was *Marbury v. Madison*.

Upon going out of office, the retiring President, John Adams, had decided to pack minor judicial offices with members of his Federalist party. Included were some justice-of-the-peace commissions that Adams had signed but which fell into the hands of the new Republican Secretary of State, James Madison. When Madison did not issue the commissions, a prospective justice, William Marbury, brought suit via a Supreme Court writ of mandamus to compel their delivery. Historically, the writ of mandamus began in England as one issued in the king's name to compel public officials to enforce the performance of a public duty. It was perpetuated in American courts as a means whereby a superior court could order an individual, corporation, or inferior court to do its duty. By a law passed at the very first session after the adoption of the Constitution, Congress had expressly granted the Supreme Court the power of issuing writs of mandamus. However, this was an untested power, and the Supreme Court was concerned that Secretary of State Madison would refuse to comply. To be disregarded in such a confrontation would seriously weaken the young Court. So the justices avoided the clash altogether by denying that Congress had the power to add actions for mandamus against public officers to the Supreme Court's jurisdiction. Superficially, the Court seemed to be restricting its own powers. However, in the long run, the decision amounted to a statement, never seriously questioned, that the Court had power to review acts of Congress and could reject their proposed legislation as unconstitutional. This enormous power, achieved indirectly, has been jealously guarded by the Supreme Court ever since.

In theory, the sources of law are twofold: previous case law, which a court may study in the annual state and federal reports; and statutes, from the Constitution and its amendments down to the most minor village regulations set out for use by the local police justice. Theoretically, a court in each particular case takes those reported cases and statutes that relate to the circumstances and applies the law. Of course the idea that a judge merely discovers and then applies the law is a fiction, likened at one time to Queen Victoria taking baths in a nightgown. The old and hallowed rule, *Stare decisis, et non quieta movere* (Adhere to the decisions, and do not unsettle things which are established), is certainly an aid to predictability, but the fact is, circumstances change, and more rapidly now than ever before. The law of negligence at the time of Edward I is inadequate to handle the situation where one of Consolidated Edison's power lines has fallen on a barbed-wire fence, thereby electrocuting a cow three miles away.

Courts are more honest about making law than they used to be, but even in 1889, when the case of *Riggs v. Palmer* was decided,[1] circumstances and the applicable law combined in such gross injustice that the court made law as follows:

Frank Palmer was a wealthy farmer who doted on his grandson

Elmer. He made the mistake of telling the boy, who clearly was a bad seed, that he intended to leave him his estate. Then the old man remarried, and though there was no indication that the grandfather had changed his mind, Elmer decided to make doubly sure and put weed poison in his grandfather's food, with the desired result. That was in 1882, and Elmer was found guilty of second-degree murder. Still ambitious, even in prison, Elmer found a lawyer to defend against a lawsuit brought by his two married sisters to cut him out of the will. As the law, statutes, and cases did not hold that murder was a barrier to inheriting under a will, Elmer won the case. The sisters appealed. By this time Elmer was free, and unless the appellate court judge made law, Elmer would gain the fruits of his crime. For authority the judge went back to Blackstone, the Code Napoléon, and even Aristotle, for there was no precedent to go on other than repulsion at the facts of the case and the old maxim, "No man shall profit by his own wrong." But the fact is, the judge was making new law, as any good judge would have done, and the logic of the decision cannot be questioned. "He caused that death, and thus by his crime made it [the will] speak and have operation. Shall it speak in his favor? If he had met the testator and taken his property by force, he would have no title to it. Shall he acquire title by murdering him?" This has been the law ever since.

Sometimes courts will overturn statutes as readily as they do older cases. The California penal code, Section 650½, prohibits a person from "willfully and wrongly committing any act which openly outrages public decency." When it came up against the prosecution of a number of topless entertainers, the statute, which until then had stood the test of time, was uniformly held to be unconstitutionally vague. The fact was, of course, that public attitudes were changing on what constituted public decency, and the statute law was obliged to change with them. Undoubtedly, in less liberal communities, the courts would uphold this statute without question.

Nowhere has the law evolved more rapidly than in the area of civil tort. A tort, by the way, is not always made of eggs and ground nuts. In the law, it amounts to a wrongful act resulting in injury to another's body, property, or reputation, for which the injured party is entitled to recompense.

The earliest tort cases in the common law involved writs in trespass. They were confined to forcible acts in breach of the King's Peace and later enlarged by a chancery writ of trespass on the case. This distinction is illustrated in *Leame v. Bray* in 1802.[2] Under an action in trespass, a person struck by a log in the highway could only bring an action against the thrower if hit by the log in flight, for here the injury was direct. If hurt while stumbling over the wood as it lay in the street, the only recourse was to action on the case. The sole concern was the injury done. Moral responsibility was of no concern to the early courts. As Chief Justice Brian said, "The thought of a man shall not be tried, for the devil himself knowest not the thought of a man." [3]

By the time American law had departed in fact, if not in spirit, from common-law jurisdiction, trespass had reached a state of strict liability. This meant that one who caused damage had no escape from penalty. The element of intention was not involved, for a person was presumed to intend the consequences of his act.

However, a rapid about-face took place during the nineteenth century. Risks of personal injury in factories and on the highways multiplied, and the old law of strict liability would have stifled infant industry and commerce. In this time of fruitful progress, men were made to share the risks and accept individual sacrifices so that free enterprise might flourish for the future good of the community. The unavoidable casualties were left to the care of friends or the poorhouse.

The early railroads had struggled with cattle on their tracks and sparks that burned farmers' fields. If a passenger held his arm out of a window, so that it was struck by a post, the railroad had been to blame for not furnishing windows that would prevent such behavior. Then, in 1853, the case of *New Jersey Railroad v. Keerwood* [4] produced the doctrine of contributory negligence on the part of the plaintiff passenger. After that he kept his arms inside, and the doctrine of strict liability remained only for damage done by sparks along the way. In some jurisdictions, even this was limited to the damage done by the first fire set, and when a fire ran through several buildings, only the owner of the first house was compensated.

On the crowded horse-and-buggy highways, defendants were soon relieved of the burden of strict liability. Now a defendant need only show that he exercised the care expected of an ordinarily prudent man in operating his vehicle. Where the danger was obvious, the plaintiff victim was held to assume the risk. Even if danger was not conspicuous and the defendant had failed to exercise reasonable care, the plaintiff still might lose his case if his conduct was shown to be contributorily negligent, or, in other words, if he failed to act as a reasonably prudent man would have acted in order to avert the injury. For the contributorily negligent plaintiff, one hope remained. This was a doctrine called last clear chance, which applied only in the most exaggerated cases. Take, for example, a plaintiff who had drunkenly stumbled into the street and stretched out with his neck on a trolley track. Clearly, such an act, should the trolley come along and behead him, would be contributory negligence. If the place where he lay was dark, not even a reasonably careful trolley driver could save him. Now suppose he lay under a street light, the driver saw him, had plenty of time to stop, but failed to do so. Here the doctrine entered, for clearly it was not good public policy to encourage vindictive people to take advantage of the helpless, however much this condition might result from personal negligence.

In that age of the entrepreneur, very little duty was placed upon a landowner for the protection of people coming upon his property. Related to the idea of the lord supreme in his castle, the only obligation was not to set traps or willfully do injury. The potential plaintiff, in other words, entered at his own risk. Through most of the nineteenth century, this limited duty was enlarged only in the case of a customer or business guest who came on the premises for the mutual advantage of himself and the landowner. In such a case, if the owner of the property knew a certain part of the floor was apt to give way, dropping his customer into a cellar below, he would be held liable for a failure to give warning. However, if a trespasser seeking shelter from a thunderstorm suffered a like fate, he would have no case.

The early nineteenth century had freed commerce from the

burdens of medieval tort liability and emphasized the interest of the group over that of the individual, but it was not long before the industrial age began to emerge from its honeymoon. In the second half of the century, the tide was turning. This reverse was initiated by landowners. In 1809, in the case of *Butterfield v. Forrester*,[5] Mr. Forrester had stuck a pole out from his property across a street, and Mr. Butterfield on horseback rode into it in the dark. The horseman was found guilty of contributory negligence and lost the action. In 1863, in the case of *Byrne v. Beadle*,[6] a new doctrine appeared. Here a barrel being loaded from the defendant's warehouse fell onto the plaintiff, a passerby below. The plaintiff received compensation when the judge announced the theory of res ipsa loquitor (The thing speaks for itself). In other words, the fault was so obvious that the plaintiff was relieved of the burden of proving the defendant negligent. This theory was extended in a case of the twentieth century to the following facts: The plaintiff was driving along a highway where escaping smog from the defendant's chemical plant entered the passing car and thereby aggravated the plaintiff's heart condition. The plaintiff won his case.[7] A dubious decision, perhaps, but one which, in our age of industrial pollution, undoubtedly should be considered.

The freedom from liability for the injury to trespassers has also broken down. An early case was *Sioux City and P.R. Co. v. Stout*,[8] in 1873. Young Stout, aged five, strayed onto railroad company property, and he was injured while playing on a turntable. The court dismissed trespass as a defense and came up with an "'implied invitee" theory, suggesting that a railroad yard offered such temptation to an infant as to amount to an invitation to an adult. From this decision has come another, that of "attractive nuisance." Most typically today is the case of the child plaintiff who strays into a neighbor's backyard uninvited and falls into the swimming pool and drowns.

The freedom of the railroad has been encroached upon in other ways. Strict liability under the last-clear-chance doctrine still holds for animals and people on its tracks, but a plaintiff who drove his car into a train standing in the station failed to collect when the judge commented wryly that a train "gives notice of its presence."

Another railroad case concerned with the limits of liability is *Palsgraf v. Long Island Railroad Co.*[9] The plaintiff, after buying a ticket to Rockaway Beach, was standing on the train's platform. Another train arrived, loaded passengers, and began to move out of the station. While the train was in motion, a man ran to catch it. Under his arm was a package wrapped in newspaper. As the man stumbled trying to board the train, one guard helped him with a push, another pulled him aboard. In the process his package fell to the tracks, and the fireworks which it contained exploded. This sent a shock wave well down the platform, causing a heavy scale hung up above the plaintiff's head to fall down and injure her. Alleging that the defendant's employees were negligent in pulling and pushing a man aboard a moving train and that in consequence of that negligence she had been hurt, the plaintiff brought suit. Clearly the defendant's employees had acted negligently. Had the passenger who stumbled aboard the train been injured, he might, apart from a defense of contributory negligence (running for a moving train), have recovered damages. Just as clearly, no defense of contributory negligence could be brought against the plaintiff. At issue was the word "foreseeable." Was the injury a foreseeable consequence of the defendant's conduct? The court said no, and held for the defendant.

Under similarly peculiar circumstances, courts have held the causal connection was sufficiently close to award damages in the following cases. *Ramsey v. Carolina Tennessee Power Co.*[10] considered a defendant negligent who was shunting railway cars off the end of a spur track into a field where they struck a guy wire of a power-line pole, causing the pole to twist. The high-tension wires made contact with low-tension wires, and several miles away the plaintiff, who was operating a laundry machine, was electrocuted. A 1917 case, *Walmsley v. Rural Telephone Assoc.*,[11] developed when the defendant's wires sagged over a highway. A man rode underneath with a shotgun on his shoulder. The gun was discharged by the contact and wounded the plaintiff, who was standing some distance away. In finding for the plaintiff, these courts had come a long way in extending responsibility.

An area where responsibility for negligent conduct has developed rapidly in the past sixty years concerns charitable hospitals.

Until 1910, such institutions were immune from suits brought by their patients. With public policy in mind, even strangers had no recourse, until a mechanic repairing a boiler in the basement of a Salvation Army building was injured. The court allowed him to recover damages because he was not a beneficiary of the charity. The first patient to recover damages did so in 1937, when injured in an auto accident while riding in the defendant's ambulance. However, this decision restricted liability to administrative acts, but not medical ones, so that if a patient was burned by a hot-water bottle he would receive compensation if it had been placed against his body by an orderly, but not if by a nurse. Not until 1957 did the courts overcome this foolish distinction.

Nowhere in this overpopulated twentieth century of ours has man's responsibility for careful conduct been so laboriously explored as in the case of the motor vehicle. Reasonable conduct requires an operator to observe front, back, sides, passing cars, crossings, side roads, stop signs and traffic signals, the machinery of his vehicle, and the endless varieties of behavior he may encounter from other drivers and from pedestrians. Courtrooms are choked with litigation, but of the myriad cases perhaps the most famous and one of the most interesting is *MacPherson v. Buick*.[12]

In 1911 the motorcar was coming of age. The cry of "Get a horse!" already had a nostalgic ring, and Ray Harroun astonished a watching world by sweeping around the five hundred miles of Indianapolis at an average speed of nearly eighty miles an hour. Donald MacPherson, a dealer in gravestones, had purchased a brand-new four-cylinder Buick runabout from the Close Brothers. Two months later, while he was tooling along at fifteen miles per hour, a left rear wheel detached itself. The car swerved and collapsed, injuring the plaintiff. Now, under the law as it then stood, MacPherson might have developed a cause of action against the dealers who had sold him the car. Going after bigger fish, MacPherson sued the manufacturer. Trial was held in Saratoga, New York, a town where the horse was still king. Clearly, the plaintiff had no cause of action in fraud, for Buick did not know of the defect in the car which caused the wheel to fall off. MacPherson's only claim was that Buick had been negligent in failing to exercise reasonable care in inspecting for defects.

The court looked to an earlier case where the manufacturer had mislabled a bottle of belladonna "extract of dandelion." In that situation, a plaintiff had purchased the drug, had been made ill, and had recovered damages from the manufacturer. Up to this point, third-party liability had been restricted to inherently dangerous items such as the belladonna, a poison, or to dynamite. An automobile had been regarded as dangerous only when defectively made. Extending this doctrine, the court now found for the plaintiff, and in the process enunciated the following law, which has since been followed: If a manufacturer's product, when negligently made, may imperil life and limb, and if the manufacturer has reason to know that this product will be used by one other than the purchaser (the dealer, in the MacPherson case) without tests being made, then the manufacturer is under a duty to make it carefully. The MacPherson case has been followed uniformly in American courts, where it has been variously extended to cover damage to the article sold and to pedestrians struck by the defective auto.

So, in the course of a century, the law regarding negligence has come full circle, from strict liability under the old trespass law, to near immunity under early tort law in the nineteenth century, to near strict liability once again. From the preference given industrialization a hundred years ago, the courts have molded their decisions so as not to lay the burdens of modern society upon its victims but upon all of us, a cost shared largely by the insurance companies. With the growth of liability insurance in the last fifty years, courts and juries have come to assume the company, not the defendant, will bear the cost. Verdicts increase in amount. Compensation is given not only for physical damage and injury, but for nervous and emotional shock. With a highway death every quarter hour and three injuries a minute, the courts are clogged with negligence cases. Delays of up to five years before a case is tried are not uncommon. The future promises only longer delays.

One likely alternative in keeping with current social trends is comprehensive motor vehicle loss insurance, commonly refered to as no-fault insurance. Insurance companies and many attorneys oppose the idea, but it has merit in terms of fairness and in order to unburden the courts. Such insurance would be for the benefit of anyone injured by an automobile except suicides, attempted suicides, or persons violating traffic regulations. In establishing a claim, the only other issue would be the extent of the injury suffered. Much time, effort, and money would be saved by the elimination of slow litigation, and compensation would arrive when it was most needed, not years later.

Recent developments in negligence law have indicated the general growth of a social conscience concerning an individual accidentally injured. Where the harm might have foreseeably and reasonably been averted, responsibility is fixed and recompense forthcoming through the courts. This might be described as a duty to act with care so as not to harm other human beings.

But what of the situation where no duty to act exists? Suppose a man is sitting on a park bench, harmlessly reading his newspaper. Children quite unknown to him are sailing toy boats in a lake. One of them falls in and begins to drown. No parent or policeman is within call, no one reasonably duty bound is able to save the child. Our newspaper reader happens to be an Olympic swimmer who could save the child with ease, yet he does not budge.

Or suppose, as happened in Kew Gardens, New York, not many years ago, apartment dwellers looking down from their windows see a man attacking a young woman. The man is evidently drunk. He stabs the girl. She cries for help. He reels off, returns, and attacks her again. The spectators, safe above, watch with interest without bothering to call the police until after the girl is dead. This was the notorious Kitty Genovese affair, which has stirred a controversy in the fringe area of the law involving the so-called good Samaritan.

In a discussion between a lawyer and Jesus, the former, when told to love his neighbor as himself, wanted to know just who that neighbor was. In reply, Jesus told the story of the man who was set upon by thieves and left beside the road injured and without means. First a priest and then a Levite passed by. Finally a Samaritan came along, bound the man's wounds, found an inn, and paid the innkeeper to look after him. Clearly, the Samaritan was a good neighbor, and Jesus admonished the lawyer by saying, "Go thou and do likewise."

How this lawyer reacted in practice has not been recorded. How the common law and its professionals have dealt with the problem is well documented, and is summed up in the observations of the Texas cowhand who was sitting in the Last Chance Saloon. He remarked to his friends, "I see Jim Hardin hung himself out by the corral." When asked whether he'd cut the body down, the cowhand replied, "Hell, no. He hasn't stopped twitching yet." More authoritative but of a similar mind is the statement of Dean J. B. Ames, which appears in a 1908 *Harvard Law Review*.[13] In commenting on a man who watched a drowning, he wrote, "He took away nothing from the person in jeopardy, he simply failed to confer a benefit upon a stranger. . . . The law does not compel active benevolence between man and man. It is left to one's conscience whether he shall be the good Samaritan or not."

In general, this is the attitude of our law today, so it is not surprising that the Kew Gardens spectators who watched Miss Genovese being murdered received no more than public scorn, a scorn tempered by doubt whether we, too, might have acted in this way. And the man who watched with interest while an infant tottered to the brink of a deep well and vanished was called a monster by the court which nonetheless held him free of liability.[14]

Although our law imposes no duty upon the stranger to act as a good Samaritan, our attitudes and our laws often place heavy burdens on the person who responds to a moral duty and intervenes. Where there is very little sense of neighborliness, well-intended help may be scorned as officious meddling. Of course, in serious situations there is usually the telephone, with the specialist, the fire department, or the ambulance at the other end. Not always. More than disinterest, there is a fear of involvement. This is no new thing, and Montaigne in his essays speaks of the farmers who came to him after observing in the woods a seriously wounded man. They had run away, fearing the police might find them there and hold them accountable for the crime. Such feelings are stronger now. Suppose, however, that a man is by nature a good Samaritan, an aspiring Don Quixote? What windmills stand in his path? He may make a mistake. On hearing a woman shouting murder from an apartment window, he gallops up four flights of dark stairs and bursts into the room only to find husband and wife in the midst of a family quarrel. He is cursed and thrown out. No real harm done, but will he not think twice when he again hears a call for help?

More serious mistakes are on record. Take, for instance, the case of *People v. Young.*[15] Two burly men were beating a boy while a crowd looked on. Young alone leaped into the fray, broke one of the attacker's knees, and put an end to the assault. Only afterward did he discover that the two men were plainclothes police officers making an arrest. The appeal court, which upheld a conviction of assault against good Samaritan Young, said, "We feel that such a policy [freeing Young for his good intentions] would not be conducive to an orderly society."

Other problems await the rescuer with good intentions who unfortunately bungles the job. What would have happened to the biblical good Samaritan if, in moving the roadside victim, he had opened a fresh wound from which the man bled to death? Probably nothing; but under our law the good Samaritan must bear the penalty for his own negligence. Take the case of *Zelenko v. Gimbel Brothers.*[16] Here a woman became ill in the defendant's department store. No bond of duty had yet been formed, but then one of the defendant's employees undertook to escort the woman to a rest room. An obligation had now been assumed, and when the woman, left to recover there, actually died, the defendant became liable to the woman's heirs for negligently failing to call a doctor.

Most difficult is the criminal situation. Even the biblical good Samaritan suffered no risk to life and limb by encountering the thieves in the course of their crime. Suppose a stranger is being attacked by thugs. What are the consequences of becoming physically involved? As well as the possibility of Mr. Young's mistake, there is the risk of physical hurt and even death. A bungling of the rescue may make the Samaritan negligently liable to the original victim. It is even possible, under such circumstances as subduing the attackers with unnecessary vigor, that he may end up liable in damages to them.

Fringe areas begin to offer some directive. If a person is actually involved in an accident, it is a crime to flee from the scene, whether responsible or not. This does not, of course, apply to casual witnesses. Also, between certain individuals, a duty does exist. Family members are generally taken to have an obligation to help one another, even in those cases in which the needed aid, such as a doctor, is against the family member's religion. Other relationships imply a duty. A ship's captain must aid a seaman in distress. Common carriers—planes, trains, buses, etc.—are obliged to look after ill or injured passengers. Policemen and firemen assume, through the nature of their employment, a duty to protect the stranger, but our law has gone no further than this.

Many European countries, recalling the Roman law of negotiorum gestio, have specific criminal-code provisions setting out a duty to rescue. In the United States, the would-be good Samaritan is often looked upon as an officious meddler, but in Europe the volunteer is described, according to the Roman notion, as "the manager of another's business," and the inclination is to reward and praise him.

Typical of such European statutes is that found in France. First proposed in 1934, the provision did not become law until 1941 under the puppet government, with pressure from the Nazi overlords. The catalyst was the murder of a German officer, which resulted in the execution of fifty hostages. The hostages were forgotten, but the Germans were concerned that a statute be passed which would oblige French citizens to prevent further crimes against the occupying military forces. With French liberation, the statute became void, only to reappear, revised as Article 63 of the criminal code. It provides that anyone who refuses to give assistance to another in danger, either personally or by facilitating the rescue, when he can act without risk to himself or anyone else, receives a punishment of not more than five years and not less than three months in jail and a fine ranging from 360 to 15,000 francs.

Under French law, the good Samaritan who bungles may still be civilly liable for damages done, though where he gives medical aid to a victim, his efforts are not measured by the level of proficiency expected of a physician but of that common to an ordinary man. Only the more recent Czechoslovakian civil code of 1964 explicitly protects the heavy-handed rescuer as follows: "Anyone who has caused damage when avoiding an immediate threat not caused by himself shall not be liable for damage unless the threat might have been avoided in another manner, or if the result caused is as serious or more serious than the one threatened."

What of the man who acts under a duty imposed by the law and is himself injured or killed? In 1955, a Paris court decided such a case.[17] Here a truck driver negligently drove onto a railway track and was struck and carried along some distance by a train. Two passersby arrived while the truck was still on the track. While they were attempting to rescue the driver from the wreckage, in accordance with the legal mandate to do so, another train came from the opposite direction. It plowed into the truck, which crashed into the rescuers and killed them both. The truck driver survived, and the court decided that the widows of the would-be rescuers had a good cause of action against the truck driver and his employer.

A German court with a similar code confronted a situation where a car went off the road into a river. The defendant could not swim, and she shouted for help. A road worker, hearing her shout, plunged into the water, rescued her, and then drowned. His widow brought action against the defendant for lack of support, and an annuity was granted to her for life and to her children until their eighteenth birthday.

It may seem excessive for a rescued person to be obliged to support a widow for the rest of her life, just as it is outrageous for a man to sit by while a baby crawls over the lip of a well. Somewhere there must be a compromise. The law has come a long way in extending the duty of care between strangers, but can it go so far as to recognize a new kind of liability without fault? The answer provides a crucial test of our moral values, and the obligations of citizens under the growing hazards of urban life. Are we, as Cain asked, to be our brother's keeper, and if so, to what extent? A possible law might impose upon a stranger the duty to act when the damage or injury is immediate and there seems to be no alternative to avoiding the threat than his own intervention. Intervention would also be conditioned on the likelihood of little or no peril to the rescuer, while his intervention would reasonably avert substantial harm being done. Should the rescuer be injured, if compensation from the victim seems an imposition, it might be possible to work out a system along the lines of workmen's compensation and compulsory motor vehicle insurance. This would spread the cost of rewarding the good Samaritan, a cost which would not be great in the light of the rarity of such impersonal heroism.

Criminal as well as civil law has undergone humanizing trends through the centuries. Originally the law concerned itself solely with the extraneous facts, with the damage done, but never with the intent. Suppose a defendant tried to murder someone by placing a pistol to his head and pulling the trigger. Nothing happened. Unknown to the attacker, who was arrested and charged with attempted murder, the gun was empty. Formerly, as in fact no murder could have been accomplished, the defendant would undoubtedly have gone free. Today, the court measures the bad intent, rather than splitting hairs over the accidental events that may block its exercise. Nowadays it would constitute fraud for a jeweler to sell to a customer a piece of glass after saying it was a diamond and collecting payment on that basis. As late as the seventeenth century, however, caveat emptor (Let the buyer beware) was a very real doctrine, and the buyer could not even get his money back unless the seller had said the following magic words, "I *warrant* that you are paying for a diamond." A more peculiar rigidity was due to the technical "forms of action" imposed in bringing each case. Suppose in the year 1400, A sued B for assault and battery. As it turned out, A had attacked B without provocation and gotten pommeled for his trouble. Today B would plead self-defense, but in early common law, A would collect for damage done. B's only recourse would be to bring another action in his own behalf.

One area of criminal law that attracts much concern today is that of the insane criminal. Until recent times there has been little understanding of the insane, but from the very beginning the notion persisted that one who is insane cannot be held criminally responsible. Only the measure of insanity and its treatment have altered. To put the criminal law into operation, there is normally a requirement of scienter (evil intent). So, if an escaping robber forces his victim to roll his trousers down around his ankles to prevent pursuit, the victim will not be held for indecent exposure in a public place. Should an epileptic during a seizure hit and injure a bystander, he will at most be civilly liable for damages done. There will be no question of criminal assault. So, too, with the insane murderer.

In the trial of Edward Arnold in 1724,[18] it was held that a man totally deprived of his understanding and memory, who does not know what he is doing any more than an infant or a wild beast, cannot be the object of punishment. From the wild-beast test came the question, Can the defendant tell right from wrong? And by 1843 the law and medicine were in agreement about insanity. Man could be fragmented, with some parts of him being sane and others not. That was the year of the famous McNaghten case in England. Daniel McNaghten believed the Pope, the Jesuits, the Tory party, and particularly Sir Robert Peel were all conspiring against him. Thinking Peel the prince of evil, McNaghten aimed at him a fatal bullet, which actually struck Peel's secretary, Edward Drummond. Drummond died and McNaghten was put on trial. The jury was asked whether or not the defendant knew he was doing a wrong and wicked act. They decided in the negative, and McNaghten got off by reason of insanity. A lively debate followed, in consequence of which the House of Lords was asked to state a rule for the courts. They produced the following: In order to establish a defense on the ground of insanity, it had to be proved that at the time of committing the act, the accused was laboring under such a defect of reason from a mental disease as not to know the nature and quality of the act he was doing; or if he did know it, that he did not know that what he was doing was wrong.

More useful on its face than the wild-beast test, the McNaghten rule, which is still followed in England as well as the United States, has come face to face with modern psychology. No longer can it be said the law and medicine are in complete accord on who is insane. Sometimes they are, as with seventy-two-year-old Emma Fox, who for no apparent reason beat her husband unconscious with her fists and carved him up with a hacksaw. She then burned the larger pieces and scattered the remaining fragments in the backyard for the birds. Mrs. Fox admitted the deed readily, and then asked the police in a sweet Helen Hayes manner, "And now may I go home?" Here no detailed examination or debate was required. She was found unfit to stand trial and was committed to an institution.

Another grisly case involved an old man named Albert Fish. In 1928 one Frank Howard, a gentle old fellow, had been employed by the Budd family as a handyman. They had allowed their ten-year-old daughter Grace to accompany him to a children's party, allegedly given by his sister. Although the child vanished, Howard gave what was regarded for the next six years as a satisfactory explanation of how they had been separated in the New York City crowd. Then, in the autumn of 1934, Mrs. Budd received an unsigned letter which told of a sea captain who had spent so much time in famine-ridden China, where stray children were apt to be eaten, that he had returned to New York and indulged in some cannibalism of his own. The handwriting was traced to old Mr. Howard, whose real name was Albert Fish. Fish promptly confessed he had taken Grace to his sister's empty house in Westchester; there he had murdered her and stewed up her remains with carrots and onions. No trace of her was left, except the bones, which the police eventually found. Once the old man was in jail, several other such murders, perhaps fifteen in all, were traced to Fish, who had a habit of beating himself with a paddle until the blood flowed and shouting from the hilltops, "I am Christ!" X rays disclosed twenty-seven needles imbedded in his body, driven there for masochistic pleasure. Naturally his defense was insanity. In his own mind he denied that the murders were wrong, for if they had been wrong, an angel would have stopped him. In psychiatric terms it is unlikely a man could be much madder than Albert Fish. Nonetheless, due undoubtedly to the hideousness of the crime, psychiatric evidence was divided—if not as to his medical, then as to his legal, sanity. The jury, taking all the evidence, found him legally sane, and Fish went to the electric chair posthaste, a man clearly mad. On the other hand, one must stretch the sense of humanity to see any purpose in keeping such a creature alive.

A more difficult case developed in 1946. William Heirens, a seventeen-year-old University of Chicago student, was arrested for burglary and confessed. This confession was quickly extended to include three horrible murders which involved dismemberment and messages scrawled at the scene in lipstick: "For God's sake, catch me before I kill again; I cannot control myself." Further investigation showed that young Heirens attributed the murders to an imaginary yet dominant companion, "George." Here the court and jury applied the compartmentalizing idea of insanity. No one denied Heirens's belief in his companion or the insane compulsion that drove him to kill, yet under the McNaghten test, Heirens was capable of understanding the nature and object of the proceeding brought against him. There was no question, either, that he knew his crimes were wrong, so Heirens was found legally sane and given a life sentence.

Sometimes, as in *State v. Moore*,[19] even the state's medical witnesses may believe in the insanity of the murderer, but the jury, confronted with the legal McNaghten test, may pronounce him legally sane and thereby guilty.

The dispute between lawyer and psychiatrist is a natural and nearly unavoidable one. The psychiatrist generally considers the lawyer rigid and out of date in his attitude regarding insanity. The lawyer labels the psychiatrist vague and uncertain. The difference springs from the separation of their roles. The doctor must think in terms of treating a disease by no means fully understood, but it is the lawyer's task to deal with justice and fix responsibility. Yet some closure of the gap has recently been achieved, thanks to more flexible tests. The American Law Institute is a board of legal experts not bound by any one decision or set of facts. It has proposed that a person is not responsible for criminal conduct if, at the time of such conduct and as the result of a mental disease or defect, he could not appreciate the wrongfulness of his conduct or was unable to conform his behavior to legal requirements. Although more flexible from the psychiatrist's point of view than the McNaghten rule, the Law Institute's model has been followed by only a few courts.

A simpler measure now being followed in a few jurisdictions came from *Durham v. U.S.*[20] Here the distinguishing-right-from-wrong test was dropped, and it was held that a defendant should not be found guilty if his unlawful act was the product of a mental disease or defect. This "Durham test," though focusing on the link between the crime and the mental disease, lacks the precision desired of a legal test. Its validity is shaken by the words of Judge Thurman Arnold, "In the determination of guilt, age-old conceptions of individual moral responsibility cannot be abandoned without creating a laxity of enforcement that undermines the whole administration of criminal law." [21]

Public concern is not with such definitional niceties, but with the newspaper headline announcing the toll of another insane rampage. Why are insane murderers allowed to walk the streets? Why, in 1966, was a madman permitted to climb to the top of a tower overlooking the University of Texas campus and shoot down twelve strangers? Psychiatrists are blamed for softness. Tough legal controls of the mentally ill are demanded, but, of course, controls sufficient to guarantee streets safe from mental breakdowns might well require incarceration of one tenth of the human race. What of the known deviant? Why does he walk the streets? The answer is human compromise and the imperfect process by which the law is civilized. Hundreds of years ago, a deranged person was either deified or burned at the stake as a witch. Among the Norsemen, the raving killer led his men into battle and was known as a "berserk"; today the insane are exempt from military service, rarely if ever go up in flames except by their own choosing, and only occasionally are deified.

Yet even in our civilized approach to the insane creator of disorder there are hidden dangers. Bizarre public behavior may often lead to a psychiatric examination. Often such an examination can be used as a punishment. Take, for example, the case of Herbert Callender, chairman of the Bronx chapter of CORE, who marched to City Hall to dramatize his cause by placing the mayor of New York under citizen's arrest. The charge against the mayor was misappropriation of public funds by allowing racial discrimination on city-sponsored construction projects. Bizarre, yes. Insane, no. But after arrest, Mr. Callender spent five days in Bellevue Hospital under psychiatric observation.

In actual practice, the fate of the insane criminal is rarely decided in the courtroom, but rather at a pretrial psychiatric examination. Though an accused criminal is held to have the right to a speedy and public trial, few of the insane receive it. At this pretrial hearing, a court-appointed panel of psychiatrists must decide whether the accused is mentally fit to stand trial; that is, can he understand the charges brought against him, the nature and object of the legal proceedings, and can he assist his counsel in preparing his defense? His state of mind at the time of the crime is not at issue, nor is the magnitude of the crime itself. If he is found incapable of standing trial due to his mental condition, the usual proceeding is to place him in a mental institution until such time as he is deemed fit to stand trial.

For every patient found not guilty by reason of insanity by a jury, dozens are confined with no trial ever having been held. Once they are institutionalized, their prospects of obtaining a trial in the future are dim. The problem is that recovery from psychosis is seldom absolute. Schizophrenics become skillful in concealing their overt symptoms. The psychiatrists who must examine such people are aware of these difficulties and the hazard of possibly setting dangerous patients at large. They tend to play safe. Thus it is rare that a person so confined will ever be deemed sufficiently recovered to stand trial. Very often, then, the pretrial hearing amounts to a life sentence. Just deserts for individuals such as our friend Mr. Fish; but what of the forgotten case of Louis Perroni, whose gas-station lease was canceled after ten years when a shopping center was proposed for the area? Mr. Perroni resisted eviction. He made the mistake of firing a gun into the air, was arrested, and found unfit to stand trial. After he had spent several years in jail, friends on the outside obtained a writ of habeas corpus. Only then was Mr. Perroni reexamined. Found sullen and withdrawn after five years in jail for disturbing the peace, Mr. Perroni was again incarcerated without trial. If not mad in the first place, he may well be by this time. There are other, more unfortunate cases than his on record. In 1966, the New York State Court of Claims awarded $115,000 to a man who had stolen a box of candy and been held in Dannemora Prison Hospital for twenty years.

Presuming the accused is judged competent by the pretrial

examiners, he then may stand trial for the crime alleged. Insanity at the time of the crime may be raised as a defense or it may not, but it is at this level that the potentially dangerous man is most often released on society, not at the time he is in the hands of the psychiatrists. Suppose, in fact, the defendant is dangerously insane. If he does not plead insanity as a defense, he may well get off entirely. If his crime was a minor one, such as assault, he will at worst receive only a limited penalty. Very soon he may be back on the streets. For this reason alone, insanity is rarely pleaded except in murder cases, though the likelihood of an insane man getting out of jail is better than out of an institution. On the other hand, what if he does plead insanity as a defense? The jury may not believe it. In this case, he will undoubtedly be found guilty, as such a defense tends to admit the crime. On the other hand, if the jury believes him to have committed his crime while insane, it is unlikely that he will get off. Insanity is rarely a temporary affair, and he will be up against the same problems as the man found unfit to stand trial in the first place. In effect, he will be institutionalized under an indefinite sentence. Occasionally there is offered the defense of temporary insanity, but courts frown on this plea. Psychiatrists rarely believe it, but juries sometimes accept it under a kind of unwritten law whereby the husband, allegedly blinded by a jealous rage, shoots his wife's lover: sane before, sane after, but witless with rage during the moment of pulling the trigger.

A variation rarely occurring in fact is the case of the sane man attempting to escape legal justice under a faked plea of insanity. The evidence surrounding the crime itself usually answers the question. Lack of motive, lack of remorse, and unnecessary brutality usually mark the insane murderer, and if they do not, his conduct under professional observation thereafter will almost infallibly distinguish him from the most skillful faker. A case in point is that of *People v. Schmidt*.[22] Dr. Schmidt's troubles began when the dismembered corpse of Anna Aaronsen turned up in the Hudson River. Brought to trial, Dr. Schmidt alleged that he had had an affair with the deceased and that God had begun telling him to kill her as an atonement and sacrifice for his sins. Dutifully, the doctor complied. Of the five psychiatrists who examined him, two said he was insane, three that he was a faker. The jury found him guilty of murder in the first degree. Subsequently, the doctor appealed, asserting that indeed he was a fake. The facts, according to his new story, were quite different. He and others had performed an illegal abortion on Miss Aaronsen which had caused her death. Confident in his ability to appear insane, Dr. Schmidt agreed to assume total responsibility for the crime if need be. In fact, this story seemed far more likely than the original one, but the appeals court held that a criminal may not play about with defenses. He was held to his original defense. The governor refused clemency, and Dr. Schmidt went to the electric chair, a more skillful but more unlucky faker than most.

Psychiatry and the law have had a short and hectic marriage, but divorce is unlikely. The future seems bright, though there is still much room for improvement. Among the many suggestions, a few follow. At the trial itself, the old advocacy system, which is at the root of our common law, casts doubt and discredit upon the psychiatrist witness. It confuses the jury. The sad fact is that expert witnesses are hired by the defense and the prosecution alike, and no unity of opinion is achieved. Testimony conflicts, and it is hard for any sensible juror to conclude that sound judgment, not money, is behind these disagreements. Justice might be better served if the fee system for medical witnesses were ended and replaced by an impartial panel of experts rendering an unbiased decision on the issue of insanity.

Another great danger, as has been stressed, is that of involuntary confinement in excess of the crime, with very little help being given the patient toward his healthy restoration into society. This is not a problem of callousness, but simply a lack of funds, which works particular hardship upon the minor deviant, such as the Peeping Tom and the exhibitionist. Public horror at the idea of the sexual psychopath walking the streets keeps these relatively harmless men in jail. In fact, with treatment, the likelihood of their becoming repeaters is statistically less than that of the average sane criminal. The possibility of one of these types of minor sexual offenders turning into a rapist is virtually nonexistent.

CHAPTER SIX

Civilizing Punishments

As long as crime has had a name, there has been punishment, and before that, there was simple vengeance: an eye for an eye. Squaring matters in kind was a dominant consideration in early punishment, so that in twelfth-century England a man who killed another by falling on him from a tree was not simply hanged. He was executed by his victim's relative, presumably a heavy one, falling on him from a tree; if possible, from the same tree.

Before the Christian notion of sin entered the picture, minor crimes were often dealt with by compensation. But sin brought a need for penance and punishment so literal that in the Dark Ages animals that had killed humans were tried. A few were acquitted. Most were hanged. At Savigny in 1457, a sow with a litter of six piglets was condemned for child murder. The piglets enjoyed a last-minute reprieve because proof of their complicity was found wanting. The last reported case of animal execution occurred in 1906, when a Swiss court found a dog guilty of having taken part in robbery-murder. (It is to be wondered if he had had rabies whether he might not have gotten off under the McNaghten rule.)

At the very root of the common law, the Magna Carta provided: "A free man shall not be fined for a small offense, except in proportion to the measure of the offense, and for a great offense he shall be fined in proportion to the magnitude of the offense." But this left the door open for hanging, drawing, and quartering, chopping off hands, slitting nostrils, and similar atrocities where the circumstances were deemed appropriate. Colonial America was perhaps less barbaric, but every community had its pillory and stocks. Public floggings were common, and as late as 1963 the Supreme Court of Delaware upheld a sentence of twenty lashes for breaking parole in a case of auto theft. In general, such penalties are now rare in the United States, due largely to the application of the Eighth Amendment, which forbids that punishments be cruel or unusual. No elaboration of cruel and unusual is given by the Constitution, but various courts of appeal have held the following to be cruel and unusual punishments:

twenty-one months in jail for bigamy when remarriage was undertaken in the belief that a legal divorce had been achieved;
thirty years hard labor for burglary without weapons and without a previous criminal record;
ninety days in jail for being addicted to narcotics.

In the last case, *Robinson v. California*,[1] the judge said that the sentence made it a crime simply to be an addict, as opposed to selling or conspicuously using drugs. "Even one day in prison would be a cruel and unusual punishment for the crime of having a common cold," was the analogy he drew.

A controversial case on the subject and one giving an insight into the process of electrocution is *Francis v. Resweber*.[2] Willie Francis, a convicted murderer, went to the electric chair on May 3, 1946. Like thousands before him, he was strapped down, prayed over, and with the words, "Good-bye, Willie," the electrician threw the switch. Then something undetermined went wrong, leaving Francis alive to give the following description:

You feel like you got a mouthful of cold peanut butter and you see little blue and pink and green speckles in front of your eyes, the kind that shines in a rooster's tail. All I could think was, "Willie, you're going out of this world. . . ." They begun to strap me against the chair and everything begun to look dazy in the room. It was like the white folks watching was on a big swing and they swung away-y-y back and then right up close to where I could hear their breathing. I didn't think of my whole life like at the picture show, just, Willie, you're going out of this world in this bad chair. Sometimes I thought it so loud it hurt my head, and when they put the black bag over my head I was all locked up inside the bag with the loud thinking. . . . Some folks say it's gold [death]; some say it's white as hominy grits. I reckon it's black. I ought to know, I been mighty close.

Recalling the electrician's parting words, Willie went on,

He could have been putting me on a bus for New Orleans the way he said it, and I tried to say good-bye, but my tongue got stuck in the peanut butter, and I felt a burning in my head and my left leg, and I jumped against the straps. When the straps kept cutting me, I hoped I was alive, and I asked the electric man to let me breathe.[3]

The machinery had failed. Willie went back to his cell, and before another attempt was made, his attorneys took an appeal based upon double jeopardy and cruel and unusual punishment. The appeal failed, but a dissenting opinion presented the following argument: If the state had deliberately put Francis into the chair, turned up the electricity not quite enough to kill, then removed him only to return him later to his death, this would be cruel and unusual torture, and as far as the victim was concerned, the want of design on the state's part made no difference. The majority view, perhaps relying upon the fact that when Captain Kidd had been hanged in 1701, the rope had broken on the first try, held that such mechanical failure was only an accidental peril. A month later Willie went back to the chair. This time the machinery worked.

Why are criminals punished? There are several reasons, which have received more or less emphasis throughout the ages. First there is retribution, an eye for an eye, which serves a need civilized people prefer to deny. More valid is deterrence, which primarily removes the offender from the public, either by prison walls or death. Also, the example is supposed to discourage others from similar behavior. Some go so far as to maintain it elevates the moral standards of society. As Plato said, "He who desires to inflict rational punishment does not retaliate for a past wrong which cannot be undone; he has regard for the future, and is desirous that the man who is punished, and he who sees him punished, may be deterred from

doing wrong again. He punishes for the sake of prevention." [4]
Most modern and hopeful of motives for punishment is rehabilitation of the criminal.

The first influential arguments against the death penalty and inhuman treatment of prisoners came from an Italian, Cesare Beccaria, in his book *Crimes and Punishment,* published in 1764. With Beccaria in mind, various methods have been attempted to improve the prisoner and his lot, as well as his social prospects. In Philadelphia an early attempt was made to break down what was regarded as the criminal's obdurate spirit by placing him in a private cell for his entire term; solitary confinement, in other words, which, in the light of more modern psychiatry, seems to have been a likely way to ensure a quota of psychopaths. Only a little less oppressive was the silent system, with the prisoners separate only at night but under enforced silence during the day. During exercise periods the prisoners were sometimes hooded to diminish the temptation of human contact.

In the United States today, these techniques have been abandoned. Prisoners share their cells and such work and recreation periods as are available. The result is that most prisons serve as schools for crime, where nonconformable elements are brought together, bitter and defiant, to share their talents. Once released, the ex-prisoner has only partly paid his debt. He remains a stigmatized felon lacking the rights and privileges of citizenship. Acceptable jobs are hard to find. His temptation to return to crime is powerful.

Improvements are to be observed in other countries, notably in Soviet Russia. There a man is generally sentenced to prison until "cured" in a practical sense. If he works well, he eats better. He may live with his wife, and take weekends away from prison. When returned to society, he is regarded as cured, and not derided as an ex-felon. The rate of criminal repeaters in Russia is statistically very low. Similarly, in Israel, prisoners who can and will work, receive a wage, most of which is put aside against their release. For those prisoners who are not regarded as a menace or likely to attempt escape, good behavior is rewarded with four-day passes home.

Reform is not likely to come, as formerly believed, through punishment. Not all prisoners can be cured, but more can be done to help them, with less mechanical and degrading conditions. In the United States, younger prisoners should be kept from the corruptive influence of hardened degenerates. Homosexuality is rampant in prisons now, and much could be achieved in this area by colonies where prisoners may live with their families. All reforms, naturally, are a calculated risk and an immediate social expense. In the long run, however, the saving might be enormous.

Of greater public concern than the rehabilitation of criminals is capital punishment; to kill or not to kill the killer. Revenge, deterrence, the harsh but not entirely unreasonable notion that it is unfair for the honest taxpayer to support the worthless who may again impose on society are arguments raised in behalf of execution. The Romans deprived their prisoners of any dignity in death by feeding them to the beasts in the arena, frequently with clown's masks over their faces. In fact, executions were still public spectacles until a hundred years ago.

Today, means of execution vary. Soviet Russia prefers the firing squad, France the guillotine. The Anglo-Saxon way has always been the hangman's noose. The art of hanging in England began with a jeering and delighted crowd around the hanging tree at the crossroads. Before its abolition it had become a science. A good hangman worked out a formula involving the weight of the criminal and the length of the rope, so that the drop would snap the neck without tearing off the head. With the trapdoor set and the rope in place, the criminal was encouraged to play dominoes in his cell with his back to the door. Thus, the executioner and his assistant could slip in and pinion his arms before he knew what was happening. Hands tied, he was walked briskly, or, if his legs failed, carried, strapped to a chair, to the execution cell. Fitting the noose with its sliding brass rings was more effective than the old-fashioned knot. Fitting it took less than a minute. With the ring under the angle of the left jaw, the head would ideally be thrown back and the spinal cord broken. If all went well, the shock of falling would cause immediate unconsciousness. The spinal cord would be torn from the brain stem, and within twenty seconds the heart would stop its automatic beating. Of course, mistakes happened. Ropes broke, prisoners hit against the side of the trap and strangled slowly. But one way or another, irrevocable justice was done. In England, the deceased was buried in the prison yard to spare the relatives, for hanging tends to leave the body with a distressingly elongated neck. In the United States, the bodies of executed criminals, however mutilated, are turned over to the next of kin.

Besides the firing squad and the hangman's noose, there are two other means of execution used in the United States; both modern, scientific, and allegedly as painless as violent death can ever be. One is the electric chair, which began as a New York experiment in 1890 with much doubt as to its efficacy. In fact, a volunteer wrote the governor of the state offering to give it a try, providing five thousand dollars would go to his family on the odd chance that the confounded thing worked. The offer was declined, however, and a murderer by the name of Kemmler was executed with much public delight at its apparent painlessness, an assumption since refuted. Apart from incidental singeing, electrocution does have the virtue of causing little mutilation.

Finally, there is the gas chamber. Here the condemned, stripped to his shorts, sits on a wooden chair in a closed cell. A stethoscope is taped to his chest so that a physician on the outside may listen for the last signs of life. Strapped down with a leather mask over his face, the prisoner waits as the room is evacuated. The last thing he hears is the plop of cyanide pellets falling into a pan of water beneath his seat.

So, for various crimes and by assorted means, society condemns and sometimes executes its criminals. Does it serve the purposes advanced by its advocates? The traditional police viewpoint is that capital punishment deters prospective murderers and discourages other criminals from using weapons. Statistically, studies comparing areas with and without the death penalty show no relationship between the possibility of execution and the murder rate. Logically, the death penalty is no deterrent to one who has already committed murder; nor is it a deterrent to the murderer who follows up his crime with suicide, as about one out of three do.

Clearly it will not cause the insane or the mentally deranged to think twice. It has no effect on those who kill in a sudden fury, who account for 85 percent of all murders.

Typical of such crimes is *Fisher v. the United States*,[5] in which the Supreme Court affirmed the first-degree murder conviction of a Negro janitor. The crime took place as follows. Fisher, who was found to be of subnormal intelligence and psychopathic personality, was accused of doing poor work by the woman librarian where he was employed. They argued. She called him a nigger. He hit her. She screamed. He hit her some more and finally stabbed her. Surely this criminal was not reflecting on the consequences, and though it might be argued that there is no social value in preserving such a life at public expense, one must look beyond to the greater concern. Taking a life because it has no value is only one step away from a program of euthanasia as practiced in Nazi Germany.

Others who are not deterred, who may be in fact encouraged by the potential death penalty, are those disturbed people who desire punishment. About 10 percent of all murderers appear to fall into this class.

Putting aside the vast majority of murderers described above, there are left only the coldly calculating killers, which include professional killers and armed robbers who kill to achieve some other crime. The calculating murderer is rarely deterred by the possibility of punishment, for he expects to get away with what he is doing. The professional burglar rarely carries a gun. Most killing resulting from violent robberies involves young toughs who imagine themselves as romantic desperadoes. The risk of death or causing death is part of the incentive.

What of the argument that murderers will be loosed upon society after a jail term and commit further crimes? True, they are eventually loosed if found to be sane, but between 1928 and 1948, of the 174 convicted murderers released in England, only one committed a second murder.

A strong argument against capital punishment is its irrevocability. An innocent man may still be extricated from prison, but not so the one who has suffered the death penalty. Dare civilized society take such a risk? Some say that the innocent man who dies in this way falls for his country like a soldier in battle, his death unavoidably serving the greater communal good. In a letter to Benjamin Vaughan on March 14, 1785, Benjamin Franklin argued passionately in opposition, saying, "It is better a hundred guilty persons should escape than that one innocent person should suffer." Are innocent people, then, often condemned? Not very often, but often enough; probably more than one in every hundred trials, for witnesses and experts are fallible. Judges and attorneys may be careless, juries prejudiced and confused. Sometimes circumstances seem to conspire against the innocent man. Take Timothy Evans, convicted in England in 1949 for strangling his wife. Evans was hanged. Later an insane murderer, John Christie, who had at the time been quietly living in the same building, admitted the murder, too late to clear anything but Evans's name.

Can the death penalty be described as cruel and unusual? The courts are leaning that way. A *cause célèbre* of recent years was Caryl Chessman, a habitual criminal found guilty of kidnapping in California. In 1948, Chessman was sentenced to death. However, he survived seven postponements. While waiting twelve years in death row, he wrote three popular books. A film, *Justice and Caryl Chessman,* was made, the "The Ballad of Caryl Chessman" became a best-selling song. Can waiting twelve years under sentence of death be anything but cruel and unusual? His final execution may have served some purpose, but the case will remain a blot on American justice and legal procedure.

Advocates of the death penalty have urged the economy of execution, a callous but practical argument which in practice can be refuted. Modern prison systems should see to it that prisoners do productive work. It is good for them as well as society, and in fact the vast population of do-nothing prisoners are not murderers. They are vagabonds, alcoholics, and petty thieves residing briefly in local jails. Strictly from the taxpayers' viewpoint, these, more logically, should be hanged.

A final objection to the death penalty is that it does not work. One can look to the Bloody Code of England for an example. Under medieval common law, the death penalty was imposed for murder, treason, arson, and rape. Then, in 1722 in Hampshire, the landowners were concerned about a band of black-masked poachers, and they got Parliament to enact a three-year emergency statute to punish them when caught. In fact, this statute was on the books for 101 years, and was gradually expanded to include 350 capital offenses; among others, the stealing of turnips, the impersonating of pensioners at Greenwich Hospital, and fraternizing with Gypsies. Why such a spread? It was largely due to the Industrial Revolution, rapid urbanization, and because England had no organized police force until well into the nineteenth century. Punishment, not the patrolman, was relied on to enforce the law. To this end, in 1808, a seven-year-old girl was publicly hanged at Lynn; and in 1833 a nine-year-old boy was sentenced to hang for pushing a stick through a cracked shop-window and pulling out printers' colors to the value of twopence. Public protest saved him, and public reaction, reflected in jury verdicts, finally doomed the Bloody Code. Severity of punishment bred impunity, for juries refused to convict where excessive punishments were prescribed by inhuman laws. This reluctance led the bankers of London to petition Parliament in 1830 to abolish the death penalty for forgery. Their motives were not humanitarian. It was simply that the prospect of the death sentence prevented conviction at all, and forgers, far from being intimidated by the severity of punishment, were encouraged by its lack of enforcement. The lesson is a simple one. The severity of punishment can breed impunity, for men are reluctant to inflict excessive punishments as prescribed by law. The really effective punishment is the moderate one that can be inflicted with certainty and with speed.

The modern trend is away from capital punishment. Despite the old biblical blood-for-blood codes, modern Israel has abolished the death penalty, and so have most European nations. Germany and Italy reinstated it during the days of Hitler and Mussolini but have now removed it once again. In the United States, several states have renounced it; Rhode Island as early as 1852. And even in those states where men remain under sentence of death, no execution has taken place in several years. Man is becoming too civilized to play God. The hangman's noose and the electric chair are not only devices for death, they are signs of brutalizing disdain for life. They stand for the institutionalized savagery that the human race must denounce if it is to survive on this crowded planet.

From *The Newgate Calendar* of 1738 still echo the last words of George Manley, speaking to a crowd at Wicklow:

> "My friends, you assemble to see—what? A man leap into the abyss of death! See what I am—I'm a little fellow. My Redeemer knows that murder was far from my heart, and what I did was through rage and passion, being provoked by the deceased. You'll say I've killed a man. Marlborough killed his thousands, and Alexander his millions. I'm a little murderer and must be hanged. How many men were lost in Italy, and upon the Rhine, during the last war for settling a king in Poland? Both sides could not be in the right! They are great men; but I killed a solitary man."

In this vein let us hope that Justice Benjamin Cardozo was right when he wrote,

> I have faith . . . that a century or less from now, our descendants will look back upon the penal system of today with the same surprise and horror that fill our own minds when we are told that only about a century ago one hundred and sixty crimes were visited under English law with the punishment of death, and that in 1801 a child of thirteen was hanged at Tyburn for the larceny of a spoon.[6]

Another criminal problem now challenging the civilizing of our laws is that of drug addiction. This problem, whether at root medical or legal, goes back long before the growing concern that followed the Second World War. Opium has been eaten since Ulysses sailed the seas, and it has been smoked for nearly five hundred years. Morphine began as a pain-killer about 1850, and today's chief problem, heroin, was derived from opium about 1900. All three derive from a species of poppy known as *Papaver somniferum* which yields raw opium and from which morphine and diacetyl-morphine (or heroin) may be extracted. All are natural opiates. Synthetic opiates such as codeine, Eucodal, and Dilaudid are now on the market.

The direct harm caused by these drugs is not criminal behavior. Their tendency is to tranquilize, not to encourage violence.

However, as they are by nature addictive, their procurement regularly takes criminal patterns where they are not legally obtainable in desired quantities. Their physical effect upon the user is slow and deadly.

Until 1914 there was no law in the United States regarding the sale of these drugs. They might be obtained as pain-killers through mail-order catalogs under a variety of soothing titles. An addict went quite unnoticed, and often as not was a respected member of the community taking her tablespoon of comfort before going to bed. The first legislation, known as the Harrison Act, was innocuous enough and served only to make the distribution of these drugs a matter of record, for tax purposes. The first case to harden this rule still did not concern itself with addiction. In a case in 1915 [7] the court held that possession of smuggled opiates was an unlawful evasion of the tax provision. Four years later, when a physician administered recorded drugs not in the course of treatment but to maintain an addict's customary use, he was found guilty of violating the law.[8] The Treasury Department had jurisdiction, since the original legislation was born as a tax measure. It set up regulations narrowing the right of physicians to prescribe opiates to elderly addicts who might die as the result of withdrawal.

The maximum penalty under the original law was ten years in prison. The 1951 Boggs Amendment doubled this. The Narcotic Drug Control Act of 1956 set up a penalty of ten years to life for selling to minors. The selling of drugs had been elevated to the level of serious crime at a time when it was also a burgeoning problem. The Second World War had interrupted the international pattern of drug traffic, but peace had reestablished it with a vengeance, and what may have been a population of 50,000 addicts during the war years grew to perhaps 200,000. Approaches to the problem might have been various, but the one taken was that of strict enforcement of the law. The problems are unique, for, unlike most crimes, there are no unwilling victims. The police have to rely on hard evidence and the occasional informer or stooge, which means a steady flow of arrests of the petty street peddlers, but seldom a victory over the system. Of course, the real criminals are not the addicts but the gangs who obtain the raw drug in bulk from abroad, then supervise at a safe distance the gradual subdivision of the drug into the refined, single, and very highly priced dose. Addicts and small-time pushers are caught, sentenced, and imprisoned, while the traffic goes on unabated. Despite harsh laws on the books, most sentences are slight. When the penalties for the possession of drugs become more severe, the tendency is for the accused no longer to "cop a plea" (plead guilty). Courtrooms become crowded. The police are forced to appear, cases drag on, and acquittals increase. Frustrated, the police then tend to charge drug offenders with the lesser crimes of vagrancy or loitering, in which a convenient guilty plea can be expected.

As matters stand, the problem seems insoluble. What are its possible resolutions? First, we may live with it and worry about it, which seems to be the present approach. Laws and their enforcement may be stiffened at vast expense, though only a slight chance of eradicating the problem exists. The addicts may be cured, again at great expense and with little hope of success. Finally, though this is in many ways repugnant, the addict may be provided with legal drugs.

Assuming that, as a society, we are not content to live with the problem, the most obvious approach and the one being tried is stiffer enforcement. However, with elaboration, it can be seen that severe enforcement will come up against the invalidating human factors which doomed England's Bloody Code. Curing addicts has been attempted with generally discouraging results, but controlling addiction via the medical profession has been undertaken with reasonable success in Britain. Of course, Britain never has had a massive drug problem, and, to control her few addicts, individual doctors under the Dangerous Drugs Act may administer drugs to their addicted patients just as they would any other prescription. They are urged to try to cure, but no more. In large measure the system seems to work, and does offer two advantages. First, the addict is under no social stigma that would tend to drive him away from society and deeper into addiction. More important from society's standpoint, the legal availability of drugs undercuts the criminal aspects of the problem. In general, only the medical problem remains. Most European countries have similar programs, with minimal addiction compared to the United States.

Should the United States, then, follow Britain's example? It is easy to say so, but how it would work with a problem as vast as exists in America's major cities is hard to say. Would addiction spread as a result? Probably not. Much glamour would be lost to the young experimenter who is resisting parents and society. The criminal side of the problem would certainly diminish. At least it would seem a good idea to appraise foreign systems of control. To begin with, a medical approach might be tried with young addicts who do not yet represent a debauched hard core of demoralized criminality.

A problem akin to drug addiction is that of marijuana. Unlike the opium derivatives and synthetics, marijuana is not physically addictive. It is an intoxicant, as is alcohol, and probably no more physically destructive to the body. Just as alcohol—when it became defined as illegal during Prohibition—became associated with other forms of crime, marijuana, through its treatment under the law, has become associated with more dangerous drugs and their availability through criminal channels.

How physically dangerous is marijuana? Like alcohol, it impairs the reflexes and may lead to automobile accidents. Is it physically dangerous in the long run? Possibly, though this has not been proved. After all, it has taken fifty years of extensive cigarette smoking to demonstrate the inherent dangers of tobacco to the body. Then how, now that it has become a habit indulged in by a substantial minority, should marijuana be dealt with? Socially, it would be well to diminish the sensationalism that gives it illicit glamour for the young. Initially, it would seem well to institute an unbiased medical study program to determine the physical and emotional dangers inherent in marijuana smoking. Assuming the detrimental effects are found to be on a par with the consumption of alcoholic beverages, then its distribution might be legalized subject to strict licensing provisions. Unsatisfactory, perhaps, but as police measures do not seem likely to remove marijuana from widespread use, at least this approach would tend to deglamorize and break the availability link with more deadly drugs.

CHAPTER SEVEN

Freedom of Speech and Press

NEVER BEFORE HAS SO MUCH NEWS BEEN SO READILY AVAILABLE and distributed by so many means: newspapers, magazines, radio, and television. Never before have people had the opportunity to speak their minds to so many potential listeners. We have long held it a cherished right and mark of civilization to speak out freely. At times discretion has been exceeded, and restraints have been called for. These may be either self-regulating, which may be too much to hope for, or imposed from above, which suggests a threat to free institutions. It is the purpose here to sketch out the legal history of free speech and press, indicate its courtroom status, and suggest some restraints that are, or might be, applied to mitigate abuse.

Ancient Greece is regarded as the cradle of Western thought, and it was there that the battle was early joined. In 594 B.C. Solon forbade speaking evil of the living and the dead. A century and a half later, Pericles, perhaps the world's first great orator, defended freedom of speech while delivering an oration in memory of the first Athenians killed in the Peloponnesian War. Such wars usually bring repressions, and within a few years the pendulum had swung, and Socrates, a martyr in the cause of freedom of speech, was sentenced to death. Plato reported him as saying on this occasion,

"If you offered to let me off this time on condition that I am not any longer to speak my mind in this search for wisdom, and that if I am caught doing this again I shall die, I should say to you, 'Men of Athens, I shall obey the God rather than you. While I have life and strength, I shall never cease to follow philosophy and to exhort and persuade any one of you whom I happen to meet.' "

Rome ostensibly defended free speech, but it was not without censorship. Poets were wise not to lampoon the emperor, and Jesus himself was punished for words more than deeds. Later, when Christianity had gained power in Rome, free expression against the orthodox position became heresy, and heresy became in time the fuel upon which the Inquisition burned for centuries, on the theory that it was better to destroy one hundred innocents than suffer one person of guilty thought and word to escape.

Freedom of speech and the printed word were at a low ebb during the early years of the common law. The statute *De Scandalis Magnatum* in A.D. 1275 concerned itself with the preservation of the realm and provided imprisonment for anyone who disseminated false tales or news which tended to bring discord between king and country. The first printing press added a new threat, so the old statute was reenacted in 1554, with the term "seditious words" added to the original phrasing. Under the jurisdiction of the court of the Star Chamber, printing and publishing in England were strictly censored, and a libel was punishable even when addressed to the dead. The concern was not with the truth or falsity of the utterances, but whether they might be deemed seditious. During the reign of Queen Elizabeth I, the Star Chamber was so efficient that one author who said in his book that he disliked actors and acting received the following sentence: life in prison, a brand on the forehead, ears cut off and nose slit, not to mention a fine of ten thousand pounds. Extreme, indeed, but it seems the Queen had recently taken part in a play and his comments were taken as an assault on the government.

Cromwell cost Charles I his head and the Star Chamber its jurisdiction. The common-law courts took over the role as moral custodians of the realm in 1641. No longer was the press censored in advance, but criticisms of the government, once unleashed, were punished harshly. The general policy was summed up in the Dean of St. Asaph's case by Lord Mansfield. "The liberty of the press consists in printing without any previous license, subject to the consequences of law. The licentiousness of the press is Pandora's box, the source of every evil." [1]

Legal attitudes toward free speech differed little in Britain's American colonies. By 1662, two licensors had been appointed, with the power to censor proposed writings, and even when this was ended in the early eighteenth century, a printer still published at his peril. The first newspaper in the colonies was called *Publick Occurrences* and was presented in Boston by Benjamin Harris. For criticizing the conduct of the Indian wars, it died after one issue. Another newspaper, in trouble almost from its first issue on November 5, 1733, was *The New York Weekly Journal*. This publication appeared in opposition to the *Gazette*, whose editorial policies were dominated by the British governor, William Cosby. The governor, recently appointed, claimed back salary for the period before he arrived from England to take office, and he juggled the local court to make sure his claim was accepted. Such was the material that became the subject of articles given to the *Journal*'s printer, Peter Zenger. Almost immediately he was arrested for printing and publishing seditious libels, defined at the time as "written censure upon public men for their conduct as such, or upon the law or upon the institutions of the country." The truth of the disputed statements was not at issue, nor indeed was the fact of the libel, which was left in the hands of the governor's picked court. Only the jury, made up of local citizens, could have been on Zenger's side, and they were allowed to decide but one issue: Did Zenger print the objectionable articles? This was undeniable; an open-and-shut case, it would seem, until eighty-year-old Andrew Hamilton from Philadelphia took it over. He admitted the publication, but attacked the phraseology of the statute, which spoke of false, scandalous, and seditious libel, particularly the word "false." Naturally the prosecution argued that the nature of the libel was a court question, and, indeed, truth would not become an accepted defense for another hundred years. But Hamilton had given the jury an out, which they very much wanted, and Zenger went free. The case established the corner-stone of liberty of the press in the United States which the years have failed to erode.

The Constitution of the United States makes no direct statement regarding "prior restraints," that is, censorship, but the First Amendment says, "Congress shall make no laws respecting an establishment of religion, or prohibiting the free exercise thereof; or abridging the freedom of speech, or of the press, or the right of the people peaceably to assemble, and to petition the government for a redress of grievances." Most of the states, however, set out terms in their individual constitutions forbidding prior restraints.

In a very few years reaction set in, but it was brief. John Adams was President. War with France was anticipated, and in 1798 a Sedition Act was established that punished with fine and imprisonment any act of writing, printing, or publishing scandalous material against the government. Except that truth was allowed as a defense, this was a complete reversion to the harsher British ways. One man convicted under the new laws was James Callender, who had written a pamphlet entitled *The Prospect Before Us*. In it he said such things as "Take your choice, then, between Adams, war and beggary, and Jefferson, peace and competency." [2] No wonder that Adams bristled. No wonder that when Jefferson became President, the law was allowed to expire and those imprisoned under it set free.

With the collapse of the Alien and Sedition Acts, there began a century of unbridled license in newspaper publishing. As early as 1801, the following criticism was voiced by Fisher Ames, "Some of the shocking articles in the paper raise simple, and very simple, wonder; some terror, and some horror and disgust. Now what instruction is there in these endless wonders? They make a thousand old maids, and eight or ten thousand booby boys afraid to be alone." The penny press spread rapidly, and by 1835 James Gordon Bennett entered the field with his New York *Herald*. It began what was later to be called yellow journalism, with a pandering to themes of sex and murder. When Dr. George Parkman's dismembered body was found in the laboratory of Harvard professor John Webster, the headlines screamed. Papers sold as never before. The courtroom was mobbed, and crowds broke into nearby houses to reach the roof in time to watch Mr. Webster go to the gallows below. Restraints, when they came, were not legal, but the result of mob prejudice. Under particular attack in the 1830's was the abolition-of-slavery press. In 1836, the Reverend Elijah P. Lovejoy had quarreled editorially with Judge Luke E. Lawless of St. Louis because the latter condoned mob violence against the Negro. Forced to move to Alton, Lovejoy again began printing his *Observer,* and its antislavery sentiments so incensed the citizens of the free state of Illinois that three times within a year the printing press was thrown into the river. Three times Lovejoy persisted, until on November 7, 1837, he was killed by the mob as he defended his new printing press.

After the Civil War, the free press was deeply involved in politics. The newspapers very nearly managed to have President Andrew Johnson impeached on preposterously prejudicial grounds, and they fanned the fires of riot during the 1886 Chicago Haymarket riots. On the plus side, when most New York papers were on Boss Tweed's Tammany Hall payroll, the publisher of *The New York Times,* George Jones, was offered five million dollars to get in line, but held firm. He said, "I don't think the devil will ever make a higher bid for me. My answer still stands." [3] The result of the *Times* exposé was prison for Boss Tweed and the collapse of Tammany Hall.

In 1895, William Randolph Hearst officially launched yellow journalism with an emphasis on scare headlines, natural disasters, sordid crimes, and doctored photographs and sketches. The Spanish-American War has been attributed largely to Hearst's hysterical efforts. One of Hearst's particular targets was President McKinley, and when Governor William Goebel of Kentucky was assassinated in 1900, the *New York Journal* printed the following verse:

> The bullet that pierced Goebel's breast
> Can not be found in all the West;
> Good reason, it is speeding here
> To stretch McKinley on his bier.

Another time, commenting obliquely on President McKinley,

the *Journal* suggested that if bad men could be gotten rid of only by killing them, then killed they should be. Few would accept this doctrine, particularly regarding the genial McKinley, but his assassin obviously did. In stark comment on the danger of an irresponsible press, McKinley's killer, when seized, had in his possession a copy of the *Journal* containing an attack on the President.

Clearly, yellow journalism had taken justice too much into its own hands. Of course there was always the possibility of redress via a libel suit, but even this sold papers. Sometimes the injured parties took matters into their own hands. Take the case of Fred Bonfils and Harry Tammen. From their office, known as The Bucket of Blood, they edited the *Denver Post* in imitation of Hearst. When one of their reporters named Polly Pry wrote a story about a prospector who had killed and eaten his partner, the prospector's attorney was so incensed he shot both editors. The pair survived the attack undaunted and swiftly turned the incident into moneymaking headlines.

Sometimes the issues found their way to court, and the case of *Near v. Minnesota*[4] carefully weighed the competing virtues and vices. Minnesota at this time (1931) had a statute authorizing the courts to forbid the publishing of malicious, scandalous, and defamatory newspapers. One J. M. Near began printing a Saturday paper in Minneapolis, the main purpose of which was slandering the Jews. A suit was brought under the statute to close down the paper. A defense of truth was alleged, and the case went up to the Supreme Court. Clearly, in a time of rising Nazism, the paper did more harm than good. Still, the Supreme Court held that the state statute was unconstitutional. Their reasoning was that if a state in effect was allowed to censor a paper, there might be no end to government telling the people what was good for them to read. It is to be remembered that along with persecution of the Jews, freedom of the press was dying in Nazi Germany. No other civil liberty was held so deeply to penetrate community life, and freedom of the press does not exist unless it is free to publish thoughts that some disapprove, reject, and detest. So the court refused to enjoin the publication of this racist journal and left the injured to seek damages for libel. Even if what is said is totally false, the community is entitled to hear and to judge.

From the passage of the Alien and Sedition Acts of 1798 until 1917, no federal law had attempted to limit freedom of the press. Then, with World War One, came the Espionage and Sedition Acts of 1917 and 1918, which made it a crime to interfere with the war effort. The first case under the new law to reach the Supreme Court was in 1919.[5] The defendants were socialists who printed and distributed to draftees pamphlets containing the Thirteenth Amendment abolishing slavery, plus a harangue against involuntary servitude in the army to benefit the men of Wall Street. Justice Oliver Wendell Holmes got down to the core of the matter when he said, "The question in every case is whether the words used are used in such circumstances and are of such a nature as to create a clear and present danger that they will bring about the substantive evils that Congress has a right to prevent."

Another test favored by the courts over the "real and present danger" test was established in *Gitlow v. New York*.[6] Here it was held that the utterances of the defendant had created a "bad tendency," regardless of the possibility of their achieving concrete results. This measure was less precise and less demanding than Justice Holmes's formula, and together with the Alien and Sedition Act brought about some startling results. One example is the case [7] in which the defendant received a ten-year sentence for presenting a film entitled *The Spirit of '76*. Objected to was a scene showing British soldiers bayoneting women and children during the Revolutionary War; this was held to incite hatred and enmity toward our English ally.

The Espionage Act of 1917 had been a wartime measure, but in 1940 the Smith Act became the first peacetime sedition act in the United States since the eighteenth century. It made it unlawful to knowingly advocate or teach the desirability of overthrowing any government in the United States by force or violence. Its principal use was not during the Second World War, but against our former Communist allies thereafter. An action was brought against ten leaders of the Communist party which resulted in a trial in 1951.[8] The defendants were accused of promoting a policy of overthrow of the government by force and violence. In upholding the conviction, the court reverted to the "clear and present danger" formula, saying that it was not the likelihood of success of such a revolt that mattered, but the likelihood that it would take place. Enlarging on the "clear and present danger" test, the court went on to say that it must be asked whether the gravity of the evil discounted by its improbability justifies such invasion of free speech as is necessary to avoid the danger. This was during the alarmist, Communist-haunted early 1950's. With the danger of Communist subversion —or at least its anticipation—receding, the court also retreated in 1957 when it held that advocacy of the government's overthrow must amount to actual incitement. The pendulum has swung from the "clear and present danger" test to the "bad tendency" rule and back to "gravity of evil." Today the courts seem to be groping for a new set of measures that would balance the interests between the right of free association and the danger of substantive harm. It is perhaps for the best that the Supreme Court does not rigidly make up its mind, for its considered opinions tend to reflect the temper and requirements of the times.

Of course, today lively issues regarding freedom of speech and press are not limited to national security. Of prime concern to the fair administration of justice are the liberties taken by newspapers, radio, and television in reporting crimes and the trials that result from them. Imagine, for instance, the effect upon the deliberations of a future juror in a trial for criminal negligence upon reading the following headline in the July 17, 1970, issue of Long Island's *Newsday:* "A man whose name and address are apparently the same as the driver in the fatal Allentown accident has a list of nine accidents, six convictions, and five suspensions on his driving record in New Jersey."

It is with such headlines before a trial—frequently before an arrest—that the newspapers first interfere with the course of justice. The California case of James W. Preston is a spectacular example of newspaper influence.[9] A robbery had taken place for which Preston was arrested. The newspapers alleged that Preston had been identified by fingerprints found on a window screen of the victim's house. These accounts were read by the victim, who later identified Preston and became the sole prosecution witness at the trial. No fingerprint evidence was offered, but after the verdict the judge referred to the incriminating fingerprints. Clearly he had read the papers. Throughout, Preston protested his innocence, and after he had served eighteen months of an eleven-years-to-life sentence, another man was arrested, identified by fingerprints, and convicted.

Not always is the pretrial influence of the newspapers a bad one. In 1922, when the police failed in an investigation of a Ku Klux Klan murder in Louisiana, the *St. Louis Post-Dispatch* reporter John Rogers investigated on his own. He produced evidence that led to trial and conviction.

The next stage for newspaper involvement is after arrest. In the case of *Rideau v. Louisiana* [10] in 1963, the defendant's confession of robbery to the police was shown on local television and witnessed by three future jurors. The court held that the defendant's right to due process had been violated, and that he was entitled to a change of venue or should be tried in an area where potential jurors had not been prejudiced. This is by no means an uncommon occurrence.

There is very little a judge can do to correct such injustices besides aborting the trial. However, his control is increased during the trial period. In the words of Lord Chancellor Hardwicke, "Nothing is more incumbent upon the courts of justice than to preserve their proceedings from being misrepresented; nor is there anything of more pernicious consequence, than to prejudice the minds of the public against persons concerned as parties, before the case is finally heard." [11]

In the United States, the right of a judge to hold a newspaper in contempt for irresponsibly influencing justice was considered in the trial of *Craig v. Harney*.[12] A contempt proceeding was brought against a newspaper that had characterized the judge's order as a "gross miscarriage of justice." The decision was that contempt will only apply when there is a clear and present danger that justice will be subverted. This danger must neither be improbable nor remote, and must constitute a direct and immediate peril. In holding for the defendant newspaper, the court said that judges must not be oversensitive to the winds of public opinion.

The celebrated case of Dr. Sam Sheppard raised the issue of

fair trial. The defendant was tried for the bludgeon murder of his wife in their lakeshore home on July 4, 1954. Allegedly, the defendant had fought with and been overpowered by a bearded stranger. All the elements of sensationalism were present. During the trial, over forty pictures of the jury appeared in the Cleveland, Ohio, papers. Photographers invaded the courtroom and even climbed into the jury box. A carnival atmosphere prevailed from start to finish. Sheppard spent ten years in jail before the Supreme Court consented to review his case on the grounds that the newspapers had destroyed an atmosphere in which a fair trial could take place.[13]

Press interference has not been limited to criminal cases. In one trial in 1962 [14] the plaintiff brought a so-called wrongful-death action in behalf of the decedent, who had been killed as the result of a truck collision. At issue was the question of contributory negligence: Had the flashlight in the cab of the decedent's truck been securely held down and fallen only as the result of the crash, or had it fallen before the accident, becoming lodged under the brake pedal, thus causing the crash? Before the jury decided, the circumstances had been published in the magazine *California Highway Patrolman*, which stated as fact that the accident was a result of the negligence of the plaintiff's decedent in securing loose equipment in the truck's cab. When the jury found for the defendant, the court on appeal was obliged to reverse, granting a new trial due to the fact that the out-of-court availability to the jurors of the magazine's opinion constituted a factor prejudicial to the plaintiff's case.

In this generation of sit-ins, public protests, and marches, the courts must exercise another careful balance of rights: on the one hand, freedom of expression in public places; on the other, the right to public peace and general order in streets and parks. When the uncontrolled demonstration meets a counterdemonstration in the streets, such as occurred during the early days of Nazi Germany, the hallowed right of free expression becomes distorted and works to destroy the first civil right of all: peace within a democratic society.

First in this line of cases were the Jehovah's Witness decisions.[15] At issue was the right of Jehovah's Witnesses to disseminate religious sentiments in public places: pamphlets in the first case, broadcast speech in the second. In both cases, the Court held that the government should not unreasonably impose arbitrary and previous restraints upon expression. The Court did not, however, outlaw reasonable and proper restraint in the interest of public order—a meeting in the middle of Times Square at the rush hour, for instance.

When the defendant at a public meeting called a police officer a "God-damned racketeer" and "a damned Fascist," the court decided a clear and present danger existed that a breach of the peace would result.[16] In 1951 a college student was held guilty of a breach of the peace for trying to arouse Negroes versus whites in a mixed crowd that had begun milling and shoving.[17] The wisdom of this decision has been seriously questioned, for if a speaker is to be arrested not so much for what he says as for crowd reaction, it becomes very simple for those opposed to his views to shove and mill, with the result that the speaker is bundled off by the police.

The better view does not measure crowd action and reaction, but allows the speaker to unburden his opinions, no matter how unsavory, as long as they are not clearly designed to cause an immediate disturbance. Such a decision involved the desire of George Lincoln Rockwell, former head of the United States Nazi party, to address a crowd in Union Square, New York, on the Fourth of July. Mayor Wagner denied his right to speak, on the theory that anything that this minor Hitler might have to say was obnoxious and could only cause trouble. Rockwell brought an action to enforce his right to speak, and the court held that

> the unpopularity of views, their shocking quality, their obnoxiousness, and even their alarming impact is not enough . . . only if Rockwell speaks criminally can his right to speak be cut off. If he does not speak criminally, then, of course, his right to speak may not be cut off, not matter how offensive his speech may be to others. Instead, his right, and that of those who wish to listen to him, must be protected, no matter how unpleasant the assignment.[18]

The decision came too late for the Fourth of July, 1960, but the following year Rockwell applied in New York to speak on April 20, Hitler's birthday, and the application was granted.

Of more widespread concern are the civil rights cases and the limits to be placed on racial demonstrations, particularly in the South. A case in 1963 [19] arose from the arrest and conviction of a group of Negroes for breach of the peace. About two hundred people had marched, without violence and without obstructing the flow of traffic, to the public State House grounds. On the grounds they paraded with signs such as "I am proud to be a Negro" and "Down with segregation." A crowd of 250 curious onlookers gathered. Rubbernecking traffic slowed somewhat, but was not impeded. After this had gone on for the better part of an hour, the police gave the Negroes fifteen minutes to disband. Instead, they stayed to hear a religious speech. To the rhythm of clapped hands, they loudly sang "The Star-Spangled Banner" and other patriotic and religious songs. The police arrested them under a statute which held that conduct that stirred people to anger, invited public dispute, or brought about a condition of unrest was to be punishable by imprisonment. The demonstrators were fined ten dollars each and sent to jail for terms of from five to thirty days. On appeal, the court held the local statute unconstitutional. However, it did not prohibit such statutes as long as they were clear, uniform, and nondiscriminatory, and so long as their protection of public order did not depend solely on an audience reaction of hostility, which had been the defect in the case of the college student in 1951.

In like manner, peaceful protest, however distasteful to popular mores, has been upheld. When defendants distributed handbills suggesting that Negroes were taking over unions, parks, and pools, a criminal conviction was denied in a 1963 case.[20] Within the protection of the First Amendment, even the claptrap of racist fanatics must be protected.

The standard whereby public protesters would be protected by the law was set down in 1965. Their rights would be upheld as long as they were "asserted within limits of not unreasonably interfering with the exercise of the rights of other citizens to use the sidewalks, streets and highways, and where the protesters and demonstrators are conducting their activities in such a manner as not to deprive the other citizenry of their police protection." [21] The court went on to insist that the police had a duty to protect peaceful protesters so that the guarantees of the First Amendment should not be defeated by the heckler's veto.

This does not suggest, however, that the rights of public protesters are unlimited. Deliberate obstruction of civic order will be condemned, and a case in 1966 [22] seems to have set the bounds beyond which the Supreme Court will not condone. In this case, Negro college students entered and remained on the premises of the county jail, demonstrating against the earlier arrest of other student protesters. The sheriff asked the students to leave and said that they were violating a state law prohibiting trespass on the property of another. When the students would not move, they were arrested. The court held this was a nondiscriminatory statute. Here, the court declined to guarantee absolute freedom of the streets for all such demonstrations and refused to deny the danger of mob pressures, which move toward complete contempt for government by law. Extremists may express themselves, but they will not be given legal license to destroy the peace and privacy of a civilization.

Some have argued that freedom of speech should be guaranteed only to important information, and that it should not be extended to the arts. Here the issue is obscenity. Does obscenity, particularly in print, impoverish the culture, or does its arbitrary supervision and restraint do greater harm? In 1915 the court upheld the validity of an Ohio statute which required that a motion-picture film be moral, educational, or harmlessly amusing. Movies were a new thing in those days. More recently, courts have refused to distinguish them from the other art forms.

In the case of *The United States v. One Book Called "Ulysses"* [23] in 1933, Judge Woolsey is remembered for his observation upon James Joyce and his epic novel. "In respect of the recurrent emergence of the theme of sex in the minds of his characters, it must always be remembered that his locale was Celtic and his season Spring." Searching the text for "the leer of the sensualist," the judge could not find it. He held that the book, therefore, was not pornographic or subject to the tariff act which confiscated books of an obscene nature.

Other means have been employed to suppress objectionable texts. In 1948, the Postmaster General deprived *Esquire* magazine of its right to second-class-mail privileges on the grounds that its contents were indecent, vulgar, and risqué. The Court [24] held this to be a prior restraint and, therefore, unconstitutional.

With the post–World War Two liberalizing trend, the Supreme Court moved on to more open tests. The questions arose whether the material taken as a whole appealed to the prurient interest of the average person, and whether, despite this, there remained some redeeming social value. In the case of *Roth v. the United States* [25] in 1957, the redeeming social value became the key. It was applied in judging the *Memoirs of a Woman of Pleasure* (better known as *Fanny Hill*) case.[26] A modicum of social value was found, and on this vague standard the judges rested. Once again the pendulum had swung in accord with the public mood, but at the same time there lingered traces of a reverse motion. This was notable in a 1966 case [27] which involved the distribution of a magazine called *Eros* and a book entitled *The Housewife's Handbook on Selective Promiscuity*. The publishers first applied to the postmaster of Middlesex, New Jersey, for mailing privileges. When the post office proved too small to handle the job, mailing took place from the towns of Intercourse and Blue Ball, Pennsylvania. This in itself indicated to the judges the salacious intent of the publication. A "leer of sensuality" was easily found, and the material was held to have no purpose other than that of purveying textual and graphic matter with no appeal beyond the erotic. The defendant went to jail, the literature vanished from the newsstands. Whether the Supreme Court will proceed in the direction of more liberality or of increased restraint remains to be seen. It is very apt to reflect the public mood.

Despite the guarantee of freedom of speech and freedom of the press, this does not guarantee the right of every utterance to go unpunished. Personal abuse is not, in any proper sense, communication of information or general opinion, nor is it an art form, and the usual recourse is to the court by way of an action of slander or libel. Speech as an instrument of coercion may become criminal blackmail and is so treated. Speech that takes the form of fraud or any other unlawful activity is dealt with by the criminal law.

The right to print news does not carry with it the right to make a mistake, and if harm results, damages are awarded. Take the case of Minnie Hatfield, spinster and churchgoer of Hutchinson, Kansas. One day Miss Hatfield read the following in the local newspaper:

RAIDED ROOMING HOUSE

Sheriff Scott Sprout yesterday raided the rooming house on First Avenue West, conducted by Ruth Newman. Two girls, Bess Stolen and Minnie Hatfield, were charged with being inmates of an immoral house, and the Newman woman with running one. They were released on $500 bail.

Our shocked reader was the only Minnie Hatfield in town. The paper offered a correction, for the real defendant turned out to be one Minnie Olsen, but the court held that a libel had been done. Mistake on the defendant's part was no justification, and Miss Hatfield recovered damages.[28]

Public officials are not always so lucky. In 1964, the police commissioner of Montgomery, Alabama, alleged that he had been libeled by an advertisement placed in *The New York Times* which accused him of violating the rights of Negroes. A local jury granted him an award of $500,000, though there was no showing of financial loss on his part. But the Supreme Court reversed the decision, in part due to the inequity of the huge award, but ostensibly on the theory that a public official must endure criticism, whether or not it springs from an honest error on the critic's part.[29] Damages can be recovered only when the libel is malicious in intent. Perhaps the plaintiff got what he deserved in this case, which was nothing more than annoyance, but the decision does leave a doubt. Where is the line drawn between the private citizen such as Minnie Hatfield and a public official? For example, where do movie actors, who seek out publicity, fit in?

Another question involves defamatory, libelous statements made about groups, such as Jews, Negroes, Catholics. What can a judge do if such a group is accused of having nasty personal habits and dirty feet? Can a judge attest to the truth or nontruth of such statements? If such group libels were allowed, would not the disseminator of the Christian Gospels, which include defamatory remarks about Jews and Christians alike, be subject to a suit for libel? Shakespeare took cracks at Danes, Jews, the French. To sternly apply a group libel statute would deplete the bookshelves. It is well that we have the Constitution and the Supreme Court to weigh the merits of each case in the light of present circumstances rather than confine our fate to the determination of the prosecutor and the discretion of individual judges.

To summarize, it is the mark of a civilized and democratic country that the right to speak out exists without censorship, for where opinions are suppressed, individual freedom is weakened and in danger. However, it is also in the nature of a civilized society to redress wrongs which, despite the old adage about sticks and stones, often include the hurt done by words alone. And it is the job of the courts to balance the merits of what is said or written against the harm inflicted. Where the principal object is not to impart information and no real individual is being commented upon, the weight given either side of the scale may be slight. Here involved are the arts and the cases concerning pornography. In the United States today, the tendency is toward freedom. Where comment has to do with a private citizen whose life is not newsworthy, the inclination of the court is to respect his right to privacy. Slander and libel suits are his recourses. Should individuals slip, however unintentionally, into public concern, then their protection lessens. The public has a right to know about crimes, and the subject of comment generally is protected only to the extent that he receives a fair trial.

Other individuals seek out public attention. On the one hand, there are actors and sports heroes. Their conduct is news, however unimportant, and their lives have been the subject of articles in such dubious magazines as *Confidential*. When comment is truthful, they have very little recourse. When lies are printed, a libel suit avails. Individuals who assume public jobs, whose decisions directly affect the lives of every one of us, cannot expect to avoid comment and criticism. Here, most heavily, the scales are weighted in favor of free press and speech, and though some officials may complain that it is prejudicial and harmful to effective government, without such free comment, government runs the risk of becoming too officious, too dictatorial.

If democracy is to exist, censorship, apart perhaps from military secrets, must be limited to self-imposed restraint. In England, judges have contempt power over newsmen publishing evidence or comment inadmissible at the trial. In the United States, that power only extends to conduct obstructing the administration of justice within or near the presence of the court. In England there is virtually no organized crime or police corruption, and lawyers and judges are relatively free from political and mob pressure; in the United States the press has often kept a watchful eye upon misconduct and exposed it. For instance, between 1950 and 1953, the Long Island daily *Newsday* went after the labor leader William C. Dekoning and exposed him as a racketeer. An investigation was forced which led to his indictment and conviction for extortion related to irregularities at Roosevelt Raceway. English methods might hamper the press in such public-spirited impulses. At times, too, when contempt power is available, it is often misused. In 1963, *The Democrat,* an Arkansas weekly, was put out of business through libel judgments after the paper had imprudently criticized political machinery headed by the local sheriff. On the other hand, when newspaper comment has interfered with the administration of justice, there is room for voluntary reform. Responsible newspapers in the past have called in the industry to set standards. During the Loeb and Leopold murder case, the *Chicago Tribune* demanded restraint, and though H. L. Mencken called such good intentions "all moonshine," the halcyon days of yellow journalism have passed. In 1965, CBS News adopted guidelines for pretrial and trial coverage by radio and television, stressing that confessions and previous criminal records were not to be mentioned until admitted in evidence at the trial. In England, a British Press Council has been formed to maintain high professional standards of journalism. In practice, it seems to have done more good than harm in reprimanding excesses. The United States press thus far has remained opposed to such self-criticizing methods, though in the long run something of the sort is likely to emerge.

The question of censorship was clearly tested when in 1971 *The New York Times* made public certain documents which the Pentagon regarded as secret. The Supreme Court refused to forbid additional publication on the grounds that it would amount to prior restraint or censorship. In fact, the disclosed material which caused the government political embarrassment did not reveal military secrets in the sense of intended troop movements or the plans for a secret-weapons system. If such had been the case, the result would have undoubtedly been very different.

Where the press may have refused to moderate its disclosures in the interests of fair trial, the police, judges, and attorneys can often control pre-judicial comment. Traditionally, the police used to disclose all to the news media. In part, this was done to gain public confidence. Prior criminal records, which are not considered proper evidence at a trial, were given out regularly, perhaps to suggest that, despite police diligence, some other branch of the judicial process had granted the criminal freedom to prey upon the public once again. However, the tendency today is to limit press interviews of suspects in custody. Judges have now adopted Canon 35 of "Judicial Ethics" as compounded by the American Bar Association, which calls for discretion in dealing with the news media. A strong reaction from the days of yellow journalism also has led to Canon 20 of "Professional Legal Ethics," which condemns lawyers' statements regarding pending litigation. Disapproved are comments regarding the defendant's character, confessions, alibis, statements on the credibility of the witnesses, use of weapons, and evidence generally to be employed at the trial. Although, in theory, violators may be disbarred from the legal profession, in practice they have seldom been criticized. However, the effect in cutting back irresponsible and prejudicial comment cannot be denied, and the trend here, as in other areas where free speech has been questioned, seems to be toward a balancing of equities in the interest of a civilized society.

CHAPTER EIGHT

Privacy and the Police

BETWEEN THE LAW AND DISORDER STAND THE POLICE AND THE COURTS. If they stand too tall, not only disorder but law as well may disappear. However, we are no longer a frontier people, and the personal justice of the mountain man is gone. The Western shoot-out as a romantic form has been relegated to odd hours on TV, and we are left with a mounting rate of sordid crime. As it grows, so must the police, for as individuals we cannot cope with it; but as individuals we must not be run over in the process.

Wherever there is a major issue in the law, a balance must be struck between competing and important rights. We are, so the Bible says, descended from Cain, not Abel, and we live in a society of burgeoning crime where a woman may well speak complacently of the peaceful residential district in which she lives, then protest as an afterthought that the only bothersome sound at night is the infrequent cry of someone being mugged. Crime must be sternly dealt with. On the other hand, we are a society devoted to the fundamental notions of life, liberty, and the pursuit of happiness, which in their very nature protest intrusion into privacy. This protest includes the police, incidental curious bystanders, and, most of all, the criminal.

Combine population explosion with modern science, and very little remains of personal privacy. Some people don't even seem to miss it. Take, for instance, a college-campus project undertaken by a sociology department, in which microphones were surreptitiously planted in the bedrooms of married students. Only later were the couples asked for permission, in the interest of science, to use their most intimate dialogues in a study. All agreed enthusiastically. Not one couple screamed about their right to privacy.

125

Most people are quite unaware of the extent of nonofficial intrusion made possible via hidden cameras, microphones, and lie detectors, and used in conjunction with computers programed to digest and utilize such information. When someone applies for a charge account, an auto loan, or insurance, the computers begin to click. Does the party drink to excess? If so, no auto insurance. The neighbors will know and are questioned. Once insurance is granted, and he claims personal injury after an accident, hidden cameras may well begin to grind in the hope of exposing a fraudulent disability. If an applicant seeks a company job, more than name, address, and social security number will usually be demanded, and more is readily available. So-called data banks are full of available information for purposes of hiring, promoting, and firing. Allegedly these "executive probes" are intended to develop a portrait of the whole man, and to this end a man's finances, credit rating, and police record are placed on file, along with his property and scholastic records, his religious affiliation, and the opinions of friends and former business associates. Is he a churchgoer, a drinker, gambler, or womanizer? Information about his wife is apt to be microfilmed, not to mention his children, on the theory that if he can't handle them, he can't handle his subordinates. All this goes into indelible records and is available to employers. Not only can such reports end up distorted or sensational in focus, they can be completely erroneous, a character smear against which an individual has little defense. One woman lost five successive jobs because her data file indicated she had once worked next to a Communist party member and was therefore a security risk. Another was turned down when an interviewer saw a set of Lenin's works on a bookshelf in the applicant's home, a set which many years before had been presented as a gift. It is a sad fact that sometimes investigators are offered bribes to slant reports pro or con.

Lie detectors are employed to check for petty theft by employees. The only limit is scientific inventiveness. Restaurants have been known to install secret microphones under customers' tables with the avowed purpose of checking on their waitresses' courtesy. Factory washrooms have been bugged so that the manager may secretly separate his friends from his enemies. Even when the cause is virtuous, privacy diminishes. Everyone is familiar with the theater collection: the appeal by some well-known actor, the busy usherettes, and the feeling of being coerced. Fund raising, usually in a good if obscure cause, bombards the mails. Give once, and your name is apt to be rented, traded, or sold to other charities. The phone or doorbell may well ring with the more direct and intrusive appeal. All in a good cause, but when the government and the police get into the act, the specter of an attentive big brother looms over one's shoulder. Individuality, if not the whole society, seems threatened, but in this area of private scrutiny there is very little recourse under the law.

Although the First, Third, and Fourth amendments protect certain areas of privacy, it took the urban industrial revolution and two promising law students, Louis Brandeis and Samuel Warren, to conjure up the specific right. The year was 1890, and the vehicle for their initial statement was the *Harvard Law Review*. It was not until nine years after this suggestion had been launched that an answer came, and at first it was in the form of a denial. On the last day of the Victorian century, December 31, 1899, the prettiest girl in the city of Rochester, New York, Miss Abigail Roberson, smiled for the strolling photographer's box camera. Weeks later, the city was saturated with posters and handbills showing Abigail's charming face along with a sack of flour. She was being used without permission or previous knowledge by the Franklin Flour Mills to advertise their product. Alleging nervous shock and humiliation due to scoffs and jeers of the public, Miss Roberson brought suit. However, the court [1] could find in the common law no right of privacy, and denied the plaintiff's case. Great was the public outcry, and though it was no help to the prettiest girl in Rochester, at its next session the New York legislature passed a statute making it unlawful to use the unauthorized picture of a living person for purposes of trade.

From that beginning, a complex body of law made up of statute and case law has developed around the notion of right of privacy. In 1940, William James Sidis, a child prodigy who graduated from Harvard at the age of sixteen, brought suit protesting an article in *The New Yorker* magazine. It seemed that after his graduation in 1910, Sidis had vanished from the public scene and lived in near squalor as a simple clerk. The magazine commented on all this, and went on to quote him as saying, "It is strange, but you know, I was born on April Fool's Day." In this case there was no question about his privacy being used for purposes of trade. Had Sidis never been a celebrity, he might well have recovered damages for the intrusion, but, since he had once been a public figure, the court decided he was still subject to legitimate public curiosity, and public figures have always been held as having given up the right to privacy.[2]

What, then, of the completely private citizen? Events alone may make him newsworthy. In the case of *Leverton v. The Curtis Publishing Company*,[3] the plaintiff had been injured in a traffic accident, and a photograph that showed her being lifted to her feet appeared in a newspaper the following day. Nearly two years later, the picture popped up in an issue of *The Saturday Evening Post*. It was accompanied by an article on pedestrian carelessness and was entitled, "They Ask to Be Killed." The court, while holding that the first publication was privileged as news, decided that the second printing was a violation of the plaintiff's privacy. Although the mere passage of time may withdraw a person from fair public consideration, in this case the court was probably more affected by the uncomplimentary nature of the article than by the lapse of time.

A variation on the theme of the right to privacy occurred in 1952.[4] The case involved a utility company which made a practice of playing radio programs through the loudspeakers of its passenger vehicles. Some of the passengers preferred silence and took the company to court on the grounds that the programs were an invasion of their privacy. The court of appeals agreed with them, but the Supreme Court reversed the opinion, denying that a constitutional right of privacy existed in public vehicles. Perhaps a correct decision under the circumstances, but what if the bus loudspeakers had been hammering home propaganda?

Today, in most of the United States, the right of privacy remains uncertain and untested, particularly in such areas of intrusion as data banks. The trend, however, is toward expansion of that new legal right in appropriate cases. Many European countries support such a right, but England, staunch in her common law, denies it. So if the Queen should be caught in the midst of air sickness and the photograph is later used in an advertisement for a motion-sickness remedy, the Queen need not grin but she will have to bear it. This is good Anglo-Saxon tradition, after all.

Although the civil law rules regarding the right of privacy are of very recent origin, laws concerned with fair play in the criminal courts go back to the Magna Carta, as enlarged in an English statute of 1355. This reads, "No man of what state or condition he be, shall be put out of his lands or tenements, nor taken, nor disinherited, nor put to death, without he be brought to answer by due process of the law."

This idea was not at first incorporated in the United States Constitution, but was added to it in 1791, along with the much-litigated Fifth Amendment:

No person shall be held to answer for a capital, or otherwise infamous crime, unless on a presentment or indictment of a Grand Jury except in cases arising in the land or naval forces or in the Militia, when in actual service in time of war or public danger; nor shall any person be subject for the same offense to be twice put in jeopardy of life or limb; nor shall be compelled in any criminal case to be a witness against himself; nor be deprived of life, liberty, or property, without due process of law; nor shall private property be taken for public use, without just compensation.

Perhaps no legal phrase has overturned more decisions, resulted in more litigation, and caused more law to be made than "due process." Initially, the application of the Fifth Amendment was limited to the federal courts. Then came the Civil War, and for the first time in sixty-one years, the Constitution was amended once again. What brought it about was the status of the ex-slave. The Thirteenth Amendment prohibited slavery, but the Fourteenth Amendment was a grab bag with five sections covering the rights of citizenship. It was so phrased that the Supreme Court applied it to the resisting Southern states directly. With the years, its application was enlarged nationally, and it became a vehicle whereby the Fifth Amendment, among others, could be applied to the states. The relevant first section of the Fourteenth Amendment reads as follows:

No state shall make or enforce any law which shall abridge the privileges or immunities of citizens of the United States, nor shall any state deprive any person of life, liberty, or property, without due process of law; nor deny to any person within its jurisdiction the equal protection of the laws.

Other important amendments to the Constitution that were formerly limited to federal proceedings have been applied, via the Fourteenth Amendment's "due process" clause, to state court procedure: the First Amendment having to do with freedom of speech and press, and the Sixth setting out the rights of an accused to speedy and public trial by an impartial jury, together with the right to counsel.

Suppose you have been arrested. The arresting officer will take you before a police magistrate. If the offense is minor and within the magistrate's jurisdiction, it may be settled on the spot with a fine or brief imprisonment. Otherwise, the magistrate can only decide whether to let you go or submit the record to the clerk of the proper trial court. In the latter case, the prosecuting attorney will submit the findings to a grand jury, which must decide whether to drop the potential case or to indict. Assuming indictment occurs, a trial follows, and here the prosecution and the defendant present their evidence to a judge and jury. If found not guilty beyond a reasonable doubt, you go free. If convicted, you may take an appeal to the appropriate appellate court. Suppose, despite your actual innocence, you are found guilty all along the line. You may well feel that the law under which you have been convicted is unjust, or, if the law is fair, the procedure used has been unconstitutional. In other words, you believe you have not been granted "due process." The usual means of raising this issue is by way of a writ of habeas corpus.

Habeas corpus has been traced back to 1215 and the Magna Carta, and it was updated in 1679 by the English Habeas Corpus Act, which the American colonists adopted. What it amounts to is a direction to one holding another confined to produce him before the proper court. Each of the United States has a statute regarding habeas corpus, and the federal courts may intervene only when a violation of the federal Constitution is found to be involved.

Coupling this writ to the individual right of due process of law guaranteed by the Fourteenth and Fifth amendments, the Supreme Court has scrutinized all aspects of arrest, trial, and punishment, and thereby preserved—some say too well—the rights of the individual. An early step in any criminal proceeding is the gathering of evidence against the accused. There are now available to the police scientific methods which unquestionably intrude on an individual's right of privacy. Where to draw the line between fair police investigation and police-state surveillance has become a long-contested issue before the Supreme Court.

There is a well-known statement which goes back to Lord Coke, the famous English jurist during the reign of James I. "The house of every one is to him as his castle." [5] In this interest, English common law has guarded against unwarranted search and seizure, as has the Fourth Amendment to the United States Constitution. In the early days, search and seizure was lawful when undertaken by government officials, even though the entry onto private property was taken as a trespass. Later, a system of search warrants was developed to facilitate lawmen looking for property in wrongful possession. The Fourth Amendment provides for such a warrant in most cases. Generally it will be issued to the police when there is "probable cause," that is, when a man of reasonable prudence and caution would believe that an offense has been committed and that the accused committed it. The subject of the search has been limited to "fruits of the crime," that is, stolen goods, not simply miscellaneous evidence. A weapon used by the defendant in committing the crime may be seized, but a letter in the defendant's possession which makes certain damaging admissions may not be taken under the rule regarding an individual's giving evidence against himself. Usually the warrant must describe the place to be searched. This is a reaction to colonial days, when the British issued general warrants for harassing purposes. Once the area to be searched has been set out, the search will be rigorously applied to that area alone. An example of this occurred in 1960, when known gamblers were seen going into a certain address in New York City. The warrant was issued and the police rushed in, only to find that the gamblers had cut through a party wall and were occupying the room next door. The gamblers and their dice and cards and other incriminating evidence were seized, but due to the specifications of the search warrant, the evidence was not allowed to be used in court.[6]

Initiated in the District of Columbia and limited to federal agents is the so-called no-knock law. Much controversy has attended this legislation, which its advocates prefer to call the "quick-entry law." Subject to a judicial warrant, federal agents within Washington, D. C., have been given the right to enter premises forcibly and without warning in order to seize destructible evidence. Illegal drugs are, of course, a principal concern. Upon the traditional command from without, "Open up, this is the police," drugs could vanish with one flush of a toilet. No doubt the no-knock law is a useful provision in the war against narcotics. But one wonders what is happening to a man's castle and recalls the even more efficient "night and fog" decrees enabling Hitler's Gestapo to snatch their "suspects" very literally and usually permanently into the night and the fog.

Although the area of police search remains limited by warrant, the breadth of subject matter in most jurisdictions has widened somewhat from the instrumentalities of the crime rule. In 1967,[7] an armed robber entered the premises of the Diamond Cab Company in Baltimore, Maryland, snatched a few hundred dollars, and ran off with two cab drivers in hot pursuit. They tracked the robber to 2111 Cocoa Lane, then notified the police that the thief was a five-foot eight-inch Negro wearing a light cap and dark jacket. The police knocked, and the occupant, Mrs. Hayden, let them in. Her husband, answering the description, was feigning sleep. In the toilet tank, a shotgun and pistol were found. In the basement, a washing machine turned up a jacket and trousers similar to those described by the cab drivers. At the trial, the issue arose whether the clothing might be put in evidence. The defense argued the clothing had been seized without a search warrant and in violation of the Fourth Amendment. The court held that the Fourth Amendment is concerned with the right of privacy, and that the idea that direct evidence could not be seized was a mere fiction and should be discredited. So the clothing was shown to the jury.

Some searches take place without a warrant. Most notable and recent is a law promoted by the New York drug traffic, the "stop-and-frisk law," which allows a policeman to search a suspect on reasonable suspicion. This eliminates the need of trumping up another charge to allow the search.

The classic case of search without warrant involves the policeman in hot pursuit of the felon who runs and hides. Here the exigencies of the situation make a warrant impossible. On this theory, searches incident to a lawful arrest have been permitted, for otherwise the suspect would have time to destroy evidence. The Supreme Court has extended the search of the suspect's person to include things within his immediate control, and this generally includes the place of arrest. The practicality of this rule is obvious, and so is the danger, for the police will tend to interpret their right of search more widely than they might under a specific search warrant.

The search of a suspect while in police custody may include fingerprints, but it is not an unlimited privilege. In 1963,[8] a woman voluntarily went to a police station to complain of an assault. To record her injuries, the police officer made her submit to photographs, which were taken in the nude. This was held to be an arbitrary intrusion on the plaintiff's right to privacy. More difficult were the cases of *Schmerber v. California* [9] in 1966, and *Rochin v. California* [10] in 1952. In the first case, the defendant was dragged from an auto wreck and taken to a hospital, where doctors took a blood sample to determine if he was medically drunk. Was this forcing the defendant to give evidence against himself? The court held such self-incrimination applied only to forced verbal admissions, and that no warrant had been necessary because delay in obtaining it would have destroyed the evidence. In the Rochin case, Antonio Rochin was seized by police without a warrant in his home. As they burst into his bedroom, Rochin crammed his mouth full of capsules and swallowed them before the police could pry his mouth open. He was rushed to a hospital, where a stomach pump obtained the swallowed drugs for evidence. However, the Supreme Court set aside this conviction, holding that the methods employed were "too close to the rack and the screw to permit of constitutional differentiation." Here again the Supreme Court thought beyond the particular circumstances, which freed a criminal, to the potential imposition of such methods on guiltless citizens.

Initially, the federal courts did not deal with search and seizure within a particular state. In fact, they held that the Fourteenth Amendment did not forbid evidence obtained by unreasonable search and seizure from being used in state courts.[11] Then along came Miss Dollree Mapp. The police had been informed that a person wanted in connection with a recent bombing was hiding on her premises. Without a warrant, they staked out her home and laid siege. She refused entry, but seven men broke in, manhandling her in the process, while holding her attorney outside. Their search for the missing bomber turned the contents of the house upside down, and in the basement they found a trunk full of pornographic pictures and an obscene pencil doodle. There were, however, no explosives. Miss Mapp was arrested for possessing lewd and lascivious books and pictures in violation of the state criminal statute. All might have been forgotten had not Miss Mapp appealed. The Supreme Court, in considering the oppressive police tactics involved, overruled the decision made in 1949 and finally brought constitutional guarantees to bear on state as well as federal methods.

Since the Mapp case, in practice a defendant may make a motion before trial to suppress evidence unlawfully seized from him; and if he can show there was no probable cause for arrest or search, the evidence is excluded and very probably the prosecution fails. At times this rule protects the clearly guilty, a danger outweighed by the protection it affords the innocent from unnecessary harassment.

These are the main rules regarding search and seizure of evidence, but there are a few interesting variations. What of automobiles? What can a policeman do if he thinks a locked car contains the fruits of a crime? There is no law against his looking through the window. This alone may offer sufficient justification to search without a warrant, so long as there remains a likelihood that the car may be moved before a warrant will be issued. However, where the automobile for some reason is not likely to be moved, then a warrant must be obtained.

What about searches which do not involve the police? Assume

a gang member wants to rat on his boss and steals evidence to bring about his arrest and conviction. Such a private theft may be a burglary, but it does not come under constitutional protection. Suppose the search has been conducted by a government agency, such as the city health inspector. Generally, it has been held that health inspectors may enter a building without a warrant to look for the breeding places of rats. Should evidence of espionage turn up and be placed in the hands of the FBI, this has been held no violation. In 1967, the FBI were investigating a case of espionage, and persuaded the city health inspector to make a surprise search of the suspect's premises for two-footed rats. The Supreme Court, perhaps worried by what bordered on police-state complicity, held that a health department search, though ostensibly of a less hostile nature than a police search, was not lawful without appropriate warrants. A strong dissent along the lines of public policy regarded the decision as jeopardizing the health and welfare of many by obstructing such "rat" hunts in the future.

A form of acquiring evidence which has come under court consideration is eavesdropping. Wiretapping began with the invention of the telegraph in the mid-nineteenth century, but it did not become a legal concern until the invention of the telephone. The first landmark case was during the days of bootlegging. Fast boats were being used to run illegal liquor between Washington State and Canada, and much of the business was done over the telephone. The defendants' lines were tapped, and a conviction resulted under the federal Prohibition law. The Supreme Court upheld the decision on the ground that there had been no physical trespass, as with unlawful search and seizure.[12]

As the telephone had not been contemplated by the authors of the Constitution, the states were initially left to make up their own decisions on the subject. Then, in 1967, came the case of *Berger v. New York*.[13] The facts had to do with a conspiracy to bribe the chairman of the New York State Liquor Authority. One Ralph Pansini, a bartender, having refused to pay a bribe to obtain his liquor license, was harassed by having his records seized. With his cooperation, the District Attorney installed on his premises a recording device which gave what seemed sufficient evidence to support an eavesdrop order from the State Supreme Court to place an electronic "bug" in the office of Berger, an attorney who presumably managed the licensing bribes. The evidence obtained resulted in the discovery of the conspiracy, and Berger was indicted. Under the New York statute, a judge had the authority to issue an eavesdrop order on reasonable evidence that a crime might be intercepted during the duration of a stipulated period for eavesdropping, the maximum being sixty days. However, this statute did not fix location limitations on the tap, on the crimes involved, or on the specific evidence anticipated. The Supreme Court held the New York statute to be so vague that it was like putting a policeman behind the curtains in a bedroom, and therefore unconstitutional.

Subsequently, wiretapping among federal agents has been limited to surveillance in cases involving national security, and it requires the Attorney General's permission. Most states have statutes preventing wiretaps, but there are other ways of eavesdropping electronically. As long as one overhears with the ear, however much that hearing is aided electronically, there is no violation of the right of privacy unless there is a physical trespass upon the suspect's domain, such as the drilling of holes. A situation of this nature developed in 1961,[14] when the police installed a "spike" microphone by penetrating a wall and making contact with a heating duct which served the suspect's house. The key to the decision was physical intrusion. Four years later,[15] the police cut peepholes, disguised as air vents, in the ceiling above the stalls in public toilets to photograph homosexual practices that were suspected of taking place there. The court found no unreasonable search, and conviction stood, creating a situation reminiscent of the scene from George Orwell's *1984:* "For a moment he was tempted to take it into one of the water closets and read it at once. But that would be shocking folly, as he well knew. There was no place where you could be more certain that the telescreens were watching continuously." Perhaps with this eventuality in mind came a case in 1967,[16] in which detectives attached electronic devices to the outside of a public telephone booth. For the first time the Supreme Court held that this eavesdropping fell within the protection granted the individual by the Fourth Amendment, even though no technical trespass had resulted. Implicitly, from this case, eavesdropping would in future be held reasonable only if authorized by a warrant.

Such electronic intrusions are new to the law. Before their advent, old tests, such as physical trespass, were adequately applied, but there is no doubt that with the rapid improvement of electronic devices, wiretapping and other physical intrusions will soon be outdated. So the law, too, must change if our privacy is to be protected against constant scrutiny.

A time-honored police method is individual surveillance, or shadowing. It is generally permitted when done discreetly and so long as it is not conducted in a manner calculated to alarm and frighten. In 1963,[17] it was held that the FBI, in shadowing an individual, must use but one car parked a block from the plaintiff's house and that FBI agents, in playing golf behind the plaintiff, must draw no closer than the second foursome. Without some limits, shadowing can become a definite harassment against which an individual would have no recourse.

Once sufficient evidence of a crime has been obtained, the usual step is arrest of the suspect. Once again, the Constitution demands the arrest be reasonable, and this generally means pursuant to a warrant issued by a judicial magistrate, which is "fair on its face." Under the common law there are circumstances in which a police officer may make an arrest without a warrant. If the crime is committed in his presence, be it felony or misdemeanor, he may undertake an arrest without a warrant. When he has "probable cause" to believe that a felony has been committed and he knows the identity of the criminal, even though the crime did not take place in his presence, he may make an arrest. This latter extension of the no-warrant rule does not apply to a misdemeanor. Regardless of the enormity of the offense, mere suspicion on the officer's part is not grounds for arrest without a warrant. An example of just such an excess as the rules contemplated occurred in 1961, when a white girl was raped in Odessa, Texas. Eighty-eight Negroes were hauled off the street for no other reason than that they were black and healthy. The victim failed to identify any one of them, and they were released. A more questionable case involved a policeman in a slum neighborhood who, after watching a man pace up and down and hop furtively into a cab, tore open the cab door and in the process of arrest found some narcotics. The court held that, although the policeman's suspicion was justified, seeing a man behave nervously in a slum area is not probable cause for arrest,[18] and the state's case failed.

What happens when a suspect resists arrest? Traditionally, an unlawful arrest may be resisted, and the arresting officer is entitled to use only reasonable force in effecting capture. Deadly force is generally condoned only when necessary to apprehend a fleeing felon. If a misdemeanor is involved, most jurisdictions regard deadly force as excessive. In all the carefully worded statutes regarding arrest and force, states vary, depending largely on local conditions. For instance, due to recent riots in which demonstrators have obstructed police efforts by going limp, some states have classified this behavior as resisting arrest. And some states, to eliminate all question, have denied citizen resistance to any arrest by a peace officer even if unlawful, with redress being left to a later point in the proceedings.

Of prime concern in limited police authority is the fear of arbitrary arrest, which is a weapon of every totalitarian government. Even in the United States, arrest is abused, particularly in the case of underprivileged groups. Of those police homicides found to be justifiable, 85 percent are of young Negro males at night, which exceeds drastically the admittedly higher rate of crime among this element of the population. A particularly abused situation is the one in which the policeman may encourage violence from a suspected troublemaker to prove that he really is a criminal and to provide grounds for removing him from the street. Often questioned here is the off-duty patrolman, who in some states must carry a gun. Very often the headlines show this man killed or killing in a barroom dispute. (In New York, for example, where all policeman are armed, an average of four are murdered in uniform each year.) In London, England, where the police carry only billy clubs, one policeman dies in action every four years. Does this indicate a more violent people? Or does the armed policeman encourage guns in the hands of criminals? The argument is as circular as whether the egg or the chicken came first.

The Fourth Amendment was initially applied only to federal arrests, but like the other privileges of the individual, it has been extended to the states by way of the "due process" clause of the Fourteenth Amendment. As already mentioned, the usual recourse against unlawful arrest is habeas corpus. This is a better guarantee on paper than it is in fact, for elaborate proceedings and attorneys' fees are involved, and the chance of recompense is small. In most cases involving the natural pariahs of our society, arbitrary arrest and the planting of evidence are simple facts of life.

Once the police have a suspect, their first and natural inclination is to obtain a confession. Confessions in the past, apart from their psychological context, were given more weight than they are today. The Inquisition used endless varieties of torment to obtain confessions of witchcraft. Even when confession was not involved, but only the defendant's unwillingness to plead guilty or not guilty, the means of coercion were spectacular. Under Queen Elizabeth I of England, "pressing" reached a peak. This involved escorting the suspect to a small, dark cell, stripping him to a loin cloth, then, with his body affixed to the stone floor, placing an iron weight on his chest. The suspect's diet consisted of three morsels of the coarsest bread every other day, interspersed with three sips of stagnant water from the pool nearest the prison gate. Should the prisoner remain mute and the iron weight fail to crush him, a sharp stone was mercifully placed under the man's back to speed death on its way. In 1721, one Nathaniel Hawes refused to plead, withstood a weight of 250 pounds for a few minutes, recanted, was tried and hanged. A more resolute Mr. Strangeways endured pressing for a much longer time. He was finally relieved of this torment when his friends were allowed to jump up and down on the weight. When the common law became too civilized for this treatment in 1772, the courts began construing a felon's refusal to plead as an admission of guilt. Not until well into the nineteenth century was silence accepted as a plea of not guilty. But although torment no longer determines the nature of a defendant's plea, it is a different matter where confession is concerned. Confession still carries great influence in court, and, though it may not be good for the soul, among police it is considered vital to conviction. Short of pressing, the police have learned numerous ways of getting the suspect into the "squeal room" and there persuading him to "'spill his guts." A fake telegram may be waved before his face, indicating that his companion in crime has confessed in another city. A fake witness may identify him, or he may be charged with bogus crimes in the hope that he will confess to the real one. Psychological pressure may be used, persistant questioning with policemen alternating, the one being tough and threatening, the other a good, understanding father figure who only wants to help. Gradually the interrogator's chair is moved ever closer, until the suspect's knees are between those of his questioner. A popular device is to persuade the suspect that things aren't so bad, that the man he shot is recovering when in fact he is dead, or that the complaining witness does not want to press charges. Short of physical torture, police methods are many and varied for obtaining convincing confessions which may or may not be genuine.

At the jury trial, the threatening atmosphere of the "squeal room" vanishes. The prosecutor reads the confession "in his own words." A tidy, likable policeman testifies that, as notary public, he saw the defendant sign. A jury is unlikely to believe coercion possible on the part of these good men and true.

It must not be forgotten that a higher value than conviction is at stake, and it is important in maintaining a free society that those with power be subject to constant challenge. The rulings of the Supreme Court that are designed to protect the individual are only effective when the case comes to court.

Many cases are decided without exposure to such rulings, as the result of uncivilized tactics used by the police. This is particularly true when the victim is poor, ignorant, confused, and perhaps ridden with guilt. Then he can be railroaded into prison before any question arises about his constitutional rights. Pressure may not only result in confession, but in a bargain with the prosecutor called a cop out, whereby the defendant agrees to plead guilty to a lesser offense. In either case, constitutional rights are not brought up.

Not until President Herbert Hoover instructed former Attorney General George Wickersham to investigate, were police practices exposed. The result was an upsurge of concern on the part of the Supreme Court to make sure that evidence of guilt be lawfully obtained. More recently the sensational case of George Whitmore, Jr., brought the abuses of police coercive power to public attention.

Whitmore was an ignorant Negro drifter, nineteen years old, who, on April 24, 1964, was conveyed to the "squeal room" of a Brooklyn, New York, police station. After twenty-two hours he had confessed to one attempted rape and three murders. Nothing unusual there, except that only after two trials, a hung jury, a reversed conviction, and a dismissed indictment was the real murderer found. This embarrassment to the New York police force came at a time when the country had manifested displeasure with the Supreme Court for its softness upon murderers, a feeling that had culminated in the trial of Danny Escobedo.[19] Escobedo had been convicted of murdering his brother-in-law. It was an open-and-shut case, but then the Supreme Court reversed it, not because his confession had been tricked or coerced, but simply because it had been made after he had been denied a right to see his lawyer.

The Whitmore and Escobedo cases did not put an end to the third degree. In the case of *People v. Portelli*,[20] it came out that the police had placed lighted cigarette butts on the back of a witness for the purpose of obtaining a statement incriminating a third party. Shades of the Inquisition. Soon to follow was the case of *Miranda v. Arizona*.[21] The defendant, an adult male with the mental age of twelve, was held incommunicado and questioned for two days regarding a rape, and finally confessed in his own writing. He was not told he might have an attorney, but there was eyewitness testimony, and conviction followed. The Supreme Court, against much opposition, granted a new trial on the grounds that the police might not question a suspect in custody until he was told he had a right to remain silent and that anything he said might be used against him. Furthermore, he was held to have a right to counsel before the interrogation took place. In point of fact, at a retrial without the confession, Miranda was again convicted and sentenced to thirty years imprisonment, but great was the outrage against this coddling of criminals. Newspapers commented wryly upon the absurd limits forced upon the police. A favorite example was the policeman who laboriously advised a dying housewife of her rights before asking who cut her throat. "My husband," she finally gurgled upon expiring.

The debate still rages, but the better-reasoned arguments seem to favor the Supreme Court position. In general, informing a suspect of his rights is a protection to the innocent and the ignorant rather than to the old pro. The FBI has enjoyed commendable success in convicting prisoners, yet it has never used violence or threats. Reliance on a suspect "spilling his guts" tends to make for police laziness in the search for other evidence, and in point of statistical fact, over half of those accused of a crime will confess even after being told of their right to keep silent. Also, in an indirect way, the suspect who keeps quiet is incriminating himself, and the confession, even when voluntary, is far less reliable than originally thought. In the Elizabeth Short murder investigation, better known as the "Black Dahlia Murders," over two hundred confessions were obtained. So great is this tendency to confess that a conviction no longer can stand on confession alone. Suppose that the body of a young woman has been found run over by a train. There is no other evidence, yet a man admits having strangled the victim and then placed her on the tracks. His footprints are not found, no trace of his fingerprints, no witness who saw him in the neighborhood. Try as he will, this man will not be allowed to commit judicial suicide.

Summed up, the arguments are these: The more current view holds that even if the privileges surrounding a suspect may sometimes shield the guilty, they are the soundest safeguards against unreliable and uncivilized methods. A dissenting opinion would say that the social cost of crime is too high to regard the Supreme Court rules as anything but a dangerous experiment.

The right to an attorney before interrogation is of very recent origin, but the right to counsel during the trial itself was first seriously considered as an element of due process in the case of the Scottsboro Boys in 1931.[22] The time was the Depression, the place a train full of hoboes, black and white. The latter group contained two young women, Ruby Bates and Victoria Price. Ruby was seventeen, Victoria twenty-five. Between stops, a scuffle took place involving the Negroes and the whites, with the white boys allegedly being thrown from the train and the girls raped. Nine blacks, aged thirteen to twenty, went on trial for their lives, a trial which began within six days after indictment. An attorney was named for the defendants on the morning of the trial. He was court appointed, clearly there as a formality, and in no way aided their cause. The defendants accused one another. The case seemed open-and-shut at first glance, yet why were the white boys not called by the prosecution to testify? Only one appeared, and he did not mention the rape. Why were the clothes allegedly torn from the girls not damaged in the struggle? On appeal from conviction, the Supreme Court of the United States held narrowly that in a capital case it was a denial of due process on the part of a state not to furnish defendants with an adequate attorney. A new trial followed, then a third, over a period of five years, during which time Ruby Bates recanted and denied the rape. The state tried to get some of the boys to confess while letting others off, and as the years passed, one by one the defendants were released on parole except for Heywood Patterson, the defense's prime spearhead in the great agitation. As a sort of official revenge, he was kept in jail until 1948. Then he escaped, killed a man in a fight, was caught and jailed again, finally to die of cancer in 1952, an unrepentant criminal, made so by court injustice.

Cases that followed, for a time, limited this right to counsel at the state level to capital crimes alone, except where defendants were faced by a situation too complex to defend themselves. Then, in 1961, Clarence Earl Gideon was charged with breaking and entering a poolroom in Panama City, Florida, to commit petty larceny. Gideon was an indigent. He asked that an attorney be appointed, and he was refused. Convicted, Gideon filed a writ of habeas corpus, which was denied by the Supreme Court of Florida. He then took the petition on to the Supreme Court of the United States.[23] Here the limitation of right to counsel to state capital cases was overthrown and extended to all cases involving felonies. A circuit court has since extended the right to counsel to misdemeanors.

Settled much earlier was the Fifth Amendment right of a defendant not to incriminate himself. This "taking the Fifth," as it has been called in our era, extends to personal books and records. The origin of the right goes back to the trial of John Lilburne, a pamphleteer of Puritan persuasion, who was brought before the

English Star Chamber in the seventeenth century and whipped because he refused to incriminate himself. When the Puritan general,
Cromwell, rose to power, the Star Chamber was dispersed and a
privilege against self-incrimination granted. This privilege has been
held to operate in civil as well as criminal cases where the divul-
gence of facts would make the party liable to punishment. The
scope of the privilege does not apply to possible civil liability or
to third persons or corporations. A person may waive his privilege
against self-incrimination, but, once the door is open to disclosure,
he may not close it. Nor does the privilege extend to a defendant in
a criminal trial once he has voluntarily taken the witness stand in
his own behalf. Such an appearance is regarded as a waiver. Also,
the privilege vanishes once the liability to punishment has been
ended by conviction, acquittal, or a lapse of time sufficient to bar
future prosecution. It vanishes likewise after executive pardon,
legislative amnesty, or where immunity is granted from the results
of any new evidence which the testimony may divulge.

With this rule there is little controversy. The only problem it
raises is a negative one. In the early 1950's, Senator Joseph Mc-
Carthy, in his witch-hunting senatorial investigations, coined the
phrase "Fifth Amendment Communism," and many an innocent
man was ruined socially and professionally by its implications.

A more pervasive, catch-all requirement of due process which
may also be traced back to the secret hearings of the ancient Star
Chamber is fair and public trial. "Public" need not mean the world,
but a reasonable number of spectators. The mood must be impartial
and dispassionate, and, where the defendant is convicted in an
atmosphere of prejudice and hysteria, the conviction must be
vacated.[24] The trial of Dr. Sam Sheppard, previously discussed under freedom of the press, is again a case in point. Questions of fairness vary widely, and should the defendant call witnesses who are
kept shackled by prosecution order throughout their testimony,
creating a suspicion of their dangerous and untrustworthy character, it may be sufficient to upset a fair trial.[25]

In all these situations, the Supreme Court has interpreted the
Constitution in the light of two competing concerns: on the one
hand, the right of the public individually to receive fair treatment
at the hands of its police and courts; on the other, recognition of the

need for effective laws in a society fraught with crime. In the particular, results may sometimes seem unfair, but considering the overall sweep of cases, it would be difficult to fault the Supreme Court for the wisdom of its decisions. Recent legislation, prompted by fear of mob violence, Negro violence, and the assassinations of Martin Luther King, Jr., and John and Robert Kennedy, has attempted to cut back the Supreme Court rulings. In particular, we have the much-criticized Omnibus Crime Control and Safe Streets Act of 1968. In its terms, a valid confession may be put into evidence if voluntarily given, whether or not the suspect has been appraised of his rights. The rules regarding wiretapping have been relaxed somewhat. How this reverse trend works out in the courts is yet to be judged, but it is an unhappy trend based on the general idea that the crime problem is to be solved by locking up more people. There is no denying such a solution works. Hitler and Stalin proved it. But in terms of civilizing the law, it is an admission of defeat and a primitive dealing with disorder which, as a society, the United States is not likely to accept.

Crime is on the rise. The streets in many large cities aren't safe at night, nor often in daylight. Something has to be done, and one approach, though expensive, is to improve the police. From Robert Peel's Police Bill in 1829, the idea has already come a long way. Before that, there had only been watchmen and local volunteer agencies to protect the public. Beginning in 1829, the English professional policeman, called Peelers and Bobbies after their founder, received fifty pounds a year, wore black chimney-pot hats, and had the sole task of patrolling the streets. The idea of a detective to prevent crime was unknown. Public order, enforced with a nightstick and, if need be, a revolver, was their concern, and cases such as that of Franz Muller, which today might be taken as everyday detective work, caused international excitement. Muller, a young German living in London in 1864, robbed and bludgeoned a London bank clerk on a railroad carriage and tipped the dying body off the moving train. In departing the train, Muller made two mistakes. He left behind his low-crowned hat, and he took the victim's gold watch and chain. Four days later he sailed for the United States. Meanwhile the English police, already upgraded from sidewalk Bobbies, were busy. Within a week, a jeweler by the name of Death reported exchanging a watch chain for another brought in by a customer. Searching further, police found a cabman who remembered his daughter had been given a gift in a cardboard box with the name of Death on it, and the gift had come from young Muller. By then, as the police lacked today's electronic aids, Muller had been several days on the high seas. Doggedly, Inspector Tanner of Scotland Yard rounded up the jeweler and the cabman and set off by steamship—the one modern invention to aid the police, for Muller had gone aboard the *Victoria* under sail in what turned out to be a windless summer. The inspector and his witnesses reached New York with twenty days to spare for sightseeing. By the time the *Victoria* arrived in New York Harbor, the entire city was alert to the persistence of Scotland Yard, and excursionists passing the *Victoria* in the harbor shouted out to Muller, "How are you, Muller the Murderer?" Evidently he did not hear them, for he walked complacently into the arms of the waiting police. He was returned to England, and the forgotten hat convicted him. Ballads were written about him after he was hanged, and the condemning, low-crowned hat became a popular style. Winston Churchill almost always wore one.

While the Peelers were earning grudging respect in London, an equally hard-fisted force, really only a bunch of strong-arm men to keep day-and-night watch, was developing in New York. These were the Leatherheads. Not until 1845, under the city's first police chief, George Washington Matsell, did the half-loved, half-hated "flatfoot," so called for his capacity for standing endlessly on street corners, emerge with a copper badge on his coat. With the badge he became a "cop," or "copper."

Until the Muller case, a criminal, to escape, had simply to outrun the flatfooted policeman. But Muller was a victim of the machine age, and other new methods were evolving. Criminology was still in its infancy, and the first big advance came when the Frenchman Alphonse Bertillon decided a criminal could be identified by a series of measurements which he called anthropometry. He also, toward the end of the nineteenth century, standardized the "mug shot" of known criminals with the front and profile views. The first efforts at recording criminal portraits were more artistic than uniform.

Another new method was soon to revolutionize police work. Curiously, fingerprints had for a long time been used in China and Japan as a way of signing banknotes. A Scottish physician named Henry Faulds, while working in Tokyo, had observed this method of identification and realized that sooty prints left at the scene of a robbery would later match those of the robber. About the same time, Sir William J. Herschel, a district magistrate in India, had begun taking fingerprints to solve paying extra allowances to Indian soldiers who often sent relatives to collect twice. Brought to the attention of the British police, the method was finally given the seal of approval in a case where the only evidence linking the criminal to the crime was a set of fingerprints on a cash box. The jury accepted this as sufficient proof, and by 1910 fingerprints had been uniformly accepted as evidence in courtrooms. In 1917, the horse- and bicycle-riding coppers of New York City received their first two-way radio car. The radio aerial was very thick and stood about twenty feet in the air, which limited its use in pursuit situations, but the floodgates of science had opened. Along with photography and the radio came the comparison of bullets, first demonstrated with no great reliability in the Sacco and Vanzetti case. Since then, the comparison microscope has improved the technique. The X ray has been perfected so that a murderer's fingerprints can be found on the flesh of his victim. Closed-circuit TV, the computerizing of information, and countless other scientific methods have enhanced the process of criminal detection.

Much has been said here and elsewhere in criticism of our local police forces. More will be said. But it must be read with the awareness that the law, and commentaries on the law, point to areas of conflict and disorder. Vast areas of harmony and good works, many of them directly attributable to the tough and capable men who staff our police forces, are passed over. Where disorder occurs, the police are an indispensable first line of defense. By and large, these men are dedicated to an often dangerous and thankless job, but just as our society and its laws can be improved, so can the guardians of its order. Apart from the progressive Federal Bureau of Investigation, established in 1908, our police establishment has lagged behind the times both in methods employed and in the quality of the men on the force, a criticism applicable to most public institutions, yet nonetheless serious on this account. In spirit, there has been only grudging change since the New York City department ignited its gas-lamp police globe in 1844. Those were the days of Captain George Walling's first strong-arm squad. Clad in plain clothes and armed with locust-wood clubs, these men dealt out elemental justice to a gang of midtown muggers known as the Honeymooners. Whenever a member of the squad recognized a gang member, he simply went up to him and slugged him unconscious. Local success was achieved. The Honeymooners moved south to the Bowery.

Naturally enough, police work often attracts those people who are not averse to the use of violence. It is common in police thinking that "wise guys" need to be shown the meaning of respect, and the usual victims are society's outcasts—pimps, gamblers, drifters, who never get to court. Running in prostitutes simply by way of harassment is a common practice. If one of them resists, she may be beaten, but the hospital record is apt to show "injured while falling out of patrol car." To make sure the record stands, the proprietor of the bar where she works may get the message that he'll be raided if she complains. Petty bribery is a constant temptation to the underpaid "flatfoot" and one to which a number of them regularly succumb. Simply by loitering around a Harlem bar, police can cut down on the number of customers, so, to avoid this situation, the proprietor may be tempted to make a small contribution to the Police Athletic League. Sometimes he may not. In one such case of resistance, the police returned to the bar, marched a female customer into the kitchen, accused her of being a man in disguise, and made her strip naked to make sure; all in the line of duty, but it was very bad for future restaurant business. Grimly amusing, perhaps, but very often results are more serious where gun-toting cops are on the job. In one reported situation a man sprinted out of a bar and down the street. The bartender followed, shouting, "Stop, thief!" and a policeman with good intentions took up the chase and ordered the fugitive to halt. When the man failed to stop, perhaps without even hearing the command, the policeman demonstrated better marksmanship than judgment and shot him dead. As it turned out, he had simply failed to pay for a drink, but the police have a way of protecting their own, and the corpse was officially charged with having "defrauded an inn-keeper." This raised a minor misdemeanor to a felony, which justified the use of deadly force. Luckily for the police, the man had a criminal record, and in accordance with the old adage that "nobody cares when you smash a rotten egg," the incident was forgotten. Of a more calculated nature was the practice developed in the early 1960's by the Dallas police called Jack-in-the-box. This called for special squads to lie in wait in buildings and warehouses likely to be burglarized and to blaze away at intruders with sawed-off shotguns. True Western justice, and effective, perhaps, but a long step down the road to the police state where it is very difficult to weigh the police against the criminals.

The review board is a self-administering method for the examination of police excesses. If a citizen complains, an officer investigates the situation. If the issue appears doubtful, a formal hearing takes place, which in turn may lead to a trial before the police commissioner. Naturally enough, the police force is prone to protect its reputation and its members, and as long as the officer can be found to have acted in the course of his duty and was not off on "a frolic of his own," no disciplinary action will follow. In 1966, Mayor Lindsay of New York set up a civilian-dominated review board to scrutinize the behavior of New York's Finest. The move was inspired by the killing of two Puerto Ricans in police custody on November 15, 1963. According to a police version, the Puerto Ricans had been placed in a paddy wagon; one had whipped out a gun and both had been killed. Questions quite naturally arose. How was this possible when the men were handcuffed? And why were two men killed when they had only one gun? There seemed to be no answers. However, the civilian-dominated review board was very quickly doomed by the campaign of the Patrolmen's Benevolent Association. Before the Civilian Review Board had a chance to prove itself, it was voted out in the next election. This was probably a mistake, for, as the Roman poet Juvenal put it, *"Quis custodiet ipsos custodes?"* ("Who shall guard the guards themselves?").

Without the Civilian Review Board, it took courageous newspaper reporting to correct the following situation. In August of 1966, just before the Civilian Review Board died, Negroes in

Brooklyn skirmished with a white group calling itself SPONGE, Society for the Prevention of Negroes Getting Everything. An eleven-year-old Negro bystander was shot dead, and Ernest Gallashaw, also a Negro, was arrested for the crime. To support the assertion of his guilt, two witnesses, one emotionally disturbed, the other mentally incompetent to testify, were brought under oath. More trustworthy testimony to the effect that a member of the SPONGE group had fired the gun was suppressed until *The New York Times* interfered with its articles.

Without a civilian review board, what recourse has a citizen against police abuse? Theoretically, he may bring an action for damages in the civil court, and for assault and battery in the criminal court. In point of fact, there are few such actions, for most complainants would be from the underprivileged classes or minority groups, very often of criminal background, whose prospects in court are poor even when they can stand the cost and inconvenience.

With or without civilian review boards, what is needed is a new breed of policemen. Saturating the streets with patrolmen is not the answer in a civilization in which major crime is organized and businesslike. The expensive solution is an upgrading of the police image. A psychiatric test of applicants might be held to screen out any borderline psychotics who may be attracted by the possibility of violence. Pay incentives and training should be designed to appeal to the better educated. Simply being tough and a good shot isn't enough in a highly crowded and technical society, and the day of the graft-prone "flatfoot" must give way to that of the professionally competent civil servant and scientist. Meanwhile, citizens of the United States are fortunate to have the Supreme Court, the Constitution, and, particularly, the Fourteenth Amendment to protect them from the excesses of their guardians. As was once said of those who devised the Fourteenth Amendment,

> They builded, not for a day, but for all time; not for a few or for a race, but for Man. They planted in the Constitution a monumental truth, to stand four-square whatever wind might blow. That truth is but the golden rule, so entrenched as to curb the man who would do to the few as they would not have the few do to them.[26]

CHAPTER NINE

Civil Rights

DUE PROCESS OF THE LAW IS TODAY MUCH INVOLVED IN ANOTHER turbulent area, that of civil rights. The issue first arose during the United States Constitutional Convention in 1787, but unanimity between North and South could not then have been achieved had slavery been abolished. A resolution regarding it was dropped from the proposed document. At the time, it seemed to make little difference. Slavery was generally regarded as moribund, even in the South, until the invention of the cotton gin.

Before the Civil War, there was only one major case concerned with slavery. This led to the notorious Dred Scott decision in 1857,[1] which became as much a proximate cause of the forthcoming war as John Brown and his raiders. The background against which this seemingly minor court struggle took place was the Missouri Compromise. With the purchase of the Louisiana Territory in 1803, vast lands were added to the dominion of the United States. A portion of this territory calling itself Missouri was the first to apply for statehood. The early settlers there had been slaveholders, and when Missouri applied for statehood, it was understood that slavery was to be lawful within its borders. However, if this was allowed, slavery would be apt to spread throughout the new lands. Northern factions argued that Congress should outlaw slavery in the territory. Southerners held that it was unconstitutional to give Congress such powers, and in the end a compromise

151

line was drawn through the new territory, north of which slavery would be forbidden. Missouri, however, was allowed to be admitted as a slave state. That was in 1820. Seven years later, Dred Scott, born a slave in Virginia, was taken by his master into Missouri and sold. Later, he traveled with his new master into free territory north of the compromise line. The issue in the case was whether, having been taken into free territory, Scott had become automatically free under the Missouri Compromise. The first action was held in Missouri in 1846, and Scott understandably lost. However, abolitionist sympathizers arranged a new case which found its way to the Supreme Court. The Court might have come to a narrow technical decision, leaving Dred Scott to obscurity, but since the majority of the judges were from slave states, they went on to declare (in 1857) not only that Scott was a slave, but that the Missouri Compromise itself violated the Fifth Amendment by depriving slaveowners in free territory of their property without due process of law. In short, Congress was without power to prohibit slavery in any United States territory. The implications of this decision were enormous. Shock and outrage spread throughout the North. Twenty-two states passed resolutions declaring the Dred Scott opinion null and void, and Lincoln's star began to rise. The Civil War was at hand.

Lincoln has been called the Great Emancipator for his proclamation of January 1, 1863, which freed the slaves. It is less widely known that he did not hesitate to trample the citizen's rights to due process of law by suspending the right of habeas corpus. This allowed the military to throw Southern sympathizers into prison. In 1861,[2] the Court denied President Lincoln's constitutional right to exercise such powers, but during the war years its opinion was ignored. In a case in 1866,[3] the fate of Lambdin P. Milligan was at stake. He was a teacher, a lawyer, and a member of a Copperhead organization devoted to Confederate victory, who had been seized for inciting disorders in Chicago. The arrest had been military, and the trial for conspiracy against the government was conducted by a military commission which sentenced him to death. Before sentence was carried out, the war was over, and Milligan appeared before the Supreme Court. Here it was held that even in time of peril, so long as the civil courts are functioning, a civilian has the right to be tried by civilians, and the military should be denied jurisdiction. One can only speculate whether this would have been the result if the war had been still in progress at the time of the Court's decision.

Whatever ills were cured or created by the Civil War, one that is generally thought to have been wiped out is slavery. Not entirely. As late as 1947,[4] a Mrs. Mary Rowe was successfully prosecuted for slavery. It seems she had a Negro servant, Dora Jones, whom she kept for many years without pay or holiday. Dora lived off table scraps, and, whenever she questioned the fairness of her lot, Mrs. Rowe reminded her "slave" of an affair she had had with her "owner's" late husband and of an abortion that resulted. Finally, when deprived even of the few coins she had received for baby-sitting in another home, Dora ran to the police.

This is a rare exception. In general, the Civil War set four million confused and milling slaves free under the Thirteenth Amendment, which gave constitutional force to Lincoln's earlier military fiat. In the next ten years, Congress enacted eleven laws and three amendments to the Constitution, beginning with the Civil Rights Act of 1866. To put teeth into the earlier declarations, the Fourteenth Amendment came along in 1868, granting due process of the law to all citizens and the right to vote to any adult male citizen regardless of race. (Women were not so privileged until the Nineteenth Amendment was passed in 1920.) An 1871 act was directed against organizations such as the Ku Klux Klan which conspired to deprive citizens of their rights.

The final law in this Republican blast at postwar racism was the Civil Rights Act of 1875, and it provided "that all persons within the jurisdiction of the United States shall be entitled to the full and equal enjoyment of the accommodations, advantages, facilities and privileges of inns, public conveyances on land or water, theatres, and other places of public amusement; subject only to the conditions and limitations established by law, and applicable alike to citizens of every race and color, regardless of any previous condition of servitude."

Unhappily, the law came years before its time. A reactionary Supreme Court in the so-called Civil Rights Cases in 1883[5] reasoned that this sort of discrimination was no part of slavery and thus beyond the reach of the Thirteenth and Fourteenth amendments, which deal with "state" discrimination but not acts of the individual. The tide had turned against civil rights, and the Court busied itself with narrowing the scope of legislation, a process that culminated in 1896.[6] At issue was a Louisiana law requiring that "all railway companies provide . . . equal but separate accommodations for the white and colored races." Actually, the hardheaded railroads found it an expensive nuisance to maintain separate cars, and they were more than ready to help along a test case by arresting one Homer Plessy for refusing to sit in a Jim Crow car. Plessy, being only one-eighth black, could have passed for a white man, and one argument used before the Supreme Court was that he had been deprived of a valuable property, that is, the reputation of being white, which was described as "the master key that unlocked the golden door of opportunity." Also questioned was the failure of the statute to apply to Negro nurses attending white children, which glaringly suggested the real evil was not in the skin color but in the subordinate role that black persons maintained toward whites. Nevertheless, the Court upheld the state statute, thereby giving birth to the doctrine of "separate but equal." Only the first Justice John Marshall Harlan prophetically dissented. "In my opinion, the judgment this day rendered will, in time, prove to be quite as pernicious as the decision made by this tribunal in the Dred Scott case." It took longer, but he was right.

This decision set the pattern in the years to follow. No longer a slave, the Negro remained subservient. The lynch mob silenced protest, and such voices as were heard followed the "improve yourself and be worthy" line advanced by Booker T. Washington. Then, with Franklin D. Roosevelt, came the New Deal. It amounted to a second Reconstruction for the American Negro, who began his move from rural Southern exploitation to urban discrimination in the North. Still, without question, prospects were opening. Jobs were becoming available, and a pattern was being set. In 1944,[7] a law designed to exclude Negro railroad firemen in the South was held to be unconstitutional.

The need for Negro manpower created by the Second World War was never entirely lost thereafter; and although in 1926 [8] white landowners were permitted to enforce restrictive convenants not to sell to Negroes, by 1948 [9] the Court, while not holding such a convenant in a deed to property invalid, decided any attempt by the state to enforce it was a participation in racial discrimination. Once again the Court was juggling ideas, but this time the movement was toward the expansion of civil rights. In that same year, President Truman passed an order demanding integration in the armed forces, and within a few years it had been substantially achieved.

Then, in 1954, came an unexpected bombshell. Five Negro minors sought admission to certain white Southern schools on a nonsegregated basis. At the federal district court level, the plaintiffs were turned down under the time-honored "separate but equal" doctrine. The consolidated cases reached the Supreme Court, bearing the title *Brown v. Board of Education.*[10] Chief Justice Earl Warren handed down a unanimous opinion overthrowing the "separate but equal" rule. Former cases had found that conditions were not always physically equal in fact, but this decision held that the very existence of enforced separation was a source of inequality. States with segregated schools were called on to integrate with "all deliberate speed." Reaction was sharply divided and strongly partisan. In Little Rock, Arkansas, where integration had seemed to be proceeding smoothly for three years, school board plans were intercepted by Governor Orville Faubus. Before the fall term of 1957 could begin with the entry of nine Negro children into Central High School, Governor Faubus called up the National Guard and placed the school off limits to blacks. For three weeks, National Guard soldiers stood shoulder to shoulder preventing even token integration, until a federal injunction had the National Guard removed. Large and unruly crowds led to the calling in of federal troops. Similar conditions developed at the University of Mississippi, when a twenty-nine-year-old Negro, James Meredith, sought admission. Governor Ross Barnett had himself appointed "special registrar" at the college, and in direct defiance of federal court orders he forbade Meredith's enrollment. It became necessary for President Eisenhower to assume federal military control. Tactics of delay are commonplace in the South, but they are generally far more subtle. Deliberation with very little speed has been the order of the passing years.

Although the recent integration campaign first focused on schools, other areas, such as job equality, the right to vote, the right to use public accommodations, all came under attack in physical fact as well as in law. With the early 1960's began the Southern sit-ins, generally at restaurants where blacks had been excluded. A 1963 case [11] questioned the constitutionality of a local ordinance which made it unlawful for Negroes to use a lunch counter at a Kress store in South Carolina. The ordinance was found wanting in that it did not afford equal protection under the Constitution, and the decision came at a time when President Kennedy was pushing a general civil rights program through Congress. Before the bill could pass, Kennedy was assassinated. The wave of emotion that followed his death swept the bill into law within two months. This Civil Rights Act of 1964 provided that a citizen had a federal right to equality of service in all places of public accommodation which have any meaningful relation to interstate commerce or are in any meaningful sense creatures of state law. Reaction in the South was mixed. There were pockets of willing compliance, but there were also murders of civil-rights workers and church burnings. Some restaurant owners armed their staffs with ax handles at the approach of hungry Negro divinity students. With the new law behind them, the students were eventually fed, but at least in one case, such a restaurant owner, Lester Maddox, was rewarded by a prejudiced electorate with the governorship of the state of Georgia.

Two major cases were considered by the Supreme Court in 1964.[12] The issue at stake was the Civil Rights Act of that year, and the question was whether Congress could legislate away the right of an individual to discriminate as he saw fit in his own business. In other words, can the federal government, in exercising its commerce clauses, that is, its interstate power, widen its interpretation to include all hotels, motels, and places of public refreshment? In light of the fact that in the South the average distance between accommodations of reasonable quality that served Negroes was 141 miles, the decision was that the situation affected the smooth functioning of interstate commerce; though one hotel might seem local in nature, its refusal to serve Negroes contributed to the national problem. Another barrier had fallen.

The federal laws have done much to guarantee civil rights among the states, but what about criminal rights? That is, what protection can the federal government offer a Negro against the criminal invasion of his civil rights by a private citizen? About all it can do under Title 18 of the federal code is provide that where two or more persons conspire against a citizen's enjoyment of his constitutional rights, they may be fined up to five thousand dollars or imprisoned for ten years, or both.

An early and ominous case was *Screws v. United States* [13] in 1945. Here Screws, a Georgia sheriff, had a grudge against a certain Negro named Hall, and had threatened to have him arrested for allegedly stealing a tire. To this end, Screws and two other officers took Hall to the courthouse and beat him to death with their fists and a solid-bar blackjack. When the state failed to prosecute, the federal district court indicted Screws under the federal law prohibiting official deprivation of civil rights, a crime carrying the maximum of one year in jail and a one-thousand-dollar fine. The district court found Screws guilty, but the issue of whether he had acted "willfully" within the terms of the statute came before the Supreme Court via a writ of certiorari. This is a writ of early English origin, and it permits a higher court to examine the conduct of an inferior tribunal. The Supreme Court granted the defendant a new trial, at which he was acquitted. This case and those before it support the axiom that in the Deep South a white man is not punished for the wrongful death of a Negro. To some extent, the rule still remains true, but the federal law has made progress. A 1966 case [14] concerned itself with the shotgun murder of a Negro educator, Lemuel Penn. He had been driving back to Washington, D. C., after serving his summer hitch as an officer in the Army Reserve, and was gunned down on a Georgia highway. Two members of a six-man group were tried by the state for murder and acquitted. Then the federal government stepped in and tried them on the following narrow federal issues: not simply whether the defendants had attacked an individual incidentally involved in interstate travel, but whether the purpose of their conspiracy was to impede the exercise of the right to indulge in such travel. The latter situation was found, and the defendants were convicted. Progress, no doubt, but still justice limited to a maximum of ten years in prison for a crime which was actually murder.

A bizarre case unto itself was *Loving v. Virginia*[15] in 1967. Mildred Jeter, a Negro woman, and Richard Loving, a white man, married in the District of Columbia and then returned to live in Virginia, where they were indicted for violating the state's ban on interracial marriage. The defendants pleaded guilty and received a one-year suspended sentence on the condition that they leave the state. Reminiscent of oratory at the Scopes "monkey trial," the remark of the judge was, "Almighty God created the races white, black, yellow, Malay, and red, and He placed them on separate continents. And but for the interference with His arrangement there would be no cause for such marriages. The fact that He separated the races shows that He did not intend for the races to mix." On being taken to the Supreme Court, the issue became whether Virginia's anti-mixed-marriage law, a provision found at that time in sixteen other states, violated the individual's right to due process and equal protection. Happily for this Loving couple and others to follow, the state statute was struck down as unconstitutional.

Yet all is far from bliss within our society. It strives on the one hand for equality, yet seems on the other to split into violent factions: white against black, black against white, black against black, the slow-moving religious traditionalist against the angry militant whose slogan has become "Burn, baby, burn!" The law moves too fast for some, too slow for others; but while it retains an aura of morality codified, there is hope. Man tends to conform, to be law-abiding, and though the present process of integration may heighten inner prejudices, in the longer run actual conduct is apt to break them down. By gradually altering the situation, hopefully before too many fires are lit, it will alter attitudes as well. Already attitudes have shifted. The image of the Negro has changed from that of a bug-eyed, shuffling Stepin Fetchit to something that is often feared and sometimes respected and which brings a kind of grudging equality in the end. Certainly the slogan "Black is beautiful" has made an impact in the pages of "white" fashion magazines and upon television. Outside the glamour world, it has been the job of the Supreme Court to educate the nation on this equality by interpreting the Constitution and adjusting old laws.

If the United States is criticized from within and from abroad, few can deny the sincerity of our efforts as a nation, and few with similar racial problems can say they have done as well. In South Africa, for example, there has developed a system of apartheid which does not even pretend to live up to "separate but equal." Under apartheid, a white man is taxed on his net income, but the black African is taxed on his gross income and without benefit of deductions or exemptions. Why? Surely not for any special favor received. In truth, he is milked by his government, which would not allow him to spend his money as he pleased anyway. This domination by a small white minority began in 1948, and it is an instructive example of what may happen in a country that lacks a binding constitution. In that year, the Nationalist Government came to power with the intent of subduing the black majority, made up of Bantus, Malays, Hottentots, and other groups. By 1951, the Nationalists had pushed an act through their parliament to disenfranchise the "coloured" voters. However, the highest court in the land, called the Appellate Division, unanimously struck down the law as not being passed by the required two-thirds majority. Infuriated, the Nationalists passed a law naming Parliament "The High Court of Parliament" and giving it the right to overrule the Appellate Division. Again, the judges staunchly called this act unlawful. It took six more years for the Nationalists to pack the Parliament so that the required two-thirds majority was gained. Then the court was bound to yield to a fraud because it conformed to the letter of the law.

The flood of Nationalist laws has deprived the South African black of most of his civil rights and protections. For instance, a sabotage act of 1962 holds that a native striking for better wages or living conditions can be held for committing the crime of sabotage, which is punishable by death. What can an honest judge do about this? It is not his job to legislate, but to enforce, the law. He might resign on principle, only to be replaced by a bigot. In general, he is helpless, and the moral of the story points to the virtue of a written constitution and bill of rights beyond the reach of the legislature and executives, for in these the judge can find his written authority to weather the storm that has raged in South Africa for many years.

Fortunately, in the United States there is such a constitution, which shields the judiciary from the morally degrading duties that have been forced on the South African courts. The Constitution and its amendments have become a measure for judging the value of public acts, and the Founding Fathers who instituted it relied on early judges like Marshall to make it a living reality. A court not otherwise empowered is limited to the consideration of earlier judicial decisions and the interpretation of legislative acts. Only when protected by a constitution can that court question the justice of the acts themselves, and where they are found wanting, cast them down.

Thus protected, the high court of the United States can shape the laws toward a more civilized goal without fear of being swarmed over by passing furies that may rage in the society at large. To the best of its ability, it has set the country on the right path regarding human and civil rights, but it cannot carry a whole society very far. In the end it can only point the way, for, as Judge Learned Hand once said, "Liberty lies in the hearts of men and women; when it dies there, no constitution, no law, no court can save it; no constitution, no law, no court can even do much to help it. While it lies there, it needs no constitution, no law, no court to save it."

CHAPTER TEN

Law Among Nations: War and Its Control

TODAY CAIN WOULD PROBABLY BE ADJUDGED PSYCHOTIC AND CONFINED for life, but he killed Abel with a rock before there was any law to govern the relationship between individuals. There was no policeman to stop him. Since Genesis, we have come a long way toward civilizing individual conduct, but among nations the inclination is still to hurl rocks or their updated equivalent, hydrogen bombs.

Before discussing international law, fact or fiction, history or prospects, there is one internal relationship relevant to war that is peculiar to the United States. Just how, legally, does the United States go about making war? The Constitution declares that the Congress shall have power to declare war and to raise and support armies, and yet for more than twenty years from the 1950's the country has been involved in two major wars with no such declaration. International policy has slipped from popular control, if, indeed, it ever resided there.

The Founding Fathers gave the war-making power to Congress specifically to keep that power out of the hands of one man. They had witnessed the example of European monarchs who had been killing and impoverishing their people in private wars, allegedly for the common good. However, when the first draft of the Constitution gave Congress the right to "make" war, the very impracticality envisioned by horse-and-buggy congressmen assembling from long distances over dirt roads to debate a national emergency caused the drafters of the rewritten version to substitute the word "declare." The right to use the armed forces to meet specific emergencies was left to the President, while the Congress retained the power of the purse over the size and nature of the armed forces. With this in mind, Thomas Jefferson remained on the defensive against the Barbary pirates in 1801 until Congress approved.

The first real issue arose in 1846, when President Polk, envisioning a western empire, sent General Zachary Taylor into territory claimed by Mexico. The war was, in fact, launched before Congress gave its approval. Much discord followed this action, and Henry Thoreau returned to Walden Pond to write his famous essay on "Civil Disobedience," which has been a guide to protesters ever since. Congressional approval was eventually obtained, but the House of Representatives qualified its vote of thanks to a victorious General Taylor by describing the war as "unnecessary and unconstitutionally begun by the President."

Half a century later, the reprehensible Spanish-American War broke out. It was the doing of a Congress impelled by Hearst's yellow journalism. Congress recognized the "belligerency" of Cuban rebels against President Cleveland's objections and his threat not to mobilize the army. Later, President McKinley attempted negotiations with Spain, but the tabloids and the inflamed Congress would have its war, which only went to show that the judgment of many is not always better than that of one.

Theodore Roosevelt, who whooped his way as a Rough Rider through the Cuban campaign, continued as President to stir Latin American affairs with a heavy hand. Needing a Panama Canal and finding the Colombian government a stumbling block, he promoted Panamanian rebels who established an independent state in the area set out for the Canal Zone. He said, "I took the Canal Zone and let Congress debate." For this and other "big stick" actions, Theodore Roosevelt has been called the first modern President. A far less militant man, President Wilson, in February of 1917 asked Congress for authority to arm merchant ships, an act certain to trigger war. When some senators filibustered, Wilson complained of a "little group of willful men," and armed the ships without congressional sanction. Two months later, war was declared. Similarly, Franklin D. Roosevelt, though opposed by much antiwar sentiment, took strong and independent executive action. Despite a congressional ban on convoying, FDR pushed through an order that amounted to shooting first at German and Italian vessels in the western Atlantic. Of course, Japan's attack on Pearl Harbor let the war horse out of the barn, but if Roosevelt had not opened the door, he had certainly undone the latch. Once again, war came before Congress could give its approval.

With the conclusion of World War Two, the United States had entered the atomic age, in which wars, declared or otherwise, might be fought and carried to a conclusion within hours. Here was a situation beyond the wildest dreams of the Founding Fathers and it has imbued foreign affairs with a new sense of urgency.

When, in June of 1950, North Korea invaded South Korea, President Truman did not hesitate to order American armed forces into the fray, and only afterward did he assemble congressional leaders "so that I might inform them of the events and decisions of the past few days." The war rolled on for three years and caused over a hundred thousand American casualties without congressional authority ever being given. Public favor vanished, and the affair was condemned as "Truman's War," and a peace-making Republican administration swept into office under President Eisenhower.

By 1964, we were already seriously involved in Vietnam. When North Vietnamese gunboats fired on an American destroyer, President Johnson first ordered retaliatory bombing of North Vietnamese bases. Then, perhaps remembering Truman's fall from grace, he went to Congress for approval. There a document was produced allowing him to take all necessary steps to render military assistance in defense of South Vietnamese freedom. This was the Bay of Tonkin Resolution, upon which President Johnson relied heavily in escalating the war. A few years later, President Nixon ordered the invasion of Cambodia. However practical from a tactical standpoint, it was a move fraught with political hazard and undertaken, once again, without congressional sanction.

Have the military demands of this atomic age outgrown the Constitution? Have we, as a country, outgrown democracy, that so vast a power should be concentrated in the hands of one man? There must be some solution within the Constitution. Some sort of updating must allow the President a lead in foreign policy, but must put some guidance in the hands of Congress. They must take part in decisions related to military participation. They must not be relegated to the role of rubber stamps. Short of an unlikely amendment to the Constitution, one approach has been suggested by Senator J. William Fulbright and his energetic use of the Foreign Relations Committee. Whether or not one shares Fulbright's pacific views is not at issue; he has managed to bring his committee to a point where it commands the presidential ear and where it has begun to operate as a balancing force in international matters. A closer working relationship between any President and a well-informed group of senators, chosen for their ability and not for their seniority, might well curb the process of moving toward war by dictatorial fiat.

Regarded historically, international law has evolved little, but it has roots buried as deep in antiquity as any other form of law. In prehistoric times, strangers must have thrown rocks, run from one another in terror, or sniffed about as dogs will do on first acquaintance. No question of law here, only natural fear, hatred, or curiosity, though unrecorded agreements based upon custom must have taken place among our tribal ancestors. The breaking of weapons, burying of hatchets, smoking of peace pipes, all were customary gestures preparatory to entering into some protolegal international type of agreement between separate and self-governing human groups. Perhaps writing, more than anything else, was to separate custom from law, and the earliest recorded international "legal" agreement is in the form of a treaty between Lagash, a Mesopotamian city-state, and the men of Umma. A stone monument dating from 3100 B.C. records the setting up of boundaries, and relies on common gods to be guarantors of their treaty of peace. The warrior Pharaoh Rameses II of Egypt and King Hattusili II of the Hittites achieved a mutual defense pact in 1279 B.C. which included an early form of extradition. Strangely, the ancient Greeks achieved very little in the international sphere, simply because they regarded foreigners as barbarians and unworthy partners to any agreement. Among themselves, elaborate alliances were developed and some frontier disputes were settled by arbitration, though in the end, war of attrition between Sparta and Athens brought on the decline of that civilization. Far better, in fact, was the international record of Chinese river pirates in the sixth century B.C., who divided up portions of the Shanghai River by conference and kept a voluntary peace for over a century. Ancient Rome, noted for its laws, left treaty-making to a group of priests called fetiales, and it was up to them to decide if a foreign nation had violated its duties toward Rome. Less treaties than expressions of Roman political expansion, these priestly decisions gave the Roman armies the assurance that the gods were on their side and led to the idea of the "just war," a concept still cherished and ironically recorded on the belt buckles of Hitler's Nazi army, *Gott mit uns* (God with us).

During the Dark Ages, a trend toward international law appeared with the revival of foreign trade. Some sort of commercial and maritime order was necessary. In a letter to Offa, King of Mercia in Saxon England, the Holy Roman Emperor Charlemagne promised protection to Mercian merchants according to the ancient custom of commerce and requested equal protection for his merchants. With custom as a base, maritime law was an area of particular international progress. A small island in the Bay of Biscay, in what was called The Rolls of Oléron, set down the rulings of a merchant court which were recognized in the Atlantic and in the Baltic Sea.

The medieval church preserved the Roman idea of the just war. Thomas Aquinas (1225–1274), in his *Summa Theologica,* announced that war against women and children was always unjust, and that, except when waged in a good cause, war was a sin. Of course, finding a "just" excuse has never been difficult, and from the perspective of our atomic age one may sadly reflect upon the Ecclesiastical Council's decision in A.D. 1139, forbidding the use of crossbows as odious to God.

The modern age is usually taken to begin about 1492 with the discovery of America, the decline in church power, and the rise of national states, especially those of Spain, England, and France. The political philosopher Machiavelli (1469–1527) spoke for the times in his book *The Prince,* which envisioned peace as resulting from the rise of the all-powerful state by ruthless means. In keeping with Machiavelli's pragmatic suggestions, the Spanish ambassador to England, Don Bernardino de Mendoza, was found to be a member of a plot to murder Queen Elizabeth I and place the Catholic pretender, Mary Queen of Scots, upon the throne. To the credit of England and the developing international law relating to the immunity of foreign ambassadors, Mendoza was protected from English trial. At the same time, however, English sea captains might apply to their monarch for letters of reprisal authorizing them in careful legal terms to go forth and seize Spanish ships of value equal to that taken from them by the Spaniards. This was deemed due compensation, and any excess was turned over to the English government, which, at least in theory, returned it to Spain. Despite such niceties, the Spanish Armada sailed against England in 1588, and, but for English seamanship and bad weather, the United States might be a Spanish-speaking nation today.

It was not until the end of the sixteenth century that philosophers began putting aside the "just war" ideas of the Romans and speaking of international law. The front-runner was Alberico Gentili (1552–1608), who wrote a three-volume treatise entitled *De jure belli* (*On the Law of War*), which dealt with causes of war, warfare itself, and peace treaties. The last, he maintained, should not be binding only on those who sign, but upon their successors, a very new idea at a time when the death of a king could be taken to repudiate his agreements. The father of modern international law was Hugo Grotius (1583–1645), author of the great work *De jure belli ac pacis* (*On the Law of War and Peace*). In spite of the fact that Europe was involved in the disastrous Thirty Years' War, his book was translated into eight languages. Grotius died three years before the Peace of Westphalia, which ended the Thirty Years' War on a hopeful note. This treaty involved all the major European nations except England and Poland, and called for an amnesty for hostile acts committed in the past. A violation of the treaty called for the offended party to submit its cause to amicable settlement, and, should this fail, other parties to the treaty would presumably take up arms to punish the offender. A kind of United Nations was anticipated, but the times were far from auspicious. The church was in a state of decline, and the sovereign nation, with its need for professional standing armies, was on the rise. The hope of peace depended upon the dubious notion of the balance of power, a new concept invented by Francesco Guicciardini (1483–1540), which has survived many wars to this day.

The seventeenth century is notable for certain idealistic peace plans, one of them put forward by William Penn and another by the Abbé de Saint-Pierre, but the cause of peace continued to have its ups and downs. Frederick the Great, one of the eighteenth century's star performers, was the first conqueror to exploit fully the newly perfected firearm. With regard to the earnest Abbé's suggestions, he commented, "His peace plan is very practical but for the fact that it needs for its success the consent of Europe, and some other bagatelles." So Frederick fought his wars and fought them well. Not to be left out, the English and French made of the eighteenth century one long war, broken by sheer exhaustion into separate chapters. If France had gotten the worst of the eighteenth century, she started the next on an upswing with Napoleon Bonaparte. Success was brief, and in 1815, Napoleon was crushed at Waterloo. Typically, after the long and hard campaign, a pious note was sounded, and the Congress of Vienna resulted in a Holy Alliance of major powers, all dedicated to peace through Christian ideals. No machinery of enforcement was developed, so, before long, the old friends were at each other's throats in the Crimean War.

However, the nineteenth century was a time of great progress in nonpolitical treaties. They received their impetus from the development of the International Telegraph Union in 1865 and the General Postal Union in 1874. It was a time of unprecedented business and capital migration, and, as the French philosopher Diderot was to suggest, "A war amid different trading nations is a fire harmful to all." Reflecting this attitude, the United States and England managed to settle the *Alabama* case by arbitration in 1872. The United States had demanded from Britain a sum in excess of $15 million for damages done by the Confederate privateer *Alabama* during the American Civil War. The basis for the claim·was that Britain, though a neutral nation, had built the *Alabama* in her shipyards expressly for the Rebels. While active, the *Alabama* had taken sixty-nine prizes until cornered in the

harbor of Cherbourg, France, by the U.S.S. *Kearsarge*. There a
challenge had been offered and accepted, and like two lace-cuffed
duelists, the ships had sailed out into neutral waters side by side
and there squared off for a battle to the death. The *Alabama* was
sunk in short order, though some of the crew escaped to England
aboard an English yacht. Seven years after the event, Britain paid
what appeared to be a just claim, and thereby avoided a potentially
nasty international situation. Later, in a Bering Sea controversy
over rights to seal-fishing grounds, a tribunal made up of British,
Americans, French, Italians, and Norwegians decided against the
United States in favor of Britain. Perhaps in consideration of
Britain's earlier cooperation, the United States abided by the
decision.

But where war was at issue, Europe still relied on the balance-
of-power theory, which was called at that time The Concert of
Europe. Until the close of the nineteenth century, the only progress made to alleviate the horrors of war was the eventual flower-
ing of an 1864 convention concerned with the suffering of the war
wounded. This organization, centered in Geneva, took as its banner
the reversed Swiss flag: a red cross on a white ground. The univer-
sally praised Red Cross organization resulted, and, after a vigorous
crusade by Clara Barton, it was joined in 1882 by the United
States.

Not until the Hague Conference of 1899 were the many propos-
als regarding peace through international law brought to the conference table. Little more was accomplished there than the prohibition of dumdum (expanding) bullets, the use of gas, and the
dropping of explosives from balloons. The airplane was still four
years away, and the men who would man the trenches in the
"war to end wars" were just being born.

Even those few restraints laid down by the Hague Conference
were violated during World War One. Not only balloons but air-
planes dropped lethal devices. Gas was blown this way and
that over the fields of France. Neutral ships were sunk. About all
that came through intact was diplomatic immunity, which had
been recognized for centuries, and the Red Cross. Never before
had the world experienced such destruction. Never before had
civilian populations been so ravaged by war, and the victors

emerged more than ever filled with brief idealism and the belief that the world had indeed finally been made safe for democracy. The January 10 peace treaty of 1920 offered the usual pious remarks. It also included something new, a supranational federation of independent states made up of a permanent assembly, council, and secretariat. The objective of this League of Nations was perpetual peace with honor. The chief members of the League were to include Russia, the United States, Great Britain, and France. Unhappily, the United States, gripped by an isolationistic backlash, never joined at all. It was an idea upon which President Wilson had set his heart, and he died a broken man. Russia was ablaze with Communist revolution, and France and Britain had different ideas about what should be done with Germany. France wanted to maintain the status quo in Europe, which would leave her top dog, well content with the spectacle of Germany safely down with her face in the mud. Britain, on the other hand, looked to a refurbished Germany which would reestablish the old balance of power. The young League had other defects. Its covenant did not outlaw war. It was European in concentration while centers of power were shifting elsewhere. A reviving Germany was able to use the threat of a Bolshevik revolution to divide Britain and France, and to promote itself as a rising bulwark against this menace. Yet for a time there was hope. A 1922 treaty sought the limitation of naval armaments, and, despite endless wrangling over such items as the ratio between six- and eight-inch guns in various fleets, a balance was achieved for a time. Unfortunately, a convention limiting submarine warfare against merchantmen was disregarded where it mattered most: by Germany, who was planning for the future.

Most specifically concerned with the function of international law was the Permanent Court of International Justice. Until its foundation, attempts at peacekeeping through the courts had been entirely decentralized and had lasted only as long as the particular case. The overwhelming task of this court was, with virtually no police power, to apply the general principles of law recognized by civilized nations. A good idea, but indeed, what universal standards were there? William the Conqueror's judges had faced no such staggering task as they went out into the shires of Anglo-Saxon England looking for customs to follow. Still, an attempt was made, and John Bassett Moore's *International Adjudications,* begun in 1929, went into seven volumes and then dried up. The world was losing interest. In 1931, Japan invaded Manchuria. Five years later, Mussolini took over Ethiopia, and all the League of Nations could do was speak words of protest, with no force to back them up. Even little Paraguay, in her 1934 war with Bolivia, defied the League's protests, and all the while Hitler's armies were growing.

World War Two was really the continuation of World War One. When the fires finally burned out, the United Nations was born in the ashes. It was in most respects a reincarnation of the shattered League of Nations, and it brought renewed hope. As President Truman remarked, "If we fail to use it, we shall betray all those who have died in order that we might meet here in freedom and safety to create it." [1] The United Nations took in a wider spectrum of members than the old League. In Article Two, Paragraph Four, its Charter renounced the use of force, and went on to describe the waging of war as a crime against peace. Chapter Seven of the Charter speaks of collective security and suggests a United Nations–directed force unknown to the League. But, like the League, the very terms of its Charter are flawed. Whereas the Preamble asserts the equality of nations large and small, the working structure is one of sovereign inequality. Although the Assembly of the League of Nations could, in theory, take political action, the General Assembly of the United Nations may only recommend. Action is up to the Security Council, comprised of permanent and changing members, with each of the permanent members retaining a veto right over all affirmative action. Boiled down, this means the juxtaposition of the United States and Soviet blocs. Seeing eye to eye, they could rule the world for good or bad, but seldom is there accord. Initially, some harmony was expected from these superpowers, but a gap swiftly widened between them. The United States proposed, and the Soviet Union, lacking as large a following, resorted constantly to the veto. With the Security Council in a stalemate, for a time the General Assembly clustered around the United States position. It could be depended on for one-sided moral support which, if nothing else, seemed to color

American recommendations with world assent. However, with the gradual increase of membership from fifty to over one hundred nations, mostly African and Near Eastern, even the General Assembly failed to achieve a majority voice. The focus of action shifted to the office of Secretary General, primarily under the skillful leadership of Dag Hammarskjöld, who turned it into a United Nations prime ministership. In 1958, for instance, he personally undertook to enlarge the United Nations observer corps in Lebanon over Russian disapproval.

This is not meant to suggest that the United Nations is a failure. It is certainly a great forum where members may shelve apparent responsibility for unpleasant decisions and thereby save face. It is a shock absorber where nations on the brink of conflict may seem to make concessions, not to their enemies, but at least to the sane voice of world neutrality. The refusal to make concessions has become embarrassing, because it no longer can appear to be a courageous reaction against an enemy. It is, rather, defiance of the political voice of civilization, and if the United Nations has prevented no wars, it has shortened several: Indonesia, Palestine in 1949, Egypt in the Suez crisis of 1956, Kashmir in 1965. Conversation between nations, even when acrimonious, creates a far healthier climate than silence.

Ideally, the International Court of Justice, which is associated with the United Nations, offers a permanent judiciary to deal fairly with the settlement of international problems. In practice, once the Court has reached a decision, there has been compliance by the parties involved. There is no police force to ensure performance, but nations as well as individuals have the inclination to moral behavior, and, by the very fact of submitting the dispute, they resolve to abide by the decision, however unsatisfactory. Unfortunately, such cases are few. The Court is lucky to hear two disputes a year, for there is no compulsory jurisdiction. The Soviet Union ideologically tends to dismiss the rule of law as contrary to the idea of Communist fulfillment, and the United States has agreed to compulsory jurisdiction on the one hand, and on the other has reserved the right to decide all cases of an "essentially" domestic nature. In practice, this includes all cases of governmental interest.

It is not through the perfidiousness of statesmen but from the very nature of international politics that international law fails of application. Wars do not come from disagreement over the law, but through some pressure for change. As the existing law tends to represent the status quo, seldom are disputes litigated. Where the rivalry is purely one of a power struggle, as between the United States and Russia, legal settlement is precluded. Peripheral cases, such as the Anglo-Iranian oil dispute, are sometimes offered to the Court by one of the parties. Here Britain put forward the case, as her rights were defined by the law. Iran, agitating for change and greater self-determination, refused jurisdiction since its political future was involved. In fact, the law of nations exists and operates only in a balance of power where a group of nations have political interests in common rather than in conflict. It was in this spirit of brief harmony and agreement that the Western Allies after World War Two were able to set up a court to preside over the Nuremberg trials. The common enemy, the Nazi, was known, and there was harmony in the belief that the leaders should be punished.

Where national egos are involved, international law is helpless. It becomes no more than an interpretive tool justifying predetermined conduct. Consider the war in Vietnam. Both sides have gone to enormous lengths to establish the legality of their positions. A short summary of a few of the legal issues an international court would have to grapple with suggests the complexities involved should the situation, however theoretically, reach its jurisdiction.

In general, the United States position is that North Vietnam, directly and through its controlled, trained, and supplied agents, the Viet Cong rebels, has been trying to subjugate the free and democratic nation of South Vietnam. North Vietnam, completely denying the political independence of the South, sees itself as aiding a spontaneous uprising against a puppet regime maintained by the United States, a foreign power which wishes to turn part of Vietnam into a military base.

The issue in law as far as this confrontation is concerned goes back to the Geneva accords of 1954. Until that time, France had been defending its colonial foothold in what was then French

Indo-China against a national uprising led by Ho Chi Minh. At the time of the cease-fire, France held the southern portion of Vietnam; the nationalists held the north. At Geneva, a provisional military demarkation line was set up between France and Ho Chi Minh, subject to final settlement by a free general election to take place in July, 1956, and to be supervised by an international commission. During this interim, many of Ho Chi Minh's followers remained south of the military line, and these the interim government in the south set about uprooting. Fighting spread, and the scheduled elections were postponed until the situation could be stabilized. Disappointed that his ends could not be achieved politically and in line with the Geneva accords, Ho Chi Minh began to supply the rebels in the south, encouraging subversion and terror tactics and building toward an armed insurrection. As this pressure grew, the United States, upon the invitation of the interim government of South Vietnam, entered the vacuum left by French withdrawal and began to provide a military balance.

The first legal issue, then, that the court would have to decide is whether or not South Vietnam was legally bound by the Geneva accords. The North Vietnamese position is that at the accords France spoke for the area of South Vietnam, thereby binding the later government to hold general elections which, if held, would have unified the nation under Ho Chi Minh. The United States view is that neither the United States nor South Vietnam was bound by the accords, to which neither gave formal agreement, and even if South Vietnam could be considered a party to the agreement, the fundamental breach was the North Vietnamese military intervention and not the postponement of elections.

Material to the United States intervention is the question of whether or not South Vietnam is an international entity, a nation; in other words, entitled to seek foreign aid. If not, the intervention from the north would only amount to civil war. Although the Geneva accords state that the demarkation line is only a temporary division of one nation for administrative purposes subject to elections, subsequent history saw North Vietnam recognized as independent by the French. In 1950, the area of South Vietnam was treated as an independent state within the French union, and has since been recognized by many other nations, despite the express statement of the Geneva accords. To support its act of intervention in response to the requests of the South Vietnamese government for aid, the United States has treated that geographical area as a de facto nation. There is strong legal support for both views.

Suppose that North Vietnam were to concede the national status of South Vietnam, which is has not done. At once, another issue arises. When rebels command a sufficient area of a nation and are conducting their fight in accordance with the rules of war, then, as defined by international law, those rebels have passed from a condition of insurgency to one of belligerency, and may be recognized and given aid by foreign states. North Vietnam would argue that the Viet Cong have established themselves as belligerents, but attorneys for South Vietnam and the United States would say that they held insufficient territory to be so designated, and that in any case the terror tactics employed by the Viet Cong were not in acccordance with the proper rules of war.

The above only begins to pose the legal issues in such a case if it appeared before the International Court. At the moment, such a possibility is a distant dream, but it is more civilized than endless war. As far as legal material to apply in such a hypothetical case, there are innumerable treaties and treatises on international law, customs insofar as major nations have abided by them, and a philosophy of natural law and morality. However, case precedents thus far are sadly lacking, and there is very little basis for applying a uniformity of international customs.

For instance, take the case of territorial waters. Every nation assumes the right to own a part of the waters that surround it. The question is, How much? Many accept the three-mile limit. Finland and Norway consider themselves entitled to four miles; Spain, India, and others to six; Mexico, nine; Albania, ten; and Iceland, the Soviet Union, and the United Arab Republic demand twelve miles. Except for the wording of specific treaties, disagreement and uncertainty are the rule and alleged violations commonplace, such as Russian trawlers in United States waters, United States fishing boats too close to Peru.

A treaty creates law between those who are party to it, though it fails to carry with it any guarantee of impartial enforcement. Still, treaties are one of the most hopeful approaches to binding international law. Chief Justice Marshall gave the following definition in 1828: "A treaty is in its nature a contract between two nations, not a legislative act. It does not generally effect, of itself, the object to be accomplished, especially so far as its operation is infraterritorial; but it is carried into execution by the sovereign power of the respective parties to the instrument." [2]

The Constitution of the United States declares a treaty entered into by the United States to be the law of the land. It is taken by the courts as equivalent to an act of the legislature, whenever it operates of itself without the aid of any legislative provision. However, when the terms of the proposed treaty suggest a contract, with the burden on either or both parties to perform a particular act, such as with the limited test-ban treaty, then the legislature must execute the contract before it can become a rule for the court. Of course, a sovereign nation retains the power, though not the right under international law, to break any treaty and suffer the consequences. Without some form of supranational government, this cannot be otherwise, and the only way in which such a treaty can be enforced is downward, such as against a violation by a state or individual. For example, if, through the federal supremacy clause of the Constitution the federal government enters an arms-control agreement, it automatically overrules any inconsistent provisions in the constitutions or laws of the states.

As far back as 1796,[3] the Supreme Court held that a treaty with Great Britain superseded a Virginia act canceling debts owed by its citizens to British subjects. Just as the federal government may enter into a treaty in behalf of the states and its individual citizens, it has the power to recognize the jurisdiction of an international court. Under past treaties, the United States has agreed to submit the claims of its citizens against foreign governments to international commissions. On the same theory, it might submit to an international court of justice issues related to agreements on arms control and inspection. Constitutionally, there would be no objection. The difficulty would lie in getting used to the idea of international officials observing the operation of our government. The idea of national sovereignty, the need for identification, the "us" idea given form only by the idea of "them," is the main barrier to functional international law today.

The legal control of arms was an issue long before the United Nations came into being, and even nationalism need be no insurmountable barrier to a civilized solution. The medieval church tried to ban the use of the crossbow and failed. Czar Nicholas II, at the Hague Peace Conference of 1899, tried to outlaw aerial bombs and poison gas. However horrible, these were weapons that the human race could survive. Now we face the hazards of the kilomegaton-bomb age, with so many stockpiled hydrogen bombs that their explosive equivalent in TNT would fill a string of freight cars stretching from the earth to the moon and back fifty times. Phrased otherwise, for each human being on earth there exists a hydrogen bomb equivalent to fifteen tons of conventional explosive. At a cost of close to $15 billion, either Russia or the United States could construct a doomsday machine. Press one button, and the world would end. A fantastic deterrent to war, but eventually many countries may possess it. No civilized human being would ever use it, but picture yourself back in the spring of 1945. With Berlin crumbling about him, how would Hitler have acted with his hand on such a switch?

The United Nations, the atomic bomb, and a new urgency for arms control entered the world at the same time. In 1946, before the Cold War set in, the Baruch Plan was put forward by the United States for an international monopoly of atomic energy. This was a serious but unrealistic step toward supranational government. It was, of course, rejected by the Soviet Union, which, if the status quo had been maintained as the plan envisioned, would have remained militarily inferior to the United States, which had bombs already stockpiled. In 1949, the situation altered when Russia set off her first atomic bomb. Stockpiling renewed, and inspection problems multiplied. Various legal plans were suggested, such as the Anglo-French "blueprint for world disarmament" and President Eisenhower's "open skies" proposal for inspection. Meanwhile, the United States and Russia inflated their respective national egos by competitive tests that tainted the atmosphere with radioactive pollution. A "balance of terror" was at last achieved, and the United States and Russia, despite their stilll-divergent ideologies and world objectives, came to agreement on a partial test-ban treaty, which has been observed ever since. How does it happen that even so limited an accord was achieved in such a sensitive area? The answer is simple: mutual interest, which, within limits, should be a guide to further arms regulations. The Rush-Bagot Treaty is a classic success story in that it provided, shortly after the American Revolution, the longest unarmed frontier in the world, that between the United States and Canada. As the parties to an agreement move away from mutuality of interests, any treaty is less likely to achieve its purpose. Such was the fate of the 1932 World Disarmament Conference, wherein France sought to remain superior to Germany and Germany wanted to catch up.

If any progress is to be achieved today, it must begin between the United States and the Soviet Union. There are those who would deny Russian good faith, but where an agreement serves a country's own best interests, there need be no anxiety. Therefore, a working arms agreement must comply with mutual self-interest. To this end it can generally be assumed that neither Russia nor the United States wants an all-out military confrontation. Both have serious domestic problems that a diminution in world tension and the shifting of expenditures would lessen. Assuming this mutuality of objective the problem becomes one of inspection and balancing arms reduction. Inspection has all along been a stumbling block. It is far more in the interest of the United States, which is a more open country with less secrets in the first place. Then, too, when it comes to limiting weapons, the United States has held the edge in nuclear weapons while Russia has had more conventional armaments. How is this to be balanced? Ten hydrogen bombs scrapped by the United States for the demobilization of one Russian infantry division? Such questions might diverge endlessly, and even fighting spirit would have to be put into the balance. France had a larger army than Germany in 1939, but it was emotionally and physically unprepared for sudden war, and was swiftly overmatched by the German will to conquer. There are no mathematical answers, only political bargaining points. If nations were willing to surrender some of their sovereignty, an impartial, dispute-settling mechanism could be undertaken by the International Court or a similar body. Article Forty-one of the statute founding the Court provides: "The court shall have the power to indicate, if it considers the circumstances so require, any provisional measures which ought to be taken to preserve the respective rights of either party." This is equivalent to a temporary injunction to stop alleged disarmament violations. The process could be undertaken very gradually, with uniform courses of conduct gradually hardening into custom and thereafter into rules of international law. For instance, the United States, might decide not to fire test missiles in the direction of the Soviet Union, even though those rockets were designed to fall short of their "target." This, in time, might become a custom that Russia would be likely to follow, and eventually, if the International Court had supervisory powers, it could become a rule of international law.

Utopian and fearful is the unilateral answer; strange, too, that one of its most vivid endorsements comes from Friedrich Nietzsche, Hitler's favorite philosopher:

> . . . and perhaps the great day will come when a people, distinguished by wars and victories and by the highest development of a military order and intelligence, and accustomed to make the heaviest sacrifice for these things, will exclaim of its own free will, "we break the sword," and will smash its military establishment down to its lowest foundations. Rendering oneself unarmed when one has been the best armed peace, as it now exists in all countries, is the absence of peace which must always rest on a peace of mind; whereas, the so-called armed peace, as it now exists in all countries, is the absence of peace of mind. One trusts neither oneself nor one's neighbor and, half from hatred, half from fear, does not lay down arms. Rather perish than hate and fear, and twice rather perish than make oneself hated and feared . . . this must someday become the highest maxim for every single commonwealth.[4]

At the moment, of course, total unilateral disarmament is a dreamer's fiction, but another related concept which might be called disengagement—that is, the unilateral initiative in taking steps toward disarmament—is not. Short of scrapping some hydrogen bombs, suppose the United States deactivated all poison gas. No great risk, but hopefully such a step would lead to a reciprocal step on the other side. The basis for such unilateral action is to take the initiative in something militarily disadvantageous but not crippling in the hope of reciprocal action. Such action should be widely publicized in advance and should not demand prior commitment on the part of the enemy. Troop reduction, the exchange of scientific information, the evacuation of unimportant military bases, such as happened after the Cuban missile crisis, all are such possible gestures. Can they help? Assume two hostile men are equally armed with pistols, knives, and fists. One man throws away his knife. He is no less lethal for having done so, and such a gesture may give his opponent pause. He, too, may discard his knife which, if nothing else is accomplished, will ensure that no one is stabbed to death. But at this point it takes a very brave, confident, perhaps foolhardy man to lay down the gun.

As idealistic and unlikely as unilateral disarmament is the prospect for a world state. Once disarmament was achieved, it would take a very small international army to police the world. Half a million men would perhaps be enough to do the job, a force small enough so that it would not become a Frankenstein monster that could take over the world. The United States and the cantons of Switzerland are examples of small units joining into larger political units. Then why not all the nations of the world? There are many reasons: no common language or traditions, diversity of customs and faiths, and, most important, the lack of a common enemy. For world federalization, there could be nothing so persuasive as an invasion from outer space.

No such one-step solutions are likely, which brings to mind Lloyd George's remark that the most dangerous thing in the world is to try to leap a chasm in two jumps. If the chasm is fifty feet across, one jump isn't going to be much use, but it might help to climb down slowly to the bottom and go up the other side one step at a time. Through the lawful supervision of the International Court, such steps toward disarmament and world peace might be taken. To assume otherwise is to share Hermann Göring's view that "in a life and death struggle, there is no legality." [5]

CHAPTER ELEVEN

The Future of the Law

IN NO PREVIOUS PERIOD OF HISTORY HAS THE WORLD CHANGED SO
rapidly. The arrival of the atomic age, the clash of world and
domestic problems, and the population explosion have created
problems of a complexity beyond the capacity of legislators to
regulate effectively by statute or of the courts to solve by case law.
Accustomed to a slow and glacial change, the courts of the United
States now stand in the midst of an avalanche, with the focus
of pressure on the Supreme Court, where important law is revised
and made.

Over one million lawsuits are undertaken in the United States
each year. Of these, perhaps two hundred, after years of lower
court haggling, will reach the Supreme Court, and only from a
fraction of these will important new law emerge. The deliberate
pace of the law's evolution in a time of social revolution creates
injustice. The fact that constitutional laws protect the individual
against the excesses of lesser laws throws a veil of protection over
the guilty. How else could "The Honored Society" of the Mafia
flourish? Its crimes are known, and its members and many of their
deeds are on record. If someone—the President, for instance—could
grant the proper authority to the Federal Bureau of Investigation,
agents could be sent out with warrants backed up with tommy
guns, and organized crime might vanish in a week. This is not a

180

unique solution. Off-duty policemen in Brazil formed what they called "Squadrons of Death" which, in São Paulo, accounted for twelve known criminals in indiscriminate revenge for the slaying of one detective. In all, the squadrons accounted for over a thousand criminals, not to mention a few cases of mistaken identity, in their anticrime drive. With less violent objectives, Presidents of the United States have tried to "pack" the Supreme Court in order to have their bidding done. Thus far, all such attempts have failed, but is not the very effort symptomatic of a legal system slowed and encumbered with decisions beyond its usefulness? Montaigne said, "There is little relation between our actions, which are perpetually changing, and fixed and unchangeable laws. The most desirable laws are those which are most rare, most simple and general; and I still believe it would be better to have none at all, than to have them in such numbers as we have." [1]

A clear and simple example of such a law, which would quickly dispose of most crime in this country, reads as follows:

> Whoever commits an act which the law declares to be punishable or which deserves punishment according to the fundamental concepts of the penal law and sound popular feeling, is punishable. If there is no penal law which directly applies to such deed, it shall be punished according to the law the basic concept of which is most applicable.

Imagine the sweeping reforms such a law envisions, and which it, in fact, effected. Crime virtually vanished from Nazi Germany. So, presently, did the Communist party, and in fact all other political parties, until only one was left, the National Socialist German Worker's party. On June 28, 1935, Adolph Hitler gave breath to this general "blank check" law with his signature, thereby putting an end to crime and to the rights of the individual. Perhaps a benevolent and godlike dictator might have turned such a statute to the good. In future, an impartial computer might do so. But, at this point in the evolution of civilization, freedom-loving people are not inclined to trust one man or one machine with complete dominion over law and disorder.

This argument is not slyly designed to excuse the common-law system for letting too many criminals roam at large. It makes no attempt to hide the fact that the individual seeking justice in his own personal affairs will find the process slow and expensive, but this is no new state of affairs. One may read in Charles Dickens of family lawsuits, contesting estates, being wrangled on through several generations, until the issue vanishing with the attorneys taking all in fees. Writing at the same period, David Dudley Field commented on the New York courts: "Speedy justice is a thing unknown; and any justice, without delays almost ruinous, is most rare." [2] At that time, 1840, court business was two years in arrears. Today, someone seeking damages in New York through a jury trial may expect to wait at least four years before that trial takes place, and longer should appeals follow. Nor have court costs diminished. A British trial in 1949 [3] lasted for sixty days and left the loser with court costs of £77,000, about $200,000 in United States currency.

Similar problems plague the criminal courts, particularly in crowded urban centers. In New York, half a million potential cases jam courts, jails, and police stations. To avoid congestion, most cases are settled by a bargain struck between the defense and the prosecution attorneys whereby the defendant pleads guilty to a lesser charge and is rubber-stamped along his way. Often jail sentences are, in effect, served before trial can take place, for a case may wait years for a hearing. However, the defendants are usually let out on bail. The jails are too packed to hold them, and, when a date is set for a trial, as often as not the defendant ignores the subpoena. Trials get postponed. Police and witnesses are forced to wait around courtrooms to testify; the police collecting overtime pay for doing nothing. Witnesses grow impatient and no longer obey the mailed subpoenas because they know the police are too busy to follow them up in person. No wonder the usual defense is not a brilliant cross-examination before judge and jury, but subtle delaying tactics, which cause a case to be postponed time and time again, until witnesses vanish and charges are dropped. Even in cases as serious as attempted murder, this has happened. It was certainly not with justice in mind, but rather in the hope of profit from delay that Charles Manson's attorney allowed his client, accused of brutally directing the murder of actress

Sharon Tate and others, to hold up a headline before the jury which indicated that the President of the United States believed him guilty.

In the future, the law, if it is to evolve as a civilizing process, must overcome delays in meting out justice. The answers are expensive but less costly than a society where law and order have lost respect. More judges, more courts are only part of the answer. An updating and mechanization of simple paper work could free the judges we now have from tasks as menial and antiquated as those performed by Charles Dickens's clerks. This is vital if arrest, trial, and conviction are to have any meaningful connection.

Equally important but more difficult of achievement will be the elimination of human error made up of preconceived and prejudicial notions. Of course, the human factor cannot be altogether eliminated, and at least at this point in our evolution the thought of computerized order is a disturbing one. But in the United States system, which emphasizes both judge and jury, and where combative rather than fact-finding attorneys are the order of the day, the risks involved are great. The innocent have been hanged before and will be again, more often than not without notice being taken. Occasionally, when the truth has come out, or when the popular prejudice was obvious from the start, cases have become notorious in legal history. A few of these are described, not to give answers, but as examples of what can happen despite guarantees of constitutional rights and a jury made up of twelve good men and true.

A modern example, and a classic in this area, is the case of Mme. Marie Besnard. She was an ordinary French housewife who suffered the grief of seeing her entire family die off, including her husband, Leon. Apparently Marie had unloving neighbors, for it was nosed about that foul play had been involved. Presently, the late husband and other relatives, eleven in all, were exhumed, and Marie was charged with multiple murder. Arsenic was found in the much-deteriorated corpses. Marie was savagely interrogated; her letters were intercepted. Other prisoners were planted to badger her into breaking down, but she held firm for two and a half years until a court considered the case. The main evidence against her came from government toxicologists. One claimed that in testing the eye of a corpse that had been dead for five years he could visually distinguish, without the aid of a magnifying glass, the difference between arsenic and antimony rings. When asked to make the distinction in court, he failed to do so. The experts persisted, although their tests had admittedly been conducted with contaminated instruments and water that itself contained arsenic. Bungled tests were corrected by falsified figures, and an explanation offered by the defense from the start was repressed: that the cemetery soil where the Besnard kin had all been buried, itself contained arsenic which the bodies had absorbed. To no avail. The first trial was aborted. A panel took six years to file a report while Marie languished in jail. A second and finally a third trial followed, wherein the court and prosecution, seeking to salvage their reputations, tried to get Marie to blame all the alleged crimes on her husband. Finally, after twelve years, a jury was allowed to speak, and the words were "not guilty."

Mme. Besnard was not a member of an oppressed minority. She had voiced no eccentric ideas; and yet malicious gossip, newspaper clamor, and the desire of examining and prosecuting magistrates to make a record of efficiency had conspired in a miscarriage of justice which, if the guillotine had intervened, would never have been exposed.

Another spectacular miscarriage of justice took place a long time ago in what was not yet the United States. The year was 1692, and the Inquisition had already subsided in Europe, when a group of teen-aged girls began to suffer mysterious pains, fits of blindness, and fainting spells. A slatternly Irish washerwoman named Glover was arrested and found sane by a panel of physicians. Then the court in its wisdom had her hanged for causing the afflictions by witchcraft. This occurred in Boston, Massachusetts, and proved to be a curtain raiser. In nearby Salem, a household presided over by one Parris, a minister of the Christian faith, included his imaginative eleven-year-old niece, Abigail Williams, and a half-breed Barbadian slave named Tituba. Tituba was full of tales of voodoo and the conjuring of demons, which were far more gripping than Parris's sermons. Presently, young Abigail and some of her girl friends began barking, convulsing, and reporting to the adults, who for the first time in their young lives took them seriously, that they were being bitten by demons. Tituba was seized upon as a witch, and a couple of old crones, Sarah Good and Sarah Osborne, were included for good measure. A confession was coerced from Tituba by means of the lash in behalf of all three women. Then Minister Parris searched the old ladies' bodies for inflamed moles of the type from which a witch's familiar (an evil spirit, often in cat shape) was said to suckle nourishment. The proper moles were found and duly recorded. Tituba kept the ball rolling before her first concerned adult audience by reporting all sorts of familiars, which included not only blood-red cats but yellow birds, the mention of which sent Abigail and her playmates into screeching contortions. So far so good, but, evidently impressed by the attention they were getting, the children next accused a couple of old and respectable churchwomen, Martha Corey and Rebecca Nurse, who had made the mistake of dismissing the circus as a childish prank. Old scores were being settled fast, and the girls now produced new evidence in the form of tiny teeth marks on their bodies. Under pressure, one Deliverance Hobbs confessed. Still others were accused, and some confessed in a courtroom where the children moved about in mimicry of the prisoners as though under complete demoniacal possession.

Soon the Salem jail was overcrowded. Lacking a proper court for trial, a new general court was set up, staffed by judges without legal background who applied an old antiwitchcraft statute. Deliverance Hobbs, appearing first before the court, testified that Bridget Bishop had tempted her to sign Satan's book; but Bridget, refusing to confess, denied all, and within the week was hanged. Within three months, eighteen more were hanged, along with two dogs believed to be witches' familiars. Once a person was accused, execution was by no means inevitable. Confession saved, and torture inclined one to it. Martha Carrier did not break down. Her two sons did, and, through filial attitudes only now to be guessed at, helped her on the way to the gallows by admitting under pressure that she had turned them into witches, or, more correctly, warlocks, the male equivalent.

The only people who emerged from this madness with any honor did so as corpses. Giles Corey, for one, to protect his estate, allowed himself to be pressed to death rather than confess, and died calling for more weights. Sarah Good, among the first accused, was urged by Minister Noyes to confess as she stood on the scaffold. "You are a liar!" Sarah shouted. "I am no more a witch than you are a wizard, and if you take away my life, God will give you blood to drink!" Sarah died on the spot; Minister Noyes died a bit later, evidently of a cerebral hemorrhage, for as he lay dying, his mouth filled and overflowed with blood.

Within a few months, a reaction of disgust had set in. Minister Parris was dismissed from his pulpit by a congregation as guilty as he. Those witches still imprisoned were pardoned by May of the following year, 1693. Yet, eighteen had died under the sentence of an unlawful court which adhered to no rules of evidence.

Admittedly, the witch trials are an extreme example. Even frontier justice, epitomized by Judge Roy Bean, self-styled "Law West of the Pecos," did a bit better. In 1882, this whiskey-peddling soldier of fortune had himself appointed justice of the peace in Eagle's Nest, in western Texas, along the route of the Southern Pacific Railway. He enforced his position with sawed-off shotguns and two ivory-handled six-guns which he used for gavels until his death in 1903. The pistols had been presented by the English actress Lily Langtry, after he renamed the town for her. Court was held usually on the front porch of Bean's saloon, named the Jersey Lily, also in honor of Miss Langtry, who was born on the island of Jersey in the English Channel. His judgments, all picturesque, span the range from Solomon to Salem, and they were often self-serving. On one occasion an unidentified body was found beneath a railroad trestle. Its only possessions were a loaded revolver and forty dollars in cash. Before burial, the Judge confiscated the gun and fined the deceased forty dollars for carrying concealed firearms. When a citizen of Langtry shot down an Oriental railroad worker, Bean searched his law books and finally dismissed the murder charge, admitting that it was a crime to kill a person but that he failed to find anything in the statutes about "Chinamen."

Best remembered of his judgments was that read over a cowering sheep thief, and it went about like this:

"Now time will pass. The seasons will come and go. Spring with its waving green grass and then sultry summer and fall with her great big yellow harvest moon, and last of all winter with its hard driving snow, but you won't be here to see any of them things because it's the order of this here court that you be fetched to the nearest tree and hanged by the neck until you're dead, dead, dead, you sheep-rustling son of a bitch."

That was Roy Bean, and if he did nothing in the cause of refining justice, he at least enriched American folklore. Somehow, his liberties are less disturbing than those that occur in an established court of law with all the forces of the police and the Constitution ranged behind them.

Such injustice, of course, still takes place, predictably in the southern United States where the issue involves color. The old adage of the common law states, "Where there's a right, there's a remedy," but the creed involving Negroes often tends to distort this into "Where there's no remedy, there's no right." However, the unsettled lynch-mob days are generally over. The Ku Klux Klan has lost most of its glamour. The Supreme Court constantly reviews patently unconstitutional legislation designed to limit Negro rights.

This does not mean that the Deep South has given up. Take, for example, the Mississippi legislature which, in the summer of 1964, faced a disturbing invasion of civil-rights workers from the North. Any direct attack would have raised a hue and cry, so the state senate quietly passed Bill 1526, which provided for local fire departments to pool their efforts in case of emergency. Very sensible; but buried in the text, such emergency was said to include civil disturbance of the peace. In fact, the basic intent of the bill was to provide a hose-wielding, mobile force to break up any gathering of civil-rights workers. Mississippi State House Bill 64 supported this measure by providing for the prevention of the introduction and spread of contagious or infectious diseases. To achieve this, a community might restrict the movement of its citizens as well as any group thereof. Whether or not the oncoming civil-rights workers carried communicable diseases other than idealism, the measures certainly served to implement police control where no riot or valid disturbance of the peace was taking place.

That same summer of 1964 saw a Negro, an honor student in high school, apply for admission to the University of Mississippi. Scholastically, his record was unblemished, but it was found he had participated in a Negro demonstration the year before. Upon arrest, he had been taken into juvenile court and released into his parents' custody. Now, anyone charged with a crime could be forbidden admission to an institution of higher learning in Mississippi, but until this time, juvenile court records were not obtainable by the University. Senate Bill 2016 was rushed through, making such records available to the University admissions department, and the Negro's application was denied on "nonracial grounds." In court, the student might question this procedure on its constitutionality, but such a court struggle would involve the irretrievable years during which he might have been getting a higher education.

Time alone regularly frustrates the federal Supreme Court in its efforts to implement the Constitution. For instance, during the "freedom-riding" summer of 1964, several hundred civil-rights workers were arrested in Mississippi on various charges. The courts required bond in each case of fifteen hundred dollars, but in Mississippi no surety company would write a policy for a civil-rights worker. A period of incarceration followed until bond could be found outside the state. Trials ensued. Expenses were heavy for lawyers and for travel in the case of students now back in classrooms in the North and West. Attendance in a Jackson, Mississippi, court was required off and on for over a year of trials, for, though each charge was identical, each worker was tried separately. Regardless of what the Supreme Court might do, after months of harassment in the state courts, it could not compensate the defendants for their expenses and troubles. Even if the laws in question were finally found to be unconstitutional, new ones, carefully worded, could easily be put through to block justice for another several years.

During that same hot summer, nine white men were arrested and pleaded guilty on the charge of having bombed three Negro homes in McComb, Mississippi. On a finding that the men were from good families and had been unduly provoked by civil-rights workers, Circuit Judge W. H. Watkins suspended prison sentences against the defendants, saying they deserved a second chance.[4] Perhaps he was remembering the fate of Judge James E. Horton, who had set aside a jury's verdict of guilty in the previously discussed trial involving the Negro Scottsboro Boys. Two years later, Judge Horton, condemned as a "nigger lover," was defeated for reelection and was never able to regain public office.

Another celebrated case determined by popular prejudice occurred in 1913, when thirteen-year-old Mary Phagan, "a beautiful and innocent child" who had recently played the part of Sleeping Beauty in a church play, was found brutally murdered in the basement of an Atlanta, Georgia, pencil factory, where it had been her job to attach the metal tips to pencils. The very nature of the victim inflamed the public. The very nature of the factory manager, a young, educated, Northern Jew and the last person to admit seeing the victim alive, brought the community and the press to the point of hysteria. Tom Watson's magazine *The Jeffersonian* felt entitled to print, almost before an arrest was made, ". . . our little girl—ours by the Eternal God!—has been pursued to a hideous death and bloody grave by this filthy, perverted Jew of New York." Other incidental facts conspired to bury justice. The city of Atlanta was in a period of industrialization. Old ways were changing; jobs were uncertain and poorly paid, and Northern domination of the city's economy was feared. Perhaps most outrageous of all, the crime had taken place on Confederate Memorial Day.

Ten thousand mourners came to Mary Phagan's funeral. Many undoubtedly felt responsible, and worried because they were sending their own young daughters to work in factories while the father, often as not, was out of work.

Yellow journalism screamed for an arrest. Actually, the initial suspect was one Newt Lee, night watchman at the pencil factory where the body had been found. A Negro and typical victim, Newt Lee was blamed at first by the crowd. The newspapers screamed,

"Lee's Guilt Proved" after he had been manacled to a chair for three days. But Lee held out, and the Mayor threatened the police with loss of their jobs if the real murderer was not found. The Solicitor General (District Attorney) had just lost two important murder cases, and the papers hinted that failure to convict in this case would finish him politically. In such a state of affairs, the police and prosecution turned their attention to the factory manager, Leo Frank.

Bloody fingerprints were found on the factory basement's back door. The police carefully sawed off that part of the door and then, unbelievably, lost it before an examination could be made. They had one witness and possible suspect, Jim Conley, a Negro sweeper at the factory, who had been found trying to wash blood from his shirt, and who admitted writing a murder note found near the victim. But the hunt was on for Leo Frank, and all this went unreported to the indicting grand jury. In the course of interrogation, Jim Conley gradually enlarged his statements, thereby becoming a chief prosecution witness. He alleged that Frank had murdered Mary Phagan in a workshop beside his office, then forced Conley to carry her body into the factory elevator and down to the basement, where Frank had bribed him to write the note. While a violent crowd milled outside, Conley, a shabby, habitual vagrant, appeared in court combed, newly outfitted, and clean shaven. He repeated his story, and during three days of cross-examination refused to contradict himself. Though the defense brought forward witnesses who swore not only to Leo Frank's good character but to the fact that he was with them during times when Conley said he and Frank were together, the jury brought in a verdict of guilty. The fact that Frank's witnesses and attorneys had been Northern, intellectual, and generally Jewish had not helped. An appeal was taken, argued back and forth, and finally rose to the United States Supreme Court by a writ of habeas corpus on the grounds that the defendant had been absent from the courtroom during part of the proceedings. In fact, for fear of riots, Frank had been put away in a jail cell at the time of the verdict, but the Supreme Court held that he had waived his due-process claim by failure to raise the issue at an earlier period. Justices Holmes and

Hughes dissented, but Frank was down to his last hope: clemency from Governor Slaton.

Here are some of the bits of information and evidence, unheard in the courtroom, but considered by Governor Slaton before reaching a decision: Hair found at the alleged murder spot, the workshop adjacent to Frank's office, had been attributed to the victim at the trial, but it was found, through scientific examination, not to have belonged to the slain girl. The murder note, which at the trial had been read to include a reference to the "night watch" and the statement that a "Negro did" the crime was reexamined. "Night watch" was found to be "Night witch," a Negro superstition undoubtedly unknown by the Northern white defendant. Although the prosecution had pointed out that a poor Southern Negro would not have used the words "Negro" and "did," but "nigger" and "done," some letters previously written by Conley did indeed include the words "Negro" and "did." A final bit of detective work persuaded Governor Slaton. Conley had admitted to detectives that he had used the factory's elevator shaft as a toilet before the murder. Policemen who were the first to examine the murder site had duly noted the presence of intact feces at the bottom of the elevator shaft. Only later, when the elevator was activated, was this evidence destroyed. If Conley's testimony had been accurate, this evidence would have been crushed by the elevator at the time he allegedly had moved the body. Before rendering a decision, Governor Slaton had Leo Frank removed from the local prison to the state prison farm. Only then did he commute the sentence to life imprisonment, trusting that presently the whole truth would come out. Immediately, a crowd marched on the Governor's home with signs reading, "John M. Slaton, King of the Jews and Georgia's Traitor Forever." The militia had to break it up.

Even this did not end the Leo Frank case. A Mary Phagan monument was erected, and near the child's grave one hundred and fifty men calling themselves "The Knights of Mary Phagan" pledged revenge on her killer. A fellow convict, William Green, very nearly did the job for them by cutting Frank's throat. The motive for this assault, according to Green, had come from a voice on high ordering him to kill the Jew. The scar on Frank's

neck had barely closed when twenty-five men stormed the prison
farm one night and seized the prisoner. They set out by car for a
distant hanging tree, and so persuasive in his statements of innocence was Leo Frank that by the time the rope was over the limb,
all but four of his would-be executioners were convinced. It was too
late to take him back to prison, though, and the four were ada-
mant. A table was kicked from under his feet. When the dangling
corpse was found, sections of the hanging rope and bits of the victim's clothing were immediately sold as souvenirs, and for years
after, photographs of the victim were available in local gift shops.
The hanging oak became an object of pilgrimage. A fund was
raised to protect the tree from desecration with a wall. There had
been no such wall around the prison farm.

Eventually, interest died down. The tree bore new leaves, and
an investigation of the Frank lynching resulted as expected: "Death
by persons unknown." They were, after all, good citizens, and
"The Knights of Mary Phagan" went on to distinguish themselves
by meeting on a mountaintop outside Atlanta where they pledged
to renew the old order of the Ku Klux Klan. Jim Conley spent one
year on a chain gang for assisting Frank. He was then released
and served assorted terms for burglary and drunkenness before
fading from sight. Governor Slaton lived in exile from the state
for several years, returning finally to practice law; and the prosecutor of the case, Hugh Dorsey, was swept along politically into the
governor's office, almost by acclamation.

The South is no unique repository for justice gone astray thanks
to popular prejudice. Massachusetts, if not the cradle, certainly
the playpen of democracy, experienced an attempted payroll robbery in the town of Bridgewater on December 24, 1919. The
crime was interrupted when a streetcar came between the payroll
truck and the robber, who took flight. Four months later, another
robbery took place in nearby South Braintree, and a paymaster
and his guard were shot. The killers fled in a car. Later, two men
were arrested for carrying concealed weapons. One man was a
factory watchman, the other a fish peddler who often carried large
sums of money. Possession of the guns was less surprising than the
fact that the calibers of the guns matched the murder weapons.

Also, a cap found at the scene of the crime resembled one worn by the watchman, Nicholas Sacco. So the Sacco and Vanzetti case, perhaps the most celebrated criminal case in American history, was launched. A ballistics expert said that Sacco's gun had fired the murder bullets, but this was an expert who later discredited himself by giving false testimony. There was a possibility, too, that the prosecution substituted for the actual murder bullet one fired from Sacco's gun into a side of beef. To correct this impropriety, the defense evidently switched barrels on one gun. Not until 1927, when the case and the defendants were history, did a comparison microscope prove for certain that the bullet at the trial had come from Sacco's gun. But was it the murder bullet, or the bullet from a side of beef? There is now no way of telling. There was little other evidence except the cap, which was much too big for Sacco anyway; but postwar Massachusetts, like most of the United States at that time, was involved in a scare which sprang from the fear of Communists, anarchists, atheists, and foreigners in general. Sacco and Vanzetti were indeed both foreigners—Italians—and they were professed anarchists. Judge Webster Thayer, presiding over the trial, asked afterward, "Did you see what I did to those anarchist bastards?" Guilty or not guilty, it was their political persuasion, not the evidence of guilt, that brought the pair to the electric chair. Experts still debate the case. A few feel that Sacco might indeed have been one of the criminals, but most regard Vanzetti as completely innocent. In any event, once again popular prejudice had triumphed over law and order.

The case of Julius and Ethel Rosenberg updated trial by prejudice after World War Two. The Rosenbergs were accused of espionage—the stealing of atomic secrets—at a time when Communist subversion was greatly feared. The prosecution offered substantial secondary evidence of guilt, but no direct evidence whatever. In fact, guilt was not so much the issue as whether or not the defendants deserved to be electrocuted. Espionage carries the death penalty only during wartime, and, though the Korean "police action" was in progress, the secrets had gone to Russia, a nominal ally. As with other victims of prejudice since the days of Socrates, many things were stacked against the Rosenbergs: the temper of the times, the Korean War, and in particular the long shadow of Senator Joseph McCarthy. A last plea for clemency failed. Civilization had taken a small but backward step.

Not to end this sad tally on a gloomy note, there is the case of *Thompson v. Louisville*.[5] Sam Thompson, a black, part-time handyman and long-time resident of Louisville, Kentucky, stopped at the Liberty End Café on his way home. There, while waiting for a bus, he played the jukebox and tapped his foot to the music. Two policemen approached him and asked him what he was doing. He told them, and without further ado they arrested him for loitering. When he protested outside the café, they tacked disorderly conduct to the charge, and before a police justice sitting without a jury, Thompson pleaded not guilty. At issue was a city ordinance reading in part, "It shall be unlawful for any person . . . without visible means of support or who cannot give a satisfactory account of himself to sleep, lie, loaf, or trespass in or about any building in the city without the consent of the owner or controller."

At the trial, the café manager testified that Thompson was a regular patron. Whether or not Thompson had purchased anything in the café he could not say. Thompson was convicted and fined twenty dollars. Still stubborn, he appealed, and to make a long story short, this minor case, brought by an insignificant handyman with twenty dollars and his principles at stake, went to the Supreme Court of the United States, where the arresting officers' statement to the effect that the defendant had protested his arrest was not held to constitute disorderly conduct affecting the city's good order. Sam Thompson had won.

The law was not in itself wrong, and the prejudice involved was small, based perhaps on the feeling that the poor and shabby are guilty by virtue of having been born. In some countries, a supreme court would be too lofty a tribunal for such cases. If some feel that the United States Supreme Court is soft on subversives and coddles criminals, a few words should be said for its defense of the minor rights of obscure individuals like Sam Thompson. The results go a long way to suggest that no man can be legally punished without evidence. Arrest and indictment are not enough, nor are his past offenses or his color sufficient to undo the just workings of a civilized system of law.

If one is dissatisfied with the workings of the law, there are a variety of ways for bringing about its change. One may campaign for specific legislation or, as has often been the case with civil rights, deliberately bring about a case which will test constitutional rights. This accords with Thoreau's famous lines, "Under a government which imprisons any unjustly, the true place for a just man is also a prison." [6] The same theme was more elaborately stated by Martin Luther King, Jr.

In no sense do I advocate evading or defying the law as the rabid segregationist would do. This would lead to anarchy. One who breaks an unjust law must do it openly, lovingly (not hatefully as the white mothers did in New Orleans when they were seen on television screaming "nigger, nigger, nigger"), and with a willingness to accept the penalty. I submit that an individual who breaks a law that conscience tells him is unjust, and willingly accepts the penalty by staying in jail to arouse the conscience of the community over its injustice, is in reality expressing the very highest respect for law.[7]

There are elements in our society that favor less passive approaches, groups that call themselves Minutemen and Weathermen and Black Panthers. They would overturn society and its laws with better authority than they might suspect, for it was Thomas Jefferson who said, "I hold it that a little rebellion now and then is a good thing. . . . God forbid we should ever be twenty years without such a rebellion." [8] Mind you, he spoke of a little rebellion, a letting off of steam. He would not improve society by tearing it down with all its laws, a prospect contemplated in Robert Bolt's play *A Man for All Seasons,* when Sir Thomas More and William Roper discuss whether or not the Devil should be entitled to the benefit of law. Imagining the Devil sheltering himself from judgment in a forest of laws, Roper argues that he would rather cut down every law in England than let the Devil hide. Then where would we be, More reminds him, when the Devil turns at bay and all the law's laid low? For one's own protection, More insists, even the Devil must be given benefit of law.

By chopping down legal trees that clog their view, many of today's more violent young rebels hope, as the prophets of old expected, to see a vision of such brilliance and beauty as to be dazzled forever. They imagine cutting away the deadwood will automatically lead to a golden age where men will live in peace, each man under his own coconut palm, because human hearts and consciences would direct them rightly. Surely, then, there would be no need of governments or courts or laws, or of police to enforce them. Such visions are older than Moses, who in his turn laid down laws. The despots of Syria and Egypt and Babylon and Rome codified their laws into systems that oppressed the fringe minorities. The only hope for justice seemed to be that it would overcome government, not that it would be discovered by it. So the millennial age was awaited when laws and governments would simply vanish. This vision has not been limited to the ancients, but has renewed itself in almost every age. Its diverse groups included the children of Hamelin, who followed the Pied Piper and found, if one equates the legend with the Children's Crusade, only death and slavery. More recently, it included the Communist followers of Marx and Engels, who believed in a kind of religion without God.

Meanwhile, practical men, living from day to day, are well advised not to cut down their institutions until better ones are planted and growing. However, they should never accept injustice, be it ever so minor, relying on the hope that it will presently "wither away." Such complacency would be only an excuse for inaction where reforms are badly needed.

And many reforms are certainly possible as well as desirable. Some are taking place, but, to borrow Bolt's analogy, others are lost in the woods. The difficulty lies in the vastness of this legal forest. One cannot cut it all down at once. To some extent, deadwood can be removed, though it usually is not. New seeds can be planted. More often than not, to facilitate quick relief, new limbs are grafted on older trees. The result is enormous confusion. It is far easier to say, "If we had birch here instead of pine, we'd be better off," than to effect the change in fact.

The following suggests only a few possible changes, and most of these are open to passionate dispute. This is inevitable wherever the rights of litigants and the revenues of their attorneys are affected.

On the one hand are the substantive rules of law, which have to do with what may and may not be done. In general, substantive law is court made and adjustable, moving with the times. On the other hand, there is adjective law. The logjam of delayed justice has more to do with the adjective law, by which is meant the rules, largely statutory, which govern the conduct of attorneys and courts in applying the substantive law. Here there is room for vast improvement that goes to the very heart of any lawsuit. What is a "litigation"? A process whereby truth is discovered by a careful sifting of facts, or a kind of combat between legal champions? Through the course of natural evolution, from the first stages where every man helped himself to justice, to the more formalized and verbal proceedings of United States courts today, the atmosphere has far too often been that of a brawl, no longer conducted with sticks and stones, but with words. The goal of this fight is to force compliance from an opponent. The means is a favorable judgment directing the police to use force if need be. In a civil court a legal right is no more than a lawsuit won, and this very often depends on one's having enough money to buy the more clever legal battler. This same mood attaches to a criminal proceeding; the defendant squares off against the state, one wins, the other loses; a sporting theory, to be sure, but not completely a civilized one. To end this approach—and many attorneys would protest from their wallets upward—the element of surprise should be eliminated from the trial, as well as factors of built-in prejudice.

In England, the prosecutor opens his case frankly, stating evidence both for and against the Crown's case. Litigation seldom depends on the American "ambush" technique of the surprise witness or the unknown document or photograph. In the United States, many a politically ambitious prosecutor would consider it ridiculous willingly to disclose evidence before trial which would be helpful to the defendant. "Would the Mets ever hand the Cardinals their signals?" In court, however, *justice*, not *winning*, should be the objective. There is a method in that direction which is beginning to find favor, and it is one that not only enhances the fairness of the outcome but tends to shorten a long and expensive trial. This is the elimination of issues through pretrial discovery proceedings. Such proceedings are usually voluntary, and, of course, less readily used where emotions are deeply involved, but the tendency is definitely toward such early appraisal of the evidence, involving both the court and the parties to the intended action.

In the future, it might serve the interest of justice for an impartial investigative body to be attached to the courts, its job to present evidence unbiased in either direction. Along this line, too, the very unsatisfactory state of expert testimony might be improved. As matters stand in the United States, whenever a medical, psychological, or technical question arises in court, both sides produce paid witnesses whose statements inevitably favor the side they represent, leaving the judge and jury to decide between them. Though some might shout it was a stab at the breast of our adversary system, how much more satisfactory would be a court-selected expert or experts who spoke without the expectation of recompense from either side.

As basic to our common law as the adversary system is the jury, "the glory of the English law," as Blackstone called it. The origin of the jury goes back to the Germanic tribes where statements were taken from leading local citizens as to the taxable wealth of the community. This was called a jurata, and their report to the king was a verdictum. In England, the Norman conquerors first used a jury, not to consider the facts in a case, but to get information from neighbors about persons accused of local crimes. Probably the system was not popular, to judge by the old saying, "God may be for him, though his neighbors be against him." By the fifteenth century, the jury had evolved into its present form. During the colonial period, in fact, the jury became a bulwark against governmental oppression, as evidenced in the London trial of William Penn. In 1670, a conventicle act declared it unlawful for persons to meet for purposes of worship other than in the Church of England. Penn was indicted for violation of this act, but four jurors, including one named Bushell, refused to agree that the Quaker Penn had violated the law. The court threatened to lock up the jurors until they came to a decision favorable to the Crown. As the jury was led out, Penn shouted, "Ye are Englishmen, mind your privilege, give not away your right!" Evidently they took this to heart, for after two days and nights without food, water, or heat, the jury was dismissed, and Bushell with his three friends was put in jail. From there Bushell obtained a writ of habeas corpus from the court of common pleas, and ever since, the jury has retained the right to judge the facts in a case.

Today, trial by jury is not guaranteed in all cases, but in the United States is limited to those rights to jury as they existed at the time of the writing of the Constitution. This, for instance, exempts cases held before juvenile courts. The trend is to make inroads into the right to a jury, with the final constitutional criterion being one of fairness under the right to due process. Even so, in criminal cases alone, about 650,000 jury trials are pursued to a verdict each year in the United States. England, where the jury system grew, has only about 5,000 annual jury cases, and where the jury has been used elsewhere in the world, it is now on the decline.

Should the jury be done away with? Some have said so, among them Erwin N. Griswold, United States Solicitor General. "The jury trial, at best, is the apotheosis of the amateur. Why should anyone think that twelve persons brought in from the street, selected in various ways for their lack of general ability, should have any special capacity for deciding controversies between persons?" [9]

Passionate arguments have been advanced on either side. Arguments against the jury system begin with the added expense and delays caused by a jury in the effort to award justice. The very process of selecting a panel of jurors suitable to both sides may take days, even weeks, and at the trial a few details of fact may be stretched into weeks of testimony. Errors in the presentation of evidence to the jury are liable to cause an appeal to a higher court, perhaps a new trial, or further appeal. Without a jury, court costs, lawyers' fees, delay—all would shrink.

A second question involved a clash of adages. If two heads are better than one, then surely twelve are better than two. On the other hand, is it more true that too many cooks spoil the broth? Whatever the answer may be, it is a fact that lawyers are exempt from jury duty, so that in every lawsuit twelve untrained heads must be selected for their ignorance of the law. They are asked to assemble a jumble of conflicting facts and opinions presented by hostile attorneys into a meaningful whole, and then to apply the law as the judge briefly describes it to them. Does this broth always have a savor of justice? Or is the proceeding better left to one trained legal expert, the judge? Griswold of Harvard definitely thought so. Some have gone further, and described the jury as the enemy of the law: They destroy its predictability, for such novices to the law cannot learn enough about the law in the course of a single trial to apply it. No jury is sophisticated enough to say to itself, "We don't like this legal rule and we will put it down." What they do is surrender the rules for their own prejudices. If totally confused or at odds, they may flip a coin in the jury room or draw straws from a hat. Both have been done, the latter in a case where a verdict of murder or manslaughter was at issue. A related criticism is that the jury is a tool of the attorneys, and by its very presence creates a combative, not a fact-finding, atmosphere. Books published on trial techniques tell attorneys how to ingratiate themselves with the jury and how to cast their clients in a sympathetic light. Such publications are in implicit accord with Balzac's definition of the jury, "Twelve men chosen to decide who has the better lawyer."

There are, of course, very good arguments on the other side of the fence. The jury system may be justly described as a bulwark against the arbitrary tyranny of a corrupt court. It has also been praised as an educator and a creator of confidence in government, as it allows the citizen to participate in the governmental process. Perhaps most important, the jury system is embedded in customs and traditions, and in the United States it is regarded as American as the Stars and Stripes and apple pie. Of course, tradition does not always guarantee usefulness. Take the South Pacific natives whose symbols of wealth began as small stone rings, which gradually grew until a ring of any worth today weighs many tons. Though theft is unlikely, commerce has slowed almost to a standstill. Stone ring or not, the jury is just as unlikely to disappear in the foreseeable future.

However one feels about this important question, it must be admitted that the jury and the judge diverge in many cases, and the difference generally boils down to that between strict law and rough equity. A judge tends to remove his personality from his decision, applying the law to the facts, but the jury is swayed by sentiment. Is the defendant sympathetic, old, pathetic, helpless? Is he cocky and conceited? Has he already been punished sufficiently by police brutality or by the very act that brought him to court? Perhaps he lost a leg in the negligent auto homicide for which he is being tried. All such factors may be relevant in a human sort of way, yet outside the legal facts at issue. In the criminal situation, the case is phrased dispassionately, the state versus John Doe, the defendant; but the jury tends to see it as John Doe versus his victim, and often is more lenient than the law when small harm has been done. Perhaps the defendant drove drunkenly but caused no injury, or perhaps the injury was only to himself. Perhaps he stole a wallet that was empty or was immediately recovered. In such cases, the jury brings into the picture an equity which the strict interpretation would deny, and this, though some would call it a denial of the law, may have its merits, too.

Whether it is good or bad in principle, there are ways in which the jury system could be more effectively applied. In many complex cases, particularly those where a contract is at issue and both sides wish to sort out the situation as quickly as possible in order to get back to business, the jury is inappropriate. Here pretrial findings of fact, a judge alone, or a board or arbitration will better serve the interests of both sides. In actual practice, such cases are rarely heard by a jury. Its presence normally is in a criminal case, or in a serious case of negligence where large sums are at stake. In the criminal situation, the jury's presence is the least open to criticism. In cases of negligence, it is the sympathetic jury's propensity for giving the victim gigantic verdicts that causes lawyers to demand trial by jury. A solution to this situation has already been suggested, but whatever the nature of the case, it is unfortunate when one stupid or dishonest juror can undo the work of the best judge. This does happen, but it would happen less often if jury standards were raised and the selection of panels put in the hands or judges rather than politicians. In practice, the more affluent, educated, and professional people get themselves excused from jury duty. The impossibility of finding quality jurors has led to virtual elimination of civil juries in England. More positively, in Los Angeles, prospective jurors must pass an aptitude test, which is a small step in the right direction.

Once a jury is impaneled, its task as a fact finder may be rendered more precise. The normal court proceeding is for all the controversial evidence to be presented on all the issues. Was the defendant negligent? Was the plaintiff contributorially negligent? How much injury in terms of dollars was suffered? All go into one bag. Then the judge ends up by instructing the jury on the law and how it applies, depending on what alleged set of facts they believe. So informed, the jury retires, debates, and comes forth with a general verdict. Sometimes, however, the jury's role is limited to findings on special issues of fact, thus leaving it entirely to the judge to apply the legal rules. Such a special verdict cuts down on the jury's freedom to apply emotions to the law. Another method, employed in England, has been the impaneling of special juries; that is, depending on the technical issues in a particular case, the jurors are selected for their special knowledge in that field.

Judges are human, too, and subject to the same imperfections as jurors. They may sometimes be tired, inattentive, or troubled by their own domestic problems.

> The hungry judges soon the sentence sign,
> And wretches hang that jurymen may dine,[10]

so goes the poem. Far beyond such digestive prejudices, under the elective system in the United States, the judge may well be woefully unqualified or corrupt. In the early days of American independence, judges were generally selected by the executive to serve during good behavior. Then, when Jacksonianism brought in the era of the common man, judges were forced to be politicians. Like everyone else, they had to run for election, with their qualifications for the job scarcely taken into account. Very quickly the quality of judges began to decline as they became obligated to local politicians such as Boss Tweed. A politician may become a good judge, but any system that forces a judge to be a politician has its drawbacks. Even if pressure is not involved, the very fact that today, as a vote-getting factor, the candidate's racial or religious background outweighs his abilities, is injurious to the law. The alternative is appointment, not by the governor or any group whose choice will be political, but through some form of selection by the Bar Association. Even if the final appointment must be political, at least this impartial legal society could present a qualified group of possible candidates, much as in England, where judges are selected from a pool of respected barristers. Such a plan is already being employed in some states, including Missouri and California. Here the governor of the state chooses from a prepared qualified list, which frees the judge from political obligations both past and future.

Thus far, only the machinery of the law has been discussed. Something must be said about the substantive law which the court applies. Let us keep in mind that each state, within constitutional guidelines, may establish its own laws. In the country as a whole, every passing month adds some twenty thousand new cases to a deposit of over two million. There are some thirty thousand new statutes annually, plus untold administrative decisions, so that there is little point in singling out any specific laws for comment. Better to plunge into the confusing whole to see if there is any way of organizing what might be called the Substantive Law of the United States.

The task would be staggering. Most law schools give up, teach the law of their particular state, and offer a course in conflict of laws, so that the future lawyer will at least know where to look when the problem arises. There remains a need for some comprehensive study influential enough to encourage a trend toward uniformity of the law. The best hope for such a review comes from programs which from time to time have been halfheartedly initiated by the American Law Institute. At least in certain areas, the Institute has published restatements of the law of contracts, property, torts, etc., giving the majority view and also any substantial minority position. Rarely today can one human brain comment significantly on the law, as Bracton and Coke have done in the past. The subject is too vast, too swiftly changing. In some countries, there exists a ministry of justice for law reform. This institution is not likely to be established in the United States, where such governmental agencies are feared as devices to enfeeble the courts and trample human rights. But a program might be initiated at law centers concentrated around the major universities, where scholars could ascertain the law as it is and should be. Working together, they might influence the course of the substantive law for the best, as did those monumental jurists of the past.

Finally, there are the law schools themselves. The manner of study, known as the case system, which amounts to the concentrated dissection of judicial case reports, was formulated long ago by Christopher Columbus Langdell. Langdell was a recluse and a keen lawyer who lived with books and legal briefs, but he never considered the practical lawyer-client relationship. When he became Dean of Harvard Law School, he evolved his methods strictly as a library science. Though valuable, it is as inappropriate as a medical school education derived solely from the printed page. Law is a practical as well as a theoretical discipline, and the law school must, as many are beginning to do, take this into account through association with programs such as the Legal Aid Society.

It has been told that Gertrude Stein, on her deathbed, asked toward the end, "What is the answer?" When only silence answered her, she laughed and said with her last breath, "In that case, what is the question?"

Hopefully, some questions have been raised here, along with proper respect for the deathless concept of law. However imperfect, it has for centuries been the main bulwark between man and the beasts. And if the world and its laws have fallen on dark days, the reasonable man can react only as did the Connecticut House of Representatives on the nineteenth of May, 1780, when the sun failed and the sky went dark. Some fell to their knees. Others cried out for adjournment, until the Speaker of the House, one Colonel Davenport, arose and said in a great voice, "The day of judgment is either approaching or it is not. If it is not, there is no cause for adjournment. If it is, I choose to be found doing my duty. I wish, therefore, that candles may be brought. . . . Ladies and gentlemen, let candles be brought."

Appendix

A Reference Note on Case Citations
As They Appear in Chapter Notes

The recording of important judgments is standard practice throughout the United States. Each state has its series of reports, and there are federal reports. Each reported judgment, running from a short paragraph to many pages, gives the judge's reasons for deciding as he did, and usually includes references to other cases that were influential in his deciding. Because they are of constant use only to lawyers in preparing cases, and judges in deciding them, these voluminous reports are not found in many libraries. An attorney may keep in his own office the reports on the state in which he practices. A library connected with the county court may include others, particularly federal reports. In major court centers, reports from all the various states may be kept. The better law schools are obliged to keep up to date with all reports.

Suppose one wants to read a particular judgment in its entirety. Take *Powell v. Alabama;* the trick is to find a library that contains the federal reports. After that it is easy enough to find the case, which carries the citation 287 U.S. 45, meaning it can be found in the 287th volume of the United States reports on page 45. Or, should you be interested in *Weems v. State of Alabama,* the citation is 224 Ala. 524, and there is nothing complicated about it except finding a library that contains the Alabama reports. Few libraries outside of the state would do so.

Chapter Notes

CHAPTER ONE: THE TRIBAL BEGINNINGS

1. Thomas Hobbes, *The Leviathan* (New York, Everyman, 1914), Chap. 13.

CHAPTER TWO: CIVILIZING THE LAW

1. Stanley A. Cook, *The Laws of Moses and the Code of Hammurabi* (London: Adam and Charles Black, 1903).
2. L R3 H:L 330.
3. Richard Nice and Peter Owen, *Treasury of the Law* (London: Solicitors Law, 1965), pp. 69–75.
4. Nice and Owen, "Forcum Judicum," *loc. cit.*, p. 249.
5. "Aus dem Irischen Recht," from the German translation of R. Thurneysen, Bonn University.

CHAPTER THREE: SOURCES OF OUR COMMON LAW

1. F. W. Maitland, ed., *Select Pleas in Manorial Courts* (London: Selden Society, 1889), II, 121.

CHAPTER FOUR: GREAT SYSTEMS OF THE LAW TODAY

1. Oliver Wendell Holmes, *The Common Law* (Cambridge: Harvard University Press, 1963), p. 1.
2. S. Van Der Sprenkel, *Legal Institutions in Manchu China* (London: Athlone Press, 1962), p. 77.

3. Quotations from Chairman Mao Tse-tung (Peking: Foreign Languages Press, 1966), p. 297.
4. *Ibid.*, p. 258.
5. "Al-Bukhari," trans. from the Arabic in Frédéric Peltier's *Le Livre des ventes du Çah'ih' d'el-Bokhâri* (Algiers: Jourdan, 1909).

CHAPTER FIVE: HUMANIZING THE COMMON LAW

1. 115 N.Y. 506.
2. 3 East 593, 102 Eng. Rep. 724.
3. Y.B. 7 Edw. IV f 2 pl. 2.
4. 21 Pa. St. 203.
5. 11 East 60 K.B.
6. 2 H & C 722.
7. Hagy v. Allied Chemical and Dye Corp., 122 Cal. App. 2d 361, 1954.
8. 17 Wall 657, 1873.
9. 248 N.Y. 339, 1928.
10. 195 N.C. 788, 1928.
11. 102 Kan. 139, 1917.
12. 217 N.W. 382, 1916.
13. 22 Harvard Law Review 112.
14. Buck v. Amory Manufacturing Co., 69 N.H. 257, 1897.
15. 210 N.Y.S. 2nd 358, 1962.
16. 158 Misc. 904, 287 N.Y. Supp. 134, 1935.
17. D 1956. 354 Note Tunc, J.C. P., 1955, II. 8774 note Esmein.
18. 16 How. St. Tr. 695.
19. 42 N.M. 135, 1938.
20. 214 F 2d 862, 1954.
21. 149 F 2d 29.
22. 216 N.Y. 324, 1915.

CHAPTER SIX: CIVILIZING PUNISHMENTS

1. 370 U.S. 660, 1962.
2. 329 U.S. 459, 1947.
3. Charles Pelham Curtis, *Law as Large as Life* (New York: Simon and Schuster, 1959), pp. 111–112.
4. Plato, *Protagoras*, trans. by B. Jowett (New York: Dial Press, n.d.), p. 324.
5. 328 U.S. 463, 1946.
6. *Selected Writings of Cardozo*, M. E. Hall, ed. (New York: Fallon Law Books, 1947), p. 381.

7. U.S. v. Jin Puey Moy, 241 U.S. 394, 1915.
8. Webb v. U.S. 249 U.S. 96, 1919.

CHAPTER SEVEN: FREEDOM OF SPEECH AND PRESS

1. 21 Howell's State Trials 847 1040 1783-4.
2. Francis Wharton, *State Trials of the United States During the Administrations of Washington and Adams* (Albany: W. C. Little, 1849), p. 690.
3. Meyer Berger, *The Story of The New York Times—1851–1951* (New York: Simon and Schuster, 1951), p. 52.
4. 283 U.S. 697, 1931.
5. Schenck v. U.S., 249 U.S. 47, 1919.
6. 268 U.S. 652, 1925.
7. Goldstein v. U.S., 258 Fed. 908, 1919.
8. Dennis v. U.S., 341 U.S. 494, 1951.
9. E. M. Borchard and E. R. Lutz, *Convicting the Innocent* (New Haven: Yale University Press, 1932).
10. 373 U.S. 723, 1963.
11. Roach v. Garvan, 2 Atk. 469, 471, 1742.
12. 331 U.S. 367, 1947.
13. Sheppard v. Maxwell, 384 U.S. 333, 1966.
14. Cote v. Rogers, 19 Cal. Reporter 767, 1962.
15. Lovell v. Griffin, 303 U.S. 444, 1938 and Cantwell v. Connecticut, 310 U.S. 296, 1940.
16. Chaplinski v. New Hampshire, 315 U.S. 568, 1942.
17. Feiner v. New York, 340 U.S. 315, 1951.
18. Rockwell v. Morris, 211 New York 2d 25, 1961.
19. Edwards v. South Carolina, 372 U.S. 229, 1963.
20. Fields v. Fairfield, 375 U.S. 248, 1963.
21. Williams v. Wallace, 240 F supp. 100, 106, 1965.
22. Adderley v. Florida, 385 U.S. 39, 1966.
23. 5 F supp. 182, 1933.
24. Hannegan v. Esquire, 327 U.S. 146, 1946.
25. 354 U.S. 476, 1957.
26. A Book Named "John Cleland's Memoirs of a Woman of Pleasure" v. Massachusetts, 383 U.S. 413, 1966.
27. Ginsburg v. U.S., 383 U.S. 463, 1966.
28. Hatfield v. Gazette Printing Co., 175 Pac. 382.
29. New York Times Co. v. Sullivan, 376 U.S. 254, 1964.

CHAPTER EIGHT: PRIVACY AND THE POLICE

1. Roberson v. Rochester Folding Box Co., 171 N.Y. 538.
2. Sidis v. F. R. Publishing Co., 113 R 2d 806, 1940.
3. 192 F 2d 974.
4. Public Utilities Commission v. Pollak, 343 U.S. 451, 1952.
5. Edward, Lord Coke's reporting of the Semayne's case 5 co. rep. 91a 91b, 1603.
6. Keiningham v. U.S., 287 Fed. 2nd 126, 1960.
7. Warden v. Hayden, 387 U.S. 294, 1967.
8. York v. Story, 324 F 2d 450, 1963.
9. 384 U.S. 757, 1966.
10. 342 U.S. 172, 1952.
11. Wolf v. Colorado, 338 U.S. 25, 1949.
12. Olmstead v. U.S., 277 U.S. 438, 1928.
13. 388 U.S. 41, 1967.
14. Silverman v. U.S., 365 U.S. 505, 1961.
15. Smayda v. I.S., 352 F 2d 251, 1965.
16. Katz v. U.S., 88 Sup. Ct. 507, 1967.
17. Giancana v. Hoover, 322 F 2d 789, 1963.
18. Rios v. U.S., 364 U.S. 253, 1960.
19. Escobedo v. Illinois, 378 U.S. 478, 1964.
20. 15 N.Y. 2d 235.
21. 384 U.S. 436, 1966.
22. Powell v. Alabama, 287 U.S. 45, 1932.
23. Gideon v. Wainwright, 372 U.S. 338, 1963.
24. Frank v. Mangum, 237 U.S. 309, 1961.
25. Minnesota v. Ernest Coursolle, 255 Minn. 384.
26. Taken from the oral argument by Roscoe Conkling in the San Mateo C. No. 106 Oct. term 1883, p. 34.

CHAPTER NINE: CIVIL RIGHTS

1. Scott v. Sandford, 19 How. 393, 1857.
2. *Ex parte* Marryman, 17 Fed. Cas. No. 9 487, 1861.
3. *Ex parte* Milligan, 4 Wall 2, 1866.
4. U.S. v. Rowe, 73 Fed. supp. 75, 1947.
5. 109 U.S. 3, 1883.
6. Plessy v. Ferguson, 163 U.S. 537, 1896, p. 559.
7. Steele v. Louisville & Nashville Railroad, 323 U.S. 192, 1944.

8. Corrigan v. Buckley, 271 U.S. 323, 1926.
9. Shelley v. Kraemer, 344 U.S. 1, 1948.
10. 347 U.S. 483, 1954.
11. Peterson v. Greenville, 373 U.S. 244, 1963.
12. McClung v. Katzenbach, 33 U.S.L.W. 2151, 1964 and Heart of Atlanta Motel v. U.S., 33 L.W. 4059, 1964.
13. 324 U.S. 91, 1945.
14. U.S. v. Quest, 383 U.S. 745, 1966.
15. 388 U.S. 1, 1967.

CHAPTER TEN: LAW AMONG NATIONS: WAR AND ITS CONTROL

1. *The New York Times* (June 27, 1945).
2. Foster v. Neilson, 2 Pet. 253 314.
3. Ware v. Hylton, Dall. 199.
4. "The Wanderer and His Shadow," in J. G. Gray, *The Warriors* (New York: Harcourt, Brace, 1959), p. 225.
5. Beverly Leman, "The Prisoners of Vietnam," *Vietnam Report* (August-September, 1966), pp. 5, 35.

CHAPTER ELEVEN: THE FUTURE OF THE LAW

1. Michel de Montaigne, *Essays*, trans. by E. S. Trechmann (New York: Oxford University Press, 1946).
2. Letter to Gulian C. Verplanck, "On the reform of the judicial system of this state (New York)," 8, 1840.
3. *Graigola Merthyr Ltd. v. Swansea Corp.*, as noted by Lord Chorley in David Dudley Field's *Centenary Essays*, 115, 1949.
4. Reported in *The New York Times* (October 24, 1964).
5. 362 U.S. 199.
6. Wm. Henry Davenport, *Voices in Court: A Treasury of the Bench, the Bar, and the Courtroom* (New York: Macmillan, 1958).
7. *Liberation* (June, 1963), p. 13.
8. *The Writings of Thomas Jefferson, 1784–1787*, P. L. Ford, ed. (New York: G. P. Putnam's Sons, 1892), Vol. IV.
9. Erwin N. Griswold in the 1962–1963 Harvard University Law School Dean's Report, pp. 5–6.
10. Alexander Pope, *The Rape of the Lock*, Canto III.

Bibliography

Alabaster, E., *Notes and Commentaries on Chinese Criminal Law*. London: Luzac & Co., 1899.

Allott, A. N., *Essays in African Law*. London: Butterworth, 1960.

Association of the Bar of the City of New York, *Freedom of the Press and Fair Trial*. New York: Columbia University Press, 1967.

Barth, Alan, *The Loyalty of Free Men*. New York: Viking Press, 1951. (McCarthy trials, loyalty.)

Bartholomew, Paul C., *Summaries of Leading Cases on the Constitution*. Paterson, New Jersey: Littlefield, Adams, 1965.

Bedau, Hugo Adam, ed., *Civil Disobedience*. New York: Pegasus, 1969.

Belli, Melvin M., *The Law Revolution*. Los Angeles: Sherbourne Press, 1968.

Berger, Monroe, *Equality by Statute: The Revolution in Civil Rights*, rev. ed. New York: Doubleday & Co., 1967.

Black, Henry Campbell, *Black's Law Dictionary*, St. Paul, Minnesota: West Publishing Co., 1951.

Brennan, Donald G., ed., *Arms Control, Disarmament, and National Security*. New York: George Braziller, 1961.

Brenton, Myron, *The Privacy Invaders*. New York: Coward-McCann, 1964.

Chevigny, Paul, *Police Power*. New York: Pantheon, 1969.

Ch'u, T'ung-tsu, *Law and Society in Traditional China*, 2nd ed. The Hague, Netherlands: Mouton, 1965.

Cohen, Louis H., *Murder, Madness, and the Law*. Cleveland and New York: World Publishing, 1952. (Insanity from a psychiatric viewpoint.)

211

Cushman, Robert E. and Robert F., *Cases in Constitutional Law.* New York: Appleton-Century-Crofts, 1968. (General case book.)

Dean, William Tucker, ed., *Annual Survey of American Law, 1950.* Englewood Cliffs, New Jersey: Prentice-Hall, 1951.

Derrett, J. Duncan, ed., *An Introduction to Legal Systems.* New York: Praeger, 1968.

de Visscher, Charles, *Theory and Reality in Public International Law.* Princeton, New Jersey: Princeton University Press, 1968.

Dickler, Gerald, *Man on Trial.* New York: Doubleday, 1962. (Famous trials: Jesus, Charles I, witchcraft, Oppenheimer.)

Dinnerstein, Leonard, *The Leo Frank Case.* New York: Columbia University Press, 1968. (Prejudice in the South.)

Endleman, Shalom, comp., *Violence in the Streets.* Chicago: Quadrangle Books, 1968. (Racial and other violence.)

Falk, Zev W., *Hebrew Law in Biblical Times.* Jerusalem: Wahrmann Books, 1964.

Feifer, George, *Justice in Moscow.* New York: Simon and Schuster, 1964. (Soviet law.)

Gillmor, Daniel S., *Fear, the Accuser.* New York: Abelard-Schuman, 1954. (Subversive activities, McCarthy.)

Gray, J. Glenn, *The Warriors.* New York: Harcourt, Brace & World, 1959. (Mentality of war.)

Green, Leon, *Traffic Victims: Tort Law and Insurance.* Evanston, Illinois: Northwestern University Press, 1958. (Negligence, juries, insurance.)

Guttmann, Allan and Ziegler, Benjamin Munn, eds., *Communism, the Courts and the Constitution.* Boston: D. C. Heath, 1964. (Free speech and civil liberties.)

Hadley, Arthur T., *The Nation's Safety and Arms Control.* New York: Viking Press, 1961.

Hale, Leslie, *Hanging in the Balance.* London: Jonathan Cape, 1962. (Capital punishment.)

Harris, Richard, *The Fear of Crime.* New York: Frederick A. Praeger, 1969. (Tyranny from fear of crime, the Omnibus Crime Bill.)

Hays, Arthur G., *Trial by Prejudice.* New York: Covici, Friede, 1933. (Early Negro, labor, Communist cases.)

Henkin, Louis, *Arms Control and Inspection in American Law.* New York: Columbia University Press, 1958.

Hoffman, Stanley, ed., *Conditions of World Order.* Boston: Houghton Mifflin, 1968.

Holmes, Oliver Wendell, *The Common Law*. Cambridge: Harvard University Press, 1963. (Historical survey with summary on various areas.)

Hook, Sidney, *Common Sense and the Fifth Amendment*. Chicago: H. Regnery, 1963. (Self-incrimination.)

Horowitz, G., *The Spirit of Jewish Law*. New York: Central Book, 1953.

Hudon, Edward G., *Freedom of Speech and Press in America*. Washington, D.C.: Public Affairs Press, 1963.

Hull, Roger H., and Novogrod, John C., *Law and Vietnam*. Dobbs Ferry, New York: Oceana Publications, 1968.

Jessup, Philip C., *A Modern Law of Nations*. New York: Archon Books, 1968.

Kalven, Harry, Jr., and Zeisel, Hans, *The American Jury*. Boston: Little, Brown, 1966.

Koestler, Arthur, *Reflections on Hanging*. New York: Macmillan Company, 1957.

Kramer, Charles, *The Negligent Doctor*. New York: Crown Publishers, 1968. (Malpractice.)

Larson, Arthur, *When Nations Disagree*. Baton Rouge: Louisiana State University Press, 1961.

Lauterpacht, H., *International Law and Human Rights*. New York: Frederick A. Praeger, 1950.

Lin, Fu-shun, ed., *Chinese Law Past and Present*. New York: East Asian Institute, Columbia University, 1966.

Lindesmith, Alfred R., *The Addict and the Law*. Bloomington: Indiana University Press, 1965.

Lofton, John, *Justice and the Press*. Boston: Beacon Press, 1966.

Mason, Alpheus Thomas, and Beaney, William M., *American Constitutional Law*. Englewood Cliffs, New Jersey: Prentice-Hall, 1968.

Medina, H. R., ed., *Radio, Television and the Administration of Justice*. New York: Columbia University Press, 1965. (Freedom of the press, invasion of privacy.)

Morgenthau, Hans J., *Politics Among Nations*. New York: Alfred A. Knopf, 1967.

Murphy, Terrence J., *Censorship, Government and Obscenity*. Baltimore, Maryland: Helicon, 1963.

Newman, Edwin S., *Police, the Law and Personal Freedom*. Dobbs Ferry, New York: Oceana Publications, 1964. (Search and seizure, etc.).

Nice, Richard, and Owen, Peter, *Treasury of the Law*. London: Solicitors Law, 1965.

Nussbaum, Arthur, *A Concise History of the Law of Nations.* New York: Macmillan Company, 1954.

Nuttall, Jeff, *Bomb Culture.* New York: Delacorte Press, 1968. (Mentality of the atomic age.)

Pollak, Louis H., ed., *The Constitution and the Supreme Court,* Cleveland and New York: World Publishing, 1966. (Vol. I: Early decisions, the rule of law in world affairs; Vol. II: Freedom of speech, due process, civil rights.)

Rattray, R. S., *Ashanti Law and Constitution.* London: Oxford University Press, 1956.

Root, Jonathan, *The Betrayers.* New York: Coward-McCann, 1963. (The Rosenberg case.)

Schneir, Walter and Miriam, *Invitation to an Inquest.* New York: Doubleday & Co., 1965. (The Rosenberg trial.)

Schwartz, Bernard, *A Commentary on the Constitution of the United States,* Part III. New York: Macmillan Company, 1968. (Personal rights, search and seizure, civil rights, free expression.)

Stone, Julius, *Legal Controls of International Conflict.* New York: Rinehart and Co., 1954.

Stroup, Herbert H., *Church and State in Confrontation.* New York: Seabury Press, 1967. (Historical survey of church and state from the time of the Bible.)

Trebach, Arnold S., *The Rationing of Justice.* New Brunswick, New Jersey: Rutgers University Press, 1964. (Police, arrest, trial, general.)

Turner, William W., *The Police Establishment.* New York: G. P. Putnam's Sons, 1968. (Law-enforcement problems.)

A Glossary of Legal Terms

acquittal:
the legal certification of the innocence of a person charged with a crime.

action:
proceeding in a court of justice by which one party prosecutes another for the protection or enforcement of a right or the punishment of a public offense.

adjudication:
the judgment pronounced in a given case.

affidavit:
a recorded declaration or statement of facts, made voluntarily and under oath before an authorized officer.

appeal:
the taking of a cause from a lesser court to one of higher jurisdiction in order to obtain a review and retrial.

appellate court:
a court having jurisdiction of appeal and review.

arbitration:
the submission for determination of a disputed matter to a private person or persons selected in agreed-to manner.

assumption of risk:
a situation where the plaintiff assumes the consequences of injury occurring through the fault of the defendant or another.

attorney:
in general, one who manages the legal affairs of another; a legal agent qualified to act for suitors and defendants in legal proceedings.

capital crime:	a crime for which the death penalty may be inflicted.
certiorari:	a writ of review, issued by an appellate court to call up the records of a lesser court to obtain more information in a pending cause.
chancery:	a former high court in England; a court of equity in the American judicial system.
common law:	unwritten law as opposed to statute law; developed in England and based on customs or on reason and fixed principles of justice.
compensation:	the payment of damages, giving a substitute of equal value.
contributory negligence:	the act, or failure to act, on part of the plaintiff which, along with the defendant's negligence, is the proximate cause of the complained-of injury.
conviction:	a criminal judgment holding the prisoner guilty as charged.
corporal punishment:	physical punishment, as distinguished from a fine.
court:	a body to which the administration of justice is delegated.
defendant:	the party against whom relief or recovery is sought in a court action.
district attorney:	the prosecuting officer of the United States in each of the federal judicial districts; under state government, the prosecuting officer who represents the state in each judicial district.
due process of law:	a course of proceedings at law that is in accordance with the law of the land.
equity:	a system of law originating in the English Chancery that was designed to dispense justice without prejudice or favoritism; a formal body of legal rules that supplement or overrule common and statute law.
escheat:	in English feudal law, the reverting of land to the lord of the fee because there were no eligible heirs; in the U.S., the reverting of land to the state for lack of heirs legally entitled to it.

evidence:	proof presented at trial.
ex post facto:	done after the fact; retroactively.
felony:	a crime of a more serious nature than a misdemeanor.
fraud:	a false representation of a matter of fact by words or conduct, an intentional misrepresentation or concealment for the purpose of deceiving someone so that he will act upon it to his legal injury.
habeas corpus:	a writ with the objective of bringing a party before a court.
hearsay evidence:	legal testimony that consists in a person's repeating evidence told him by someone else; secondhand evidence.
homicide:	the killing of a human being; it may be a criminal, justifiable, or negligent act.
indemnity:	an insurance that protects against hurt or anticipated loss or damage.
injunction:	a prohibitive writ issued by a court directing a defendant to refrain from some act.
judgment:	the official decision of a court upon the respective rights and claims of parties to an action.
jurisdiction:	the authority by which courts and judicial officers decide cases; the legal right by which that authority is exercised.
jurist:	someone versed in law.
jury:	a body of men and women selected according to law and sworn to give a verdict based upon the evidence legally presented; a member of a jury is a juror.
justice of the peace:	a judicial officer of low rank having jurisdiction limited by statute.
larceny:	the stealing of personal property; called grand larceny if the value of the property exceeds a certain amount, and petit larceny if below that value.
last clear chance:	a doctrine evolved in behalf of a plaintiff who is clearly contributorily negligent, but helplessly so under circumstances where the defendant

	has a chance to avert the injury, *e.g.*, the drunkard lying in the road but clearly visible to the oncoming motorist.
liable:	to be bound or obligated by law to make restitution.
litigation:	the practice of taking legal action; the contest in a court of justice for the purpose of enforcing a right.
magistrate:	a public official entrusted with the administration of the laws.
mandamus:	the prerogative writ issued under English law by the King's Bench in the absence of any other legal remedy; a writ issued under constitutions and regulated by statute when there is no other adequate remedy at law, in equity, or under statute.
misdemeanor:	an offense regarded as less serious than a felony and subject to lesser fines or imprisonment.
negligence:	the failure to exercise the care that a prudent person would exercise under the given circumstances.
negotiorum gestio:	management of business.
plaintiff:	one who brings an action and is so named on the record.
plea:	an action or cause in court; a written statement made by a party to a suit in support of his cause; an accused person's answer to a charge or indictment against him in criminal practice.
praetor:	an ancient Roman magistrate ranking below a consul.
precedent:	a judicial decision, a proceeding or a course of action that serves as a rule for future determinations in similar cases.
prima facie evidence:	evidence sufficient in law to raise a presumption of fact or establish the fact in question unless rebutted.
probate:	the judicial determination of the validity of a will.

procedural law:	the rules which set out the machinery for conducting a suit.
prosecution:	in criminal law, a proceeding to determine the guilt or innocence of a person charged with a crime.
proximate cause:	a cause that directly, with no intervening cause, produces an effect; a cause arising out of a person's negligence and producing an injury.
quorum	the number of the members of a given body, such as a court, that is legally competent to transact business in absence of the other members.
rebuttal:	introduction of evidence showing that a statement of a witness is not true.
res ipsa loquitor:	literally, "The thing speaks for itself," the presumption that the defendant was negligent, arising from proof that the cause of the damage was under defendant's sole control, and that the accident was not one which ordinarily occurs without negligent conduct.
sedition:	insurrectionary activity moving toward treason but lacking the overt act.
sheriff:	the chief executive and administrative officer of a county chosen by popular election, whose duties include aiding the criminal and civil courts by serving process, calling juries, etc.
slander:	the speaking of defamatory words tending to damage someone's reputation.
statute:	the written law of a legislature as distinct from common law.
strict liability:	this rule is applied when the defendant is using something so inherently dangerous that it may cause damage to others even where the defendant uses reasonable care—explosives, for example. In that case it is not necessary in court to prove negligent use.
subpoena:	a writ commanding a person to appear in court and give testimony under a penalty for failure to comply.

substantive law:	a branch of law that prescribes the rights, duties, and obligations of persons toward one another as to their conduct and property and that determines when a cause of action for damages has arisen.
suit:	an action or process in a court for the recovery of a right or claim.
tort:	a private or civil wrong or injury; a wrong independent of contract.
trial:	the mode of examining of facts and disposal of issues in a court of law.
verdict:	the decision of a jury on the matter legally submitted to them in the course of a trial.
warrant:	a writ authorizing an officer to make an arrest, a seizure, or a search, or to do other acts incident to the administration of justice.
witness:	a person who gives evidence in court under oath.
writ:	a written order issued by a court or judicial officer and commanding the person to whom it is directed to perform or to refrain from performing an act specified therein.

Index

acquittal, definition of, 215
action (proceeding), definition of, 215
adjective law, 197
adjudication, definition of, 215
affidavit, definition of, 215
African law, 65. *See also specific countries*
Alabama case, 167
Albania, blood feuds, 15
Alien and Sedition Acts, 110
amendments. *See* Constitution, U.S.
American Law Institute, 89, 203
Andaman Island, law of, 11
Anglo-Hindu law, 57
appeal, definition of, 215
appellate court, definition of, 215
arbitration, definition of, 215
Arnold, Edward, 87
assumption of risk, definition of, 215
attorneys
    definition of, 215
    education, 203
    right of defendants to, 141, 142
"attractive nuisance," doctrine of, 77
Australia, Gringai tribe law, 12

Berger v. New York, 135
Bertillon, Alphonse, 146
Besnard, Marie, 183
Bible, 22
Bloody Code, 101
Brazil, "Squadrons of Death," 181
Brown v. Board of Education, 155
Butterfield v. Forrester, 77

Callender, James, 110
Cambacérès, Jacques Régis, 30
Canal Zone, 162
capital crime, definition of, 216
capital punishment, 98
censorship. *See* press, freedom of the; speech, freedom of
certiorari, definition of, 216
chancery, definition of, 216

Chessman, Caryl, 101
China, development of law, 57
Church of England, 48
civil law. *See* written law
civil rights (U.S.), 151
    racial demonstration cases, 118
    Southern attitudes, 187
Civil Rights Act of 1875, 153
Civil Rights Act of 1964, 156
Civil War (U.S.), 152
Code Napoléon, 29, 30, 56, 64, 65
Comanche Indians, 13
combat, trial by, 34
Commentaries on the Laws of England, 52
common law, 41, 216. *See also specific topics*
compensation, definition of, 216
confessions, 139, 145. *See also* Inquisition
Confucius, 58
Constantine the Great, 28
Constitution, U.S.
    First Amendment, 130
    Fourth Amendment, 131, 132, 138
    Fifth Amendment, 129, 131, 143
    Sixth Amendment, 130
    Eighth Amendment, 95
    Thirteenth Amendment, 153
    Fourteenth Amendment, 129, 131, 134, 153
    Nineteenth Amendment, 153
    treaties as law of the land, 175
    war-declaring powers, 161
contributory negligence, 116, 216
conviction, definition of, 216
corporal punishment, definition of, 216
Corpus Juris Civilis, 28
courts
    definition of, 216
    development of, 21
    International Court of Justice, 169, 171, 178

and trial by combat, 37
U.S., 72, 180, 181, 182
 see also judges; juries; specific
  countries
Craig v. Harney, 115
criminal law
 humanizing trends in, 86
 protection of Negro rights, 157
criminology, 146
customs, as form of law, 11
Czechoslovakia, good Samaritan laws,
 84

death penalty. See capital punishment
Declaration of Independence, 52
defendant, definition of, 216
Dharmasastra, 56
disarmament, 176
district attorney, definition of, 216
domestic relations
 adultery among Comanches, 13
 child-custody case (Japan), 55
 Code of Hammurabi, 19
 Lipit-Istar, 18
 miscegenation, 158
 Twelve Tables, 25
Draco, 21
Dred Scott decision, 151
drug addiction, 95, 103
due process, 130, 152, 216
dueling, 37
Durham v. U.S., 89

eavesdropping, 135
Ecuador, Jibaro Indian law, 14
equity, 45, 216
escheat, definition of, 216
Escobedo, Danny, 141
Eskimo song duels, 12
Espionage and Sedition Acts, 113
Evans, Timothy, 101
evidence, definition of, 217
ex post facto, definition of, 217
Exchequer, 42, 45

Federal Bureau of Investigation, 142,
 147
felony, definition of, 217
fingerprinting, 147
Fish, Albert, 88
Fisher v. the United States, 100
Fox, Emma, 87
France
 capital punishment, 98

Code Napoléon, 29, 30, 56, 64, 65
good Samaritan statutes, 84, 85
Inquisition, 32
Francis v. Resweber, 95
Frank, Leo, 190
fraud, definition of, 217

Gentili, Alberico, 166
Germany
 death penalty, 102
 good Samaritan statutes, 85
 trial by combat, 34
Gideon, Clarence Earl, 143
Gitlow v. New York, 113
good Samaritan cases, 81
Great Britain
 Bloody Code, 101
 capital punishment, 98
 common law, development of, 42
 courts, 42, 43, 108, 197
 drug addiction in, 105
 police, 138, 139, 145
 press censorship, 108, 123
 privacy, right of, 128
 trial by ordeal, 33, 37
Greece, ancient, 20, 21, 107
Grotius, Hugo, 166
Guicciardini, Francesco, 167

habeas corpus, 50, 130, 139, 152, 217
Hague Conference (1899), 168
Hammurabi, Code of, 19
Hatfield, Minnie, 121
hearsay evidence, definition of, 217
Hebrew law, 23, 60
Heirens, William, 89
Hindu law, 56
homicide, definition of, 217
Howard, Frank, 88

indemnity, definition of, 217
India, development of law, 56
injunction, definition of, 217
Inquisition, 31, 108
insanity, of criminals, 86
International Court of Justice, 169,
 171, 178
international law, 164. See also International Court of Justice
Islamic law, 60, 61
Israel
 ancient laws and courts, 22
 death penalty abolition, 102
 prisons, 97
Italy, death penalty, 102

Jehovah's Witness decisions, 116
Jesus Christ, trial of, 24
Jewish law, 23, 60
Joan of Arc, trial of, 32
judges, 202
judgment, definition of, 217
juries, 198, 217
   Athens, ancient, 21
   Britain, development of, 33, 43
   prejudice of, 183
   see also courts
jurisdiction, definition of, 217
justice of the peace, definition of, 217
Justinian Code, 28

Kenya, 65
Koran, 62
Korean War, 163

Langdell, Christopher Columbus, 204
larceny, definition of, 217
last clear chance, doctrine of, 76, 77, 217
Latin America, 63. *See also specific countries*
law, definition of, 11, 29, 54
League of Nations, 169
Leame v. Bray, 75
Leverton v. The Curtis Publishing Company, 128
liability, doctrine of, 75
liable, definition of, 218
libel, 121
Liberia, trial by sasswood, 34
Lilburne, John, 143
Lincoln, Abraham, 152
Lipit-Istar, Laws of, 18
litigation, definition of, 218
Lovejoy, the Reverend Elijah P., 111
Loving v. Virginia, 158

McNaghten rule, 87
MacPherson v. Buick, 79
magistrate, definition of, 218
Magna Carta, 46, 47, 50, 94
mandamus, definition of, 218
Mapp, Dollree, 134
Marbury v. Madison, 72
marijuana, 106
Meredith, James, 155
Mexican War (1846), 162
Mexico, 63
Milligan, Lambdin P., 152
Minos, King, 21

Miranda v. Arizona, 141
miscegenation, 158
misdemeanor, definition of, 218
Mishnah, 23, 60
Muller, Franz, 145

Napoleonic Code. *See* Code Napoléon
natural law, 52
Near v. Minnesota, 112
negligence, doctrine of, 75, 218
   contributory, case of, 116
   good Samaritan cases, 81
negotiorum gestio, definition of, 218
Negroes. *See* civil rights; slavery
New Jersey Railroad v. Keerwood, 75
New York, 146, 147, 148, 149, 182
Nietzsche, Friedrich, 178
Nigeria, Tiv tribe law, 17
no-knock law, 132

obscenity, 119
Omnibus Crime Control and Safe Streets Act (1968), 145
ordeal, trial by, 32, 59

Palsgraf v. Long Island Railroad Co., 78
Patterson, Heywood, 143
Pentagon papers, the, 124
People v. Portelli, 141
People v. Schmidt, 92
People v. Young, 83
Pericles, 107
Phagan, Mary, 189
plaintiff, definition of, 218
plea, definition of, 218
Plessy, Homer, 154
police, 131
Pothier, Robert Joseph, 30
praetor system, 26, 218
precedent, 73, 218
   ancient Rome's lack of, 26
   in Britain, 44
press, freedom of the, 108, 119
   libel, 121
Preston, James W., 114
prima facie evidence, definition of, 218
prisons, 97
   Roman Empire, 23
privacy, personal, 125
probate, definition of, 218
procedural law, definition of, 219
prosecution, definition of, 219

proximate cause, definition of, 219
punishment, law-imposed
of animals, 94
of heretics, 31
of legally insane criminals, 91, 93
see also capital punishment; *specific codes; specific countries*

Ramsey v. Carolina Tennessee Power Co., 78
"real and present danger" test, 113, 114
"reasonable man" doctrine, 53
rebuttal, definition of, 219
religion. *See* Church of England; Hindu law; Islamic law; Jewish law; Roman Catholic Church
res ipsa loquitor, definition of, 219
Rideau v. Louisiana, 115
Riggs v. Palmer, 73
Roberson, Abigail, 127
Robinson v. California, 95
Rochin v. California, 133
Rockwell, George Lincoln, 117
Roman Catholic Church
and Justinian Code, 29
influence on development of laws, 30, 47
Inquisition, 31, 108
Roman Empire, 23, 24
Rosenberg, Julius and Ethel, 193
Roth v. the United States, 120
Russia, 65, 97, 98
Rylands v. Fletcher, 20

Sacco and Vanzetti case, 193
Schmerber v. California, 133
Scottsboro Boys case, 142
Screws v. United States, 157
search-and-seizure laws, 131
sedition, definition of, 219
Sheppard, Dr. Sam, 115
sheriff, definition of, 219
Sidis, William James, 127
Sioux City and P.R. Co. v. Stout, 77
slander, definition of, 219
slaves
in ancient Rome, 28
in U.S., 151, 153
Smith Act (1940), 113
Socrates, 21, 107
Solon, 21, 107
songs, as law customs, 12, 17
South Africa apartheid, 159
Spanish-American War, 162

speech, freedom of, 107, 117, 120
Star Chamber, 108, 144
State v. Moore, 89
statute, definition of, 217
"stop-and-frisk-law," 133
strict liability, definition of, 219
subpoena, definition of, 219
substantive law, 197, 220
suit (action), definition of, 220
Summa Theologica, 165
Sunda Island, 12
Supreme Court, U.S., 72, 180, 181
surveillance, individual, 137

Talmud, 23, 60
Textus Roffensis, 41
Thompson v. Louisville, 194
torts, 74, 220
treaties
Geneva accords, 172, 173
international, 164
Rush-Bagot, 177
U.S., as law of the land, 175
trespass, 75
trials, 197, 220
Twelve Tables, 25

Ulpian, 25
United Nations, 170
United States v. One Book Called "Ulysses," 119

verdict, definition of, 220
Vietnam war, 163, 172

Walmsley v. Rural Telephone Assoc., 78
warrant, definition of, 220
wars, 161
Comanche armies, 13
Jibaro inclination for, 15
see also specific wars
waters, international, 174
Whitmore, George, Jr., 140
wiretapping, 135, 145
witch trials, 184
witness, definition of, 220
World War One, 162
World War Two, 163, 170
writs, 44, 220. *See also specific writs*
written law, development of, 18, 41, 44, 46, 47

Zelenko v. Gimbel Brothers, 83
Zenger, Peter, 109